The Professional Librarian's Reader in Library Automation and Technology

Introduction by Susan K. Martin

Knowledge Industry Publications, Inc.
White Plains, NY

Professional Librarian Series

The Professional Librarian's Reader
in Library Automation and Technology

029.7
P964

Library of Congress Cataloging in Publication Data
Main entry under title:

The Professional librarian's reader in library automa-
    tion and technology.

    (Professional librarian series)
    Bibliography: p.

    1. Libraries — Automation.   2. Library information
networks.   3. Machine-readable bibliographic data.
4. Microforms.   5. Libraries — Security measures.
I. Series.
Z678.9.P76   021.6'5   80-11636
ISBN 0-914236-59-8
ISBN 0-914236-57-1 (pbk.)

Printed in the United States of America

80-4546

Contents

Introduction, *by Susan K. Martin* iii

Part I: Networking and On-line Services

    I.   Networks for Libraries: An Evolving Resource, *by Susan K. Martin* 1

    II.   The Scope of Networking, *by Susan K. Martin* 11

    III. Bibliographic Data Base Producers, *by Roger Christian* 21

    IV. Bibliographic Data Base Distributors, *by Roger Christian* 39

    V.   Bibliographic Data Bases in the Library: Start-up Considerations,
         by Pauline Atherton and Roger Christian 55

Part II: Technologies and Applications

    VI. Minicomputers and Their Uses, *by Audrey Grosch* 77

    VII. Computer Application: Integrated vs. Individual Approach,
         by Audrey Grosch 89

    VIII. Computer-Supported Catalogs, *by S. Michael Malinconico and Paul J. Fasana* 97

    IX. Automated Library Circulation Systems, *by Alice H. Bahr* 121

    X.   Criteria for System Acquisition, *by Alice H. Bahr* 139

    XI. Microforms: Traditional Uses, *by Alice H. Bahr* 145

    XII. Microforms: Innovative Uses, *by Alice H. Bahr* 153

    XIII. Book Theft and Library Security Systems, *by Alice H. Bahr.* 163

Selected Bibliography 197

List of Figures and Tables

Table V-1:   On-line Start-up, University of Nebraska—Lincoln Libraries............................57

Table V-2:   On-line Start-up, Northwestern University Library Computer
Assisted Information Services..57

Table V-3:   Checklist for Observing Events in Pre-Search Interview................................72

Table V-4:   Checklist for Observing Interpersonal Communication During
Pre-Search Interview.. 74

Figure VI-1.   MILS Software Organization.. 84

List of Illustrations

The New York Times Information Bank 34

Using a VDT for on-line searching...43

PDP 11 series minicomputer..94

Hardware for a minicomputer system...95

Eclipse S/100 hardware for DataPhase systems 125

Using the Checkpoint/Plessey portable terminal to record a checkout 131

Exit gate with Checkpoint sensing screens..169

Components of the Gaylord/Magnavox Book Security System 174

Sensing units for the Knogo Book Detection System 178

Tattle-Tape's book check unit..187

Sentronic's S-76 model...191

Introduction

by Susan K. Martin

PURPOSE OF THIS BOOK

During the past two decades, the use of computer and information technology has increased tremendously in U.S. libraries of all kinds and sizes. The amount spent annually by U.S. libraries for technological equipment or computer services was estimated in 1976 to be over $20 million; in 1980, with the combination of inflation and increased use, the figure is likely to be double that amount. Despite this ongoing commitment and investment, relatively little is published about the concepts and details of information technology for the benefit of librarians.

This book is intended to fill part of this publication gap. It is not detailed, at the mechanical level, but focuses on concepts, description of applications, and possible future developments. To successfully grapple with technological issues and applications, librarians and library school students must understand the concepts which form the foundation of the profession's acceptance of technological solutions to existing problems. *The Professional Librarian's Reader in Library Automation and Technology* identifies areas where technologies are being used to advantage in libraries; it briefly describes these applications, as well as remaining problems and prospective developments. The book is composed of selected chapters from the following monographs, all published by Knowledge Industry Publications, Inc.

Automated Library Circulation Systems, 1979-80, by Alice Harrison Bahr

Library Networks, 1978-79, by Susan K. Martin

Librarians and Online Services, by Pauline Atherton and Roger Christian

Microforms: The Librarians' View, 1978-79, by Alice Harrison Bahr

The Electronic Library: Bibliographic Data Bases, 1978-79, by Roger Christian

Minicomputers in Libraries, 1979-80, by Audrey N. Grosch

The Future of the Catalog: The Library's Choices, by S. Michael Malinconico
and Paul J. Fasana

Book Theft and Library Security Systems, 1978-79, by Alice Harrison Bahr

For more in-depth information about the technologies themselves or their specific application, the reader may wish to consult these monographs and other relevant literature, including publications listed in the bibliography.

That libraries should understand why they are using technological tools is not an idle wish. They must understand these tools, as well as the library applications, if they are to retain control of related decisions within the library. Other control points, such as budget and staff allocation, should be firmly held by the library administrator. If the assignment of technological "decision-making" is given to a nonlibrary administrator (for example, the computer center director, the purchasing officer, or even a statewide administrative office), the library administrator may no longer have the knowledge or the power to effect change in his or her library. Ultimately, a vast amount of resources will be allocated to the use of information technology. An outside agency may not make the best or most informed decision in selection of technology (for example, which kind of circulation system to buy, or whether it should be created as a home-grown product).

The librarian must be knowledgeable and involved. Certainly, this approach means that each individual must spend time and effort; management of technology is an area which, rather than replacing existing duties, overlays them. However, the decade of the 1980s will see economic problems for libraries, and at the same time growth in technological capability. Each librarian must be sufficiently knowledgeable to manage the resultant juggling act to his or her library's best interest.

CHANGES IN THE APPROACH TO TECHNOLOGY

Machines have been used in libraries for decades. Early professional literature, amusing to today's librarians, argues the merits and faults of the contraption called the typewriter. Today's literature will undoubtedly be equally amusing to the librarians of the 21st century, as they read about our concerns with computer capabilities.

In the early 1960s, computer applications in libraries began to proliferate. No national standards existed; each library wrote its own programs, designed its own machine-readable format, and identified the areas of development most important for it. Librarians did research to support their decisions, and published articles describing the computer applications in the library press.

In 1968, the *Journal of Library Automation* (JOLA) joined the *Journal of the American Society for Information Science,* providing a forum for exchange of information and research results. For several years, the articles were technical and detailed, or theoretical and research-oriented. In many issues of JOLA, for instance, one can find articles describing research on the file structure of bibliographic data bases and their related indexes. With these articles we trace the development of search key techniques currently in use in many systems.

For at least five years, the library profession was able to learn "how we did it good" in specific institutions, or often how we promised to do it good. Sharing of information was the theme, and librarians and/or programmers cooperated to make information available. Only one major book was published (with the exception of proceedings of institutes): this was Becker and Hayes' *Handbook of Library Automation.* Becker and Hayes covered principles of data processing, as well as concepts of library applications.

In the early 1970s, networking became a reality with the establishment of the Ohio College Library Center's shared cataloging system. Also, vendors of automated library systems began to flourish; these systems included circulation systems, computer output microform (COM) catalogs, and security systems. By their very nature, these organizations did not encourage the publication of their trade or proprietary information. As more libraries relied on them, and fewer libraries formed systems offices or did in-house technical work, less technical literature was produced. Significant developments in the use of technology took place, but the technical details were not revealed. In turn, librarians focused more on the philosophical, conceptual, and political aspects of applying technologies to information services.

As a result of less local development and the evolution of library applications, published literature is radically different in approach and scope from the literature of 10 years ago. While this change is not necessarily bad, it does mean that a researcher wishing empirical data to support a new project must either gather these data directly, or must use data published up to 15 years ago. The private sector's expanding role in library technologies places librarians in a more passive posture, and this is reflected in their writings.

While this selection of readings cannot alter the situation, it does bring together recent commentary on a wide variety of library technologies.

USE OF TECHNOLOGIES IN LIBRARIES

While much can and has been said about information technologies, three points are particularly relevant for the reader of this volume:

- Libraries are increasing their use of computer and other information technologies. It is clear that even small libraries can afford computer terminals with the concomitant services. It is likely that within the next few years no library will be able to afford operating *without* some form of technological assistance.

- As stated above, there is a scarcity of detailed information. Librarians are inadequately informed about the equipment and systems they use or wish to use, and library schools do not train their students to wisely manage and work in an environment which contains computer equipment, microforms (including COM), microcomputers, and associated transactions (for example, evaluating bids, negotiating service contracts, etc.).

- Despite nationwide computer and other services, local needs for technological applications continue to exist. Few libraries have staff capable of dealing with these needs, which usually include manipulation of bibliographic or fiscal data to provide local products not available through vendors. In this area, the profession has a generation gap. The "technologists" of the 1960s have gone on to administrative positions, but they have not yet been replaced by younger librarians. In 1980, we are just beginning to feel the effects of this gap; many libraries have positions available for systems librarians, with no success in filling them. A corps of experts in library technology is once again needed, in libraries rather than in companies or network organizations.

TRENDS FOR THE FUTURE

Some obvious patterns of technological developments in libraries can be outlined:

- Libraries will use more technological aids, at a relatively lower price. Systems and services will be widely available, either to individual libraries or to consortia.

- The sheer volume of bibliographic data in machine-readable form will increase rapidly. At some point, it may be necessary to adopt standards for identifying, controlling, and storing bibliographic records which exist in multiple copies and in varying quality.

- The reference data bases (those produced by abstracting and indexing services) will be linked to bibliographic data bases, allowing links among serial titles, journal articles, and holding locations. The resultant system will allow a user to search a data base, identify desired titles, and locate the document in one step.

- Home computers will be used in libraries, and the computers in the library and the home will allow communication between the two.

- A balance will be found between on-line and off-line data storage (i.e., microform). This balance will become increasingly significant as data bases grow; it is possible that 20% of the data base will provide 80% of the use. For both economic and functional reasons, it will be necessary to use more than one storage medium.

Many questions remain to be asked, and solutions sought, in the application of technology to libraries and other information organizations. This book is intended to summarize the current situation and give an indication of the issues at hand, to assist those becoming acquainted with the field. It is hoped that these selections will stimulate further in-depth reading, and foster active participation in the development and management of library technologies.

Part I

Networking and On-line Services

I

Networks For Libraries: An Evolving Resource

by Susan K. Martin

Nearly a decade has passed since a 1970 conference at Airlie House in Warrenton, VA, set goals for library cooperation. That conference, sponsored by the U.S. Office of Education and the American Library Association, provided an intellectual groundwork for library networking. Shortly thereafter, the National Commission on Libraries and Information Science (NCLIS) was established. During the decade that followed, more than 2000 libraries in North America have become involved in on-line bibliographic processing as a means to streamline such internal tasks as cataloging. Yet in 1978, the goal of a comprehensive bibliographic network was still beyond the resources of the library community. Such a network would provide every library with access to first quality cataloging information as well as to information on the holdings of member libraries in order to facilitate a free exchange both of bibliographic information and of books, journals and other materials.

DEFINITION OF NETWORKS

In modern usage, a network can be defined as a group of individuals or organizations that are interconnected. The linking must include a communications channel, and many networks exist for the express purpose of fostering a certain type of communication among their members. In the library world, institutions form networks primarily to achieve better sharing of resources — resources consisting both of bibliographic information and of collections — and better service to patrons. It must be emphasized that the particular focus of this monograph will be on-line networks, those using computers and linking members to the computer resource by means of telecommunications connections.

A distinction must be made between networks used only for information retrieval and those used for input and modification of data as well as for retrieval. Emphasis will be placed on the latter (networks for technical processing) although some discussion of the former may be found in Chapter II.

Reprinted from *Library Networks, 1978-79* (White Plains, NY: Knowledge Industry Publications, Inc., 1978).

HISTORY OF NETWORKS

In the United States, a loosely structured library network began to form over a century ago with the founding of the American Library Association (ALA) and the increasing national activities of the Library of Congress (LC). In 1901, with the initiation of the LC catalog card production and distribution service, the nationwide network of libraries received its first significant communication tool.[1] During the first half of the century, librarians developed the bibliographic controls necessary to allow sharing of data among institutions. Fortunately, by the time of the information explosion of the 1950s and 1960s, rules for cataloging and classification had for the most part been widely adopted; the majority of libraries no longer needed to be self-reliant in processing materials. A library "network" existed, with the Library of Congress book catalog and the National Union Catalog as supporting tools, and a standardized interlibrary loan procedure facilitating exchange of materials. Regional and local networks proliferated, formed by librarians taking advantage of these national tools and attempting to improve services for their patrons.

In the late 1950s and early 1960s, librarians became increasingly aware of the potential of data processing equipment – punched card equipment and especially computers – for library automation. The Library of Congress took the lead in designing a format for machine-readable bibliographic records. This five-year effort culminated in the national and then international acceptance of the MAchine-Readable Cataloging (MARC) format.[2,3] With the computer as a processing tool, the information community now had MARC as a common data structure with which to communicate.

In 1969 LC began distributing machine-readable cataloging data. One year later the Ohio College Library Center performed its first off-line processing for 54 members, and in 1971 it started on-line operations, the first organization to do such processing. By 1978, OCLC had undergone a tremendous expansion in number of libraries served, as well as significant changes in structure and operations.

NETWORK CHARACTERISTICS

The on-line network has several characteristics worthy of mention: it requires a significant level of financial and organizational commitment from participants; it is usually based upon agreement within the group of participants that specific tasks should be performed and specific guidelines adhered to; and it provides an immediate facility for access, through computer and communications technologies, to data bases in both the public and private sectors of the information community. Because involvement entails a sizable financial commitment, libraries which are network participants must actively use the network's services in order to derive benefits commensurate with their level of expenditure. Changes in internal organizational structure are common among networking libraries; these accommodations are made in order to maximize the usefulness of the network to the user library. An even more important factor has been the consensus among participants on objectives and goals for the network. Libraries have been faced with the question of conforming to a group decision; a library that does not conform risks either grossly uneconomical use of the network or a judgment by peers that the library is engaged in poor practices.

Because the consequences of network participation are so far-reaching, individual libraries are undergoing a change in attitude toward network organizations and toward network computer systems. Increasingly, these systems are viewed as vendors who are vying for the library's business, even though the library still desires a voice in network governance. Thus, in 1978, both the Research Libraries Group (then consisting of New York Public Library and the universities of Harvard, Yale and Columbia) and the University of California system invited competitive bids as a way of making decisions on which computer system to use.

The issues and problems posed by these and other characteristics of on-line library networks are less than a decade old, and are changing rapidly. They are symptomatic of a dynamic field characterized by new technologies, and the vulnerability of libraries to society's economic trends. The problems will require considerable effort on the part of libraries. Although on-line technology in libraries is still young, the combination of technological, political and economic problems is almost beyond the scope of a single person's ability to comprehend.

THE NETWORK AS A RESOURCE

Networks are organizations, either formal or informal. Among the well-known library networks are the New England Library Information Network (NELINET), in Wellesley, MA, the California Library Authority for Systems and Services (CLASS) in San Jose, CA, the Midwestern Library Network (MIDLNET) in Green Bay, WI, the Washington Library Network (WLN), in Olympia, WA, and the Research Libraries Group (RLG) in New Haven, CT. An article by Butler has distinguished between the network as an *organization* and the network as a *resource.*[4] (Other writers have used the term "utility" to describe those organizations providing computer services.) The networks listed here illustrate this distinction very handily. All five networks are formal organizations, with member libraries, advisory boards and central staffs. Only one, however, provides computer processing services to its members from the central offices; this is WLN. Other network organizations have contracted externally for the supply of *network resources* to their member libraries. For example, NELINET and the Pittsburgh Regional Library Center (PRLC) have contracted, on an annual or biennial basis, with OCLC for the provision of on-line services to libraries which are members of NELINET and PRLC. (As a result of its restructuring in 1978, the Ohio College Library Center became OCLC, Inc. and ceased to have individual members as such, though individual libraries may still use its services. Its board is composed of representatives from the networks which use OCLC services; the Ohio members who began OCLC have now formed their own network, OHIONET, with similar representation.)

In the early days of computerized library networking (if one may use such an expression for a phenomenon which is only seven years old), embryonic network organizations looked toward OCLC as a model and attempted to make plans to either develop a similar system or to "replicate" the OCLC system by transferring the OCLC computer programs to their own computers. After two or three years' deliberation, most networks came to the conclusion that they do not need their own computers and may rely on outside contractual arrangements to satisfy their computer and system requirements. Network organizations may, therefore, consider a broadening field of available resources as potential tools for their member libraries. OCLC is still the most widely used. Among others are Stanford University's Bibliographic Automation of Large Library Operations using a Time-sharing System (BALLOTS), the University of Chicago's on-line processing system, the University of Toronto Library Automation System (UTLAS), the WLN system, and emerging commercial systems such as the new Brodart acquisition and processing system (IROS) and the on-line system designed for the British Library and offered by Blackwell/North America.

In addition to wider choices of network resources, libraries are also finding that computer software is transferable, despite doubts to this effect in the late 1960s and early 1970s. Where appropriate, software transfer is taking place, both between libraries and from libraries to networks. The widespread use of standard IBM software and hardware, together with the apparent desire of computer manufacturers to remain compatible with IBM-based systems, is clearly responsible for the ease with which many exchanges are occurring. For example, the Hennepin County Library in Minnesota and the Washington Library Network have both used software developed by the New York Public Library.[5,6] The State University of New York at Albany library has obtained a circulation system from the Ohio State University Libraries, and the University of Illinois in Urbana-Champaign was to adopt the same system in late 1978. The system software developed by Guelph University in Ontario is being used by other libraries in the province. Such software transfer carries some risks, but the visible successes encourage further efforts of this nature. Of course, it is recognized that on-line networks themselves obviate the need for software transfer among members.

Many of the existing network organizations were formed as middlemen between OCLC and the user libraries. Some of these organizations continue to provide no function or service other than arrangement of OCLC use. Since this situation creates two financial obligations on the part of the libraries (to OCLC and the network organization), it is unlikely that in the future networks will be able to survive unless they provide some service or benefit to their members other than merely facilitating on-line processing.

NETWORKS: SCOPE AND POTENTIAL

Every function in the operation of a library can be assisted either entirely or in part by automated procedures. Automation in individual libraries has touched acquisitions, cataloging, serials control, fiscal control, circulation, reference, collection development and management reporting. In network organizations, thus far, emphasis has been placed almost exclusively on shared cataloging, the production of catalog copy and queries for interlibrary loan. At its inception, the OCLC administration announced that a series of modules would be developed over a period of several years, beginning with cataloging and moving to serials check-in, acquisitions and circulation.[7] The scheduled dates for implementation of these modules have slipped badly, partly because of additional commitments taken on over the years. The serials check-in module, originally scheduled for implementation in 1972, began pilot testing in one library in late 1975, was implemented on a limited scale in 125 libraries in 1977, and was acknowledged to require further development by the OCLC administration in mid-1978.[8,9] Further work will identify the requirements for revising and re-implementing the check-in module.

The BALLOTS system has developed several capabilities beyond that of cataloging. The expansion of the system to libraries other than Stanford began in 1975; the long-awaited network file design was to streamline the system's operation in late 1978 or early 1979. Subject searching is available on the system; the acquisitions module has been in operation for several years but is still limited to the Stanford University Libraries.[10]

Technological experts are questioning the wisdom of placing a heavy load of locally oriented transactions on an already busy central computer (Chapter II). Applications such as circulation and serials check-in are high-volume functions, and the information contained in the transactions is of interest primarily to the holding library. For this reason, it may prove more practical for individual libraries or networks to install minicomputers to communicate with central network computers. NELINET is experimenting with a configuration which would use a Digital Equipment Corp. minicomputer, communicating with OCLC's computers. The Dallas County Community College, in using a DataPhase circulation and processing system, brings cataloging records in machine-readable form directly from the OCLC system to the Data General minicomputer at Dallas.

More consideration will be given to the question of network scope in Chapter II.

Impetus for Growth

The trend toward networks, consortia and related ventures has been accelerated by a number of factors.

The quantity of material from which librarians must select for local collections has soared. Each year, between 35,000 and 40,000 books are published in the United States alone. In addition, serials, government documents, foreign publications and an increasing variety of special materials must be considered by the librarian selecting for a collection. In past years, libraries have attempted to serve their clienteles from their own collections as much as possible, utilizing interlibrary loan mechanisms as a supplement. Decreasing purchasing power and increasing service goals have, in recent years, caused many libraries to view a "collection" as being not only the materials possessed by the individual library, but the materials owned by other institutions. Interlibrary loan, photocopying and reciprocal borrowing privileges form the bases of these "extended libraries."

The Airlie House Conference in 1970, followed by the report of the National Commission on Libraries and Information Science, advocated the formation of a national bibliographic network, allowing access by all to all library collections — a concept that has come in for increasing skepticism.[11] To create the extended library, libraries need assistance in the form of union catalogs giving information about each other's holdings. The attraction of a network is that individual members can use on-line terminals to query the computer about the identification of a book, its location, and in some cases its availability. Often the cost of an interlibrary loan transaction and the telecommunications link is less than the purchase price of the material, or even of a photocopy. Before and after passage of the 1976 copyright law, the Information Industry Association, the Authors' League and the Association of American Publishers objected strenuously to the potential loss of revenue caused by networks' effect on resource sharing.[12] Although several studies have been performed to analyze the publishers' claims, the situation has not been resolved, and resolution is unlikely to occur until the first formal evaluation of the effect of the copyright law in 1983.

Although the costs of most library services have mushroomed in recent years as part of the general inflation, computer equipment costs have remained stable or decreased slightly, while staff and materials costs have risen sharply. In the 1960s, the federal government began providing significant sums of money to libraries. Through programs such as the Library Services and Construction Act (LSCA), the funds from Washington rose from $7.5 million in 1956 to well over $100 million in 1966. Networks began to flourish; many innovative and valuable programs were initiated. In the early 1970s, however, federal funding for various programs was either reduced or failed to keep pace with inflation. In many ways this environment provided new opportunities for networks to develop. Libraries could no longer hope for funds to carry out ambitious individual projects. Rather, they saw in cooperative arrangements the possibility of providing new services whose cost would be spread over many institutions.

In 1978, the federal government again infused funds into academic and research libraries. Title IIC of the Higher Education Act will provide $5 million for support of library programs. Only individual libraries may apply, so that networks will benefit only if they can provide needed local services.

In 1978, libraries were showing renewed awareness that their first obligation was to local patrons. The increasing pace of installation of minicomputers for local systems is a strong indication that library efforts will be focused on local requirements first, and regional and national networking activities only second. This attitude is spreading at the same time that the symptoms of a nationwide taxpayers' revolt are emerging. But it is too early to say whether the new economic conservatism will be constructive or regressive for library networks.

Telecommunications Technology

Improvements in telecommunications technologies have also spurred the growth of networks. The use of telecommunications in libraries is not new. In 1927 the Free Library of Philadelphia used a teletypewriter as part of a closed circuit to communicate information from the loan desk in the main reading room to and from the stacks. In the 1940s, Michigan librarians connected two different city libraries with a teletypewriter.[13]

Teletypewriter-like terminals are still widely used in library networks, since their maximum rate of transmission — 30 characters per second — is within the range of ordinary telephone line capacity. However, the most efficient transmission of digital computer data requires a broader bandwidth than that of the ordinary telephone line. By conditioning telephone lines and adding ancillary equipment, communications carriers have the capability of transmitting within ranges of 30 to 1000 characters per second or even more.

In 1976 and 1977, the library community conducted a major effort to produce a draft telecommunications protocol for library and information networks.[14] The project was initiated by the American Library Association and carried out by NCLIS and the National Bureau of Standards. This protocol is designed to standardize the form in which computer messages are encoded and transmitted. By means of such standardization, communication between different computer systems, e.g. OCLC and WLN, should eventually be feasible, thereby allowing the users of one network to query the data base of another network.

The future telecommunications system for library use in networking may integrate audio, digital and video signals into a single system. A technical development in this decade called the value-added network (VAN) offers data transmission at greater speeds, lower error rates and lower costs than do ordinary telephone facilities. Several companies have sought and received the Federal Communications Commission's permission to raise the quality of normal telephone line to the level of value-added networks. Some of these companies are Tymshare, Telenet and Graphnet Systems. Tymshare's Tymnet system is widely used as the communications link for libraries with networks such as OCLC or BALLOTS, or with on-line data services such as those offered by Lockheed, System Development Corp. (SDC) or Bibliographic Retrieval Services (BRS). Telenet is already an alternative for some of this traffic.

Video discs, which were scheduled for commercial introduction in the U.S. in late 1978 or 1979, give promise of a low-cost storage medium for video and eventually for digital information. Another promising development are teletext systems for disseminating information to offices and homes via ordinary phone lines or by a terminal attached to a TV set. Two such systems, CEEFAX and viewdata, have been introduced in Great Britain and are undergoing tests in the U.S. It is interesting that OCLC is one of the sponsors of research into the applicability of this technology in the U.S.[15] Finally, satellite communication is being tested, with ALA sponsoring several conferences via satellite.

CONCLUSION

A combination of economic circumstances, evolving technologies and the need to deal with the increased flow of published information has provided the major incentives for libraries and other information processing organizations to seek out new organizational structures for processing materials and providing access to these materials for patrons and customers. The library network which deals with the "housekeeping" aspects of library procedures is a significant outgrowth of this search. Large networks seem destined to handle certain processing jobs that rely on shared bibliographic data, while other more local library tasks will be handled on minicomputers in individual institutions.

FOOTNOTES

1. David C. Weber, "A Century of Cooperative Programs Among Academic Libraries," *College & Research Libraries* 37:205-221 (May 1976).

2. *Books: A MARC Format.* 5th ed. (Washington, DC: Library of Congress, 1972).

3, International Organization for Standardization, *Documentation — Format for Bibliographic Information Interchange on Magnetic Tape.* (Geneva, Switzerland: ISO, 1973), (ISO 2709, 1973 [E]).

4. Brett Butler, "The State of the Nation in Networking," *Journal of Library Automation* 8:200-220 (September 1975).

5. Maurice Freedman, "Cataloging Systems: 1973 Applications Status." In *Library Automation II: State of the Art,* ed. by Susan K. Martin and Brett Butler. (Chicago: American Library Association, 1975).

6. S. Michael Malinconico and James Rizzolo, "The New York Public Library Automated Book Catalog Subsystem," *Journal of Library Automation* 6:3-36 (March 1973).

7. *OCLC Newsletter* 1, 1970.

8. *OCLC Newsletter* 93:1 (January 14, 1976).

9. *OCLC Newsletter* 115:3 (April 7, 1978).

10. BALLOTS Center. *Status Report on BALLOTS* (BALLOTS Center, Stanford University, April 1978).

11. Richard De Gennaro, "Copyright,Resource Sharing, and Hard Times: A View From the Field," *American Libraries* 8:430-435 (September 1977).

12. "AAP and Authors Counter CNLA Copyright Stand," *Advanced Technology/ Libraries* 7:1,5 (January 1978).

13. "Detroit Urges Use of Teletypewriters," *Library Journal* 52:1190 (August 1951).

14. "Protocol for Computer-to-Computer Communication," *Journal of Library Automation* 9:167-176 (June 1976).

15. "Viewdata Sparks Interest at OCLC and Telenet," *Advanced Technology/Libraries* 7:7-1 (July 1978).

II

The Scope of Networking

by Susan K. Martin

AUTOMATION AND NETWORKING

Computerized networking was a natural outgrowth of library automation, and followed the development of major automation programs by only a few years. A study of the literature will show that librarians began to write about automation in the early 1960s and about automated networking in the late years of that decade. The *Annual Review of Information Science and Technology* has had a chapter on library automation almost every year since its inception in 1966, and began to include chapters on networking in 1971.[1]

The distinction between automation and networking is becoming ever more tenuous. It is increasingly difficult to discuss library automation without mentioning library networks, just as it has been almost impossible for a number of years to discuss library networks without considering automation. Once again, as in the previous chapter, the difference between a *network organization* and a *network resource* should be emphasized. The network organization is the administrative structure which links a group of libraries; the network resource is the computer system which supports networking functions.

SCOPE OF NETWORK POTENTIAL IN LIBRARIES

Although each library considers itself unique, the basic operations of any library tend to follow a common pattern. The technical service functions of the library are selection, acquisition and organization of materials in order to make materials accessible to users. The procedures used to fulfill these functions are amenable in varying degrees to network operation.

Reprinted from *Library Networks, 1978-79* (White Plains, NY: Knowledge Industry Publications, Inc., 1978).

Those functions most suitable for networking are those which are least subject to local variation, require the smallest number of transactions against the library's files and stand to gain the most by using other institutions' data. This is because these functions use the communications and computer resources most efficiently and maximize the use of shared data. An examination of several library functions which appear to be good candidates for networking will illustrate this statement.

Cataloging

There is little doubt that cataloging is well suited to a network operation. A manually based cataloging operation in a small or medium-sized library may entail purchase of card sets from dealers or book jobbers, with the library staff checking each new acquisition to ensure conformity of names, subject headings and call numbers with previously assigned data. A larger library may obtain cards from the Library of Congress, generate them itself, or purchase them from dealers, among other alternatives. For all types and sizes of libraries, manual catalog production involves much checking, typing, filing and other routine clerical work. The advent of on-line systems and the rapidly growing bibliographic data bases allow some streamlining of labor-intensive cataloging procedures. In most libraries, cards must still be filed into catalogs, but the computer can print the overtyped headings and sort the cards into alphabetical order automatically. In addition, as the data base grows, the cataloger may examine an increasingly large segment of the individual library's holdings or of the holdings of all the users of the network without leaving the computer terminal.

Since libraries are accustomed to using cataloging data provided by an outside source, the network concept makes sense here. An on-line cataloging network such as OCLC provides LC cataloging data to its users; ideally, the only records which must be input by a library are those outside the scope of the MARC Distribution Service which have not yet been cataloged by any other user library. The data base is a mixture of LC MARC records and records in the MARC format which were originally input by others, plus information about additional locations reported whenever a library uses an existing record. If all libraries used a standard cataloging code, the system would be relatively simple.

However, not all libraries use standard cataloging rules. Variations may result from individual practices and idiosyncrasies; one of the simplest of these is the user library's inability to use an LC-assigned classification and Cutter number because it has already been used within that library for an originally cataloged volume. More complex are the problems arising from differences in name and subject authority files; the library may deliberately or inadvertently create a second record for an item already in the data base because of a divergence of cataloging practice. Only the Washington Library Network has resolved the problem of authorities, although BALLOTS, UTLAS and OCLC all plan to or are considering incorporating either authority files or authority contol in the near future.

Another problem of the cataloging application in networks is the pricing of the service. OCLC and BALLOTS charge user libraries only for cards produced (about four cents a card) when they input original records; if they use a record already in the data base ("First Time Use," or FTU), they must pay between $1.60 and $1.85 in addition to the card costs.[2] In OCLC and UTLAS, there is no incentive to use existing records, and every incentive to save money by creating original but duplicate records. In conjunction with its pricing structure, BALLOTS has asked user libraries to sign an agreement to use existing records if possible and to follow nationally accepted cataloging standards. Through its pricing and standards, BALLOTS has tried to discourage libraries from creating duplicate records. In other networks, much consideration has been given to the balance of input between large and small libraries, or academic and public libraries. Thus far, each network seems to be experimenting with slightly different approaches to the problem.

Despite these obstacles, it is apparent that shared on-line cataloging is a reasonable and justifiable function of a network. The benefits to participating libraries vary with the level of effort to accrue such benefits, but there is no doubt that the approach can produce either savings, added services, or both.[3]

Acquisitions

Acquisitions procedures are also adaptable to networking, for reasons similar to those mentioned for cataloging. A few differences should be identified, however. The question of accurate bibliographic authority is not as pressing for an acquisitions record as for a cataloging record, since by definition the acquisitions record is temporary. Sources of bibliographic information for purchase orders are of varying quality, and it may be difficult or impossible to generate precise bibliographic information until the item has arrived in the library. What effects does this situation have for the network resource?

First, it is possible — and valuable — for a library to query the data base and use an existing catalog or order record, if it exists, for a purchase order. Second, with locally input records for acquisitions data, the quality and quantity of bibliographic data will inevitably be at a lower level than LC or other cataloging data. Third, it is possible for networking libraries to rely on the common data base to share resources by interlibrary loan; one facet of sharing is the decision *not* to purchase, reached by examining the holdings of other libraries.

As an example, in its design for automation of acquisitions, the BALLOTS system at Stanford creates a data base called the In-Process File (IPF) which contains all bibliographic records which have not been cataloged.[4] This technique allows full searching of all machine-readable records, but still keeps separate those items which need further processing before being incorporated into the Catalog Data File (CDF). The Library of Congress, with its Multiple Use MARC System (MUMS), will allow other institutions access to its Process Information File (PIF), representing items not yet fully cataloged.[5]

Interlibrary Loan (ILL) and Network Inventory

For years, libraries have been relying on a system of telecommunications to transmit interlibrary loan requests and responses. The supporting bibliographic tools have been catalogs such as the *National Union Catalog*, or regional and local catalogs. An obvious by-product of an on-line shared cataloging system is the facility for transmitting data regarding interlibrary lending. Although no network has yet formally incorporated ILL into its on-line system, many users of OCLC search the huge data base before embarking upon an interlibrary borrowing transaction, and OCLC is in the process of designing an interlibrary loan module.

Many library cooperatives have made detailed studies of interlibrary lending patterns, and the actual and desired behaviors of libraries engaged in interlibrary borrowing are well documented. Although the possibility exists for an automated ILL system to spread the burden of lending and reduce the number of "net lenders," OCLC's preliminary system design will apparently not attempt to reach this objective. Rather, it will allow each library to designate, without formal agreement from the other libraries, up to 12 libraries from which it prefers to borrow. Each ILL query would then display names of any of the 12 libraries which had the desired item.

The utility of a shared on-line system for interlibrary borrowing information is unquestionable. With a single data base, a librarian needs only one look-up to determine the location of the nearest copy of desired material. Future ILL modules in on-line systems will not only provide location information, but also transmit the request in on-line or batch mode to the holding library. It remains to be seen whether this approach will be considered coercive or cooperative.

The concept of the library as a resource is changing, as a function of continuing high rates of publication and the fact that fewer libraries can afford to maintain comprehensive collections. The interlibrary or network data base is gradually making available an inventory of material which is regarded by some as a shared resource on a regional or even national basis. Again, *quid pro quo* arrangements must be developed, and certain group rules established (for instance, no academic library should be expected to lend materials which are on reserve for a course). The computerized network provides the tool with which libraries can implement hitherto unmanageable projects.

Reference

Paradoxically, libraries have more experience with on-line reference services than with the on-line processing done through networks, but still have limited understanding of the cost and impact on patrons of the reference services. In the last decade, when the large abstracting and indexing services began to put all their data into machine-readable form for manipulation and publication in hard copy, an obvious by-product was sale of the machine-readable data. The first service was batch-mode selective dissemination of information (SDI), followed closely by on-line services offered either by the generator of the data base or by brokers such as System Development Corp. (SDC), Lockheed or Bibliographic Retrieval Services (BRS). These services continue to be relatively costly; each search may cost $30 or more, exclusive of telecommunications cost.[6,7] In addition, a well-formulated search takes a significant amount of preparation, staff time and machine time. For these reasons, the transaction loads for on-line reference services have not been overwhelmingly heavy in proportion to the overall reference use of libraries.

However, data bases which support technical services are beginning to be considered as searching tools for reference purposes. As more libraries have more of their holdings in machine-readable form, it may become easier to use a terminal than the card catalog. One terminal is able to gain access to all the data bases available to the library. For instance, an OCLC user could use the dedicated telephone line to query the OCLC data base, then use Tymnet to search the SDC or Lockheed files with the same keyboard equipment. The Ohio State University Libraries have continued with limited patron use of on-line terminals for catalog searching, and the University of Pennsylvania Library's circulation system has several patron access terminals for inquiry about the location of known items. Many special libraries allow their users to formulate and input their own data base searches.

Since 1975, much concern has been expressed in the library profession over the increasing tendency of libraries to charge patrons for data base services, either as partial or total cost recovery.[8] On the one hand, library services are intended to be free to all; on the other hand, these services are extremely expensive and cannot be easily paid for from the existing library budget. Certainly parent agencies can be asked for additional funds to support these information services. However, in an age when every tax or tuition dollar is bitterly resented, librarians must face the fact that computer-based reference services are so visible and so individually oriented that most libraries will undoubtedly be forced to charge for them for the foreseeable future.

LIMITATIONS OF NETWORKING

Because networks involve a communication process, there exists the possibility of bottlenecks in the system if too many demands are placed on a single resource. With inadequate telephone lines, communication speeds or "polling" mechanisms, the response time of an on-line system may degenerate to the point that the system is almost useless. Worse yet, the computer may rebel against the load and "crash" the system, causing excessive down time. Organizations such as airlines or banks which rely heavily on industry-wide computer networks are able to justify investment of large sums of money to ensure that adequate facilities will be on hand to meet the highest possible workload — they buy two computers in case one develops a problem.

Libraries and library networks are moving toward a position where investment in auxiliary equipment for computer systems can be justified. However, it is necessary as part of this justification to identify those functions which are strictly local

or have very high transaction levels. These functions will be less suited to networking; test programs may experiment with one or more of these functions on a networking basis, but it still appears that local processing is more economical.

Circulation

The circulation function seems in some ways appropriate for networking, since
it uses bibliographic data which may be shared and is associated closely with interlibrary loan. However, three major problems impede the development of networked
circulation systems: transaction load, patron files and local functions.

In most libraries, the check-out and check-in transactions occur more often
than any other single transaction in the library. Widener Library at Harvard University averages 2000 transactions daily, six days a week. The Moffitt Undergraduate
Library at the University of California, Berkeley, circulates 500,000 items annually,
for a transaction load of over 1 million. The average library may circulate 10 times
the number of items it catalogs annually. It is not at all clear that a centralized
computer system would be able to easily handle 10 times the traffic given it by the
catalog departments of all network members.

In addition, the circulation process requires a record of the borrower. Existing on-line circulation systems for single libraries have the capability of storing
on-line a library's entire patron file. If this capability were also required of a
network computer facility, it would pose an added traffic burden as well as create
problems with privacy of personal files. Differences in types of libraries imply
different proportions of patrons file sizes as well; while an academic library may
have many bibliographic records, it is likely to have a small number of patrons.
Public libraries have many copies of relatively few bibliographic items, but large
numbers of patrons.

Finally, local functions such as overdue notices, recalls and replacement bills
must be accommodated by a circulation system. A network would either request conformity among its members regarding these practices, or would be required to deal
with variant practices and printed forms.

A circulation network has been created by CL Systems, Inc. (CLSI), for several
regional libraries in northern Illinois and in California. These "networks," however, do not rely upon a single central computer. Each library system owns a minicomputer and a self-contained on-line circulation system. When inter-regional information or transactions are desired, telecommunications channels connect two or more
of the independent systems. In this way, shared data are available, but local transaction loads, files and practices are dominant.

A final caution on networking circulation stems from figures recently derived
at the University of California, Berkeley and the University of Pennsylvania,
showing that the percentage of all circulation transactions involving interlibrary

lending or borrowing may be as small as .2%.[9] It may be unreasonable to build a network circulation system when such a tiny proportion of materials circulated involves more than one library at a time.

A system which combines minicomputer processing for local functions and brief temporary records with the powerful network processing of a shared bibliographic system may present a reasonable alternative. The University of Toronto Library Automation System (UTLAS), with its on-line catalog and minicomputer circulation system, is exploring this possibility.[10]

Serials Check-In

Another area of high transaction level is the checking-in and control of serial issues and volumes. Many of the same problems arise as with the circulation function: the ratio of annual transactions to titles held is high; local data exist, and local practices and forms must be accommodated.

For example, assuming an average frequency of quarterly, a library with 10,000 serial titles would receive 40,000 pieces to be checked in annually, or over 150 pieces daily. Such procedures as claiming, cancelling, binding and payment are strictly local. The binding title and address of vendor also vary from one library to another, as do the bindery, claim and cancel forms.

As described in the previous chapter, OCLC has conducted a one-year test of a serials check-in system, involving up to 125 OCLC users. Based on this test, OCLC has withdrawn the system until additional modifications and improvements can be made.[11]

Fiscal control

Fiscal control is another problem area for network designers.

Fiscal transactions do not represent a tremendously high workload within any single library. Nor do they require large supporting files such as patron files in the case of circulation. They do, however, represent a point of contact for each library with its parent organization, in which the library must usually conform to the codes, practices and printed forms of the parent agency.

Therefore, each library has its own fund codes, which are normally dictated by a government agency, university or company, and which follow no standard pattern. Invoices, vouchers and accounting forms of various types must be used, and cannot be controlled by a library network. It is unlikely that a network organization could convince the business officers of an organization to relinquish control of their library funds to a computer owned by an independent agency. The feasibility of incorporating into a network system the programming necessary to manipulate unlimited formats of fund codes and names is also questionable.

An exception, of course, would be networks whose member libraries report to the same governing body. Examples of these are the State University of New York libraries and the libraries of the California State University and College system.

CONCLUSION

The scope of networking is potentially all-encompassing within the framework of library functions. To accommodate all functions in a satisfactory manner, however, a significant investment would be necessary in terms of hardware and communications, as well as software — an investment that is probably beyond the capability of most library networks at this time. It is therefore reasonable to examine each function in terms of 1) its direct cost and indirect drain on system resources, 2) its contribution to the overall network capabilities, and 3) its capacity for shared data or transactions. Weighing these factors, the network manager should be able to remove from consideration those functions which are not economical at present. Similarly, the manager of the local library should identify those functions which are most suitable for automation locally, with potential links to networks in the future.

FOOTNOTES

1. Edwin E. Olson, Russell Shank, and Harold A. Olsen, "Library and Information Networks" in *Annual Review of Information Science and Technology,* v. 7, ed. by Carlos Cuadra. (Washington, DC: ASIS, 1972).

2. *OCLC Newsletter* 97:1 (April 2, 1976).

3. Anne Marie Allison et al., "The Impact of OCLC on Cataloging Departments — A Study" *Network* 2:11-16 (January 1975).

4. BALLOTS Center. *Status Report on BALLOTS,* op. cit.

5. "Library Launches On-Line Distribution Service," *Library of Congress Information Bulletin* 37:49, 52-53 (January 20, 1978).

6. Michael D. Cooper and Nancy A. DeWath, "The Cost of On-Line Bibliographic Searching," *Journal of Library Automation* 9:195-209 (September 1976).

7. Michael D. Cooper and Nancy A. DeWath, "The Effect of User Fees on the Cost of On-Line Searching in Libraries," *Journal of Library Automation* 10:304-319 (December 1977).

8. Fay M. Blake and Edith L. Perlmutter, "The Rush to User Fees: Alternative Proposals," *Library Journal* 102:2005-2008 (October 1, 1977).

9. Richard De Gennaro, "Copyright, Resource Sharing, and Hard Times," op. cit.

10. University of Toronto Library Automation System, "Collection Inquiry Reporting and Control System" (Toronto: UTLAS, 1977).

11. *OCLC Newsletter* 115:3 (April 7, 1978).

III

Bibliographic Data Base Producers

by Roger Christian

RISE OF COMPUTER-BASED BIBLIOGRAPHIC SERVICES

As anticipated when the first edition of *The Electronic Library* was published in 1975, the field of computer-based bibliographic services has undergone vigorous change and development. Then, there were slightly more than 100 machine-readable data bases available, fewer than half of them on-line. By early 1978, there were more than 360.[1]

Similarly, in mid-1975, Lockheed and System Development Corp., the two nation-wide vendors of whole collections of on-line data bases, together offered fewer than 30 data bases. In early 1978, Lockheed alone offered more than 70 and SDC provided access to at least 35. Moreover, a third major vendor — Bibliographic Retrieval Services — joined the fray in January 1977 with a fee schedule sharply lower, for high-volume users, than those of Lockheed and SDC; both promptly modified their fee structures to provide advantages to customers who are in a position to commit themselves in advance to a heavy volume of searching.

Direct costs per on-line search have dropped in the past three years from an average of about $50 to more like $25 now — and one vendor's ads even claim that we are now in "the era of the $5 search." While these figures and their underlying assumptions are not directly comparable, it is nevertheless clear that typical, direct on-line search costs have fallen dramatically during this period.

In 1975 there was only one major data communications company in the U.S., aside from AT&T itself: Tymshare. The size of this company's communications network has burgeoned from about 40,000 miles in 1975 to more than 100,000 miles in 1978. Here, too, other suppliers — notably Telenet — have entered the market with valuable services.

Among the other significant changes: Only a couple of dozen academic libraries were offering on-line services to their scholarly communities in 1975, but three years later at least 400 are doing so. Specialized magazines have been launched to serve those

Reprinted from *The Electronic Library: Bibliographic Data Bases, 1978-79* (White Plains, NY: Knowledge Industry Publications, Inc., 1978).

in the on-line industry; and an entirely new specialist — the freelance reference librarian, or "information on demand" broker — has come into being, in large part because of the advent of machine-readable data bases and the accompanying increased awareness, on the part of both researchers and business executives, of the power and value of information. All these are merely examples of the ferment in the field. Change — exciting change — is everywhere and ongoing.

Computer-based bibliographic services are a response to a combination of trends and developments that are forcing major changes in the way libraries operate. Chief among these is the ever increasing avalanche of scientific and technical literature and the steep increases in the cost of acquiring that literature. For instance, in the six years between 1970 and 1976 — a period during which consumer prices increased 47% — the average price of chemistry and physics journals increased 86%.[2] The price of technical books rose with comparable speed.

Moreover — to no one's great surprise — both the proliferation and the cost trends continue. A study sponsored by the National Science Foundation and released in 1976 indicates that the number of scientific and technical books published rocketed from 3379 in 1960 to 14,442 in 1974. In the decade of 1964-1974 alone, the number of books published *per scientist* shot up 63%, while the number of periodicals per scientist rose 19%.[3]

As to the inexorable rise in literature cost, a British study tells the story. According to the Library Management Research Unit of the University of Loughborough, the price of scholarly books in Great Britain zoomed 96% in the two and a half years ending in 1977. More specifically, the average price of a scholarly book there was $7.80 in 1974, but $15.25 in 1977. Books in the sciences were, of course, even more expensive, averaging more than $24 each in 1977.[4] Similar trends in the U.S. have forced many libraries to concentrate their funds on the increasing number of periodicals, to the neglect of books. (Indeed, the National Center for Education Statistics found that in a recent two year period, library expenditures for periodicals rose 36% while those for books inched up only 2.8%).[5]

Because of the increasing flood of new books and journals, each at painfully rising prices, the acquisition costs alone for a library trying to maintain a constant fraction of the available literature doubles every five years. Staff and operating costs are also rising every year.

Faced with lean, and in many cases shrinking, budgets, libraries have stepped up the amount and variety of resource sharing they practice. This is reflected not only in the burgeoning traffic of photocopies and interlibrary loans, but also in new cooperative networks and information centers.

Another trend favoring machine-readable bibliographic data bases is the switch to photocomposition and other computer-aided production techniques on the part of publishers of conventional abstracting and indexing (A&I) services. Finding themselves with extensive files of bibliographic data in machine-readable form (initially as a by-product of the photocomposition process), publishers discovered it was a short step to supplement their traditional product line with magnetic tapes containing much the same information for search and retrieval by computer.

Among the many other developments favoring data bases are:

• Technological progress in computer programming, storage, terminals and communications;

• The dramatic decreases in the cost of the necessary equipment;

• The massive declassification of government documents with important technical information;

• The increased acceptance by librarians of electromechanical equipment; and

• The availability of sophisticated commercial services to provide efficient, nationwide access to various individual data bases.

Behind all this has been the powerful prestige and financial support of the National Science Foundation's Office of Science Information Service (OSIS), now called the Division of Information Science and Technology (DIS&T), which is charged by law with fostering technological transfer and the dissemination of scientific and technical information. In performing this function, OSIS funded the foundation of new information services and regional centers to provide data base services on a not-for-profit basis; the conversion to computer-readable form of a number of substantial files of scientific and technical bibliographic data, and a host of other significant innovations.

As a result of this financial encouragement to the industry, there are now at least 40 abstracting and indexing services providing machine-readable bibliographic services to the scientific and technical communities, and well over 360 distinct data bases available for computer search.[6]

ADVANTAGES AND SHORTCOMINGS

What benefits do data bases offer that make their development of interest to so many people? The advantages to the researcher are that:

• A computer-aided search takes only a fraction of the time of a manual search and, according to some studies, is only half as expensive.

• A researcher can be more confident that he or she has not overlooked important citations.

• Owing to the storage density, economy, convenience and processing speeds of machine-readable media, such bibliographic data bases are normally more comprehensive, more deeply indexed and more readily updated than printed bibliographic tools.

• An interactive, machine-aided search can be expanded, narrowed or redirected instantly on the basis of results achieved.

• A skilled searcher can combine terms, concepts and strategies in ways that are extremely difficult or even impossible during a manual search.

• A single search can cover both current and past literature.

The principal shortcoming of data bases — one that is also true of conventional bibliographic tools — is that once relevant citations or abstracts have been isolated, there is still the problem of tracking down the full text of the document.

Another disadvantage is that the user fees associated with computer-aided searches may dampen enthusiasm for data base services, particularly when the fees represent full cost recovery. Prices for a search vary greatly, depending on a number of factors, the most important being the sponsoring library's ability to afford data base services and its willingness to subsidize the individual requesting the search. But the direct, identifiable costs usually fall in the vicinity of $25. Few libraries can justify absorbing such costs, plus the associated overhead, to serve one patron once. As a result, the direct, incremental cost must normally be passed along to the individual requesting the search — a notion many librarians find hard to accept.

For the most part, academic, special and a small number of public libraries currently providing data base services treat them much as they do books and periodicals: that is, they acquire the resource (by means of an on-line terminal in this case), introduce it to their patrons, help them get the most out of it, and that is all. Very few libraries acquire, maintain and process the data bases themselves — that would require a vast investment and heavy on-going expenses. Even offering access to machine-readable data bases is a clear add-on expense, and one that can significantly increase the staff's workload.

Moreover, these services typically increase the demand for more conventional library services — interlibrary loans, microfiche, photocopies, supplemental manual research, etc. The number of technical journals and printed abstracting and indexing services carried usually cannot be reduced (and may well have to be increased), and the staff members who work with the data base source and the individual patron require special skills and training. All this has been a real obstacle to public libraries with painfully limited resources.

For all these reasons, the individual libraries prefer to function as local "windows" into the data bases made available by other organizations.

PROBLEMS AND FUTURE TRENDS

In addition to a chaotic competitive situation (see below), high visible costs and the continuing flood of scientific and technical literature — which appears to be growing faster than abstracting and indexing (A&I) services — the data base industry faces a number of other challenging problems. Among them are the tendency of electronic data bases to erode the market for the underlying printed services that subsidize them, redundant coverage of the core literature, copyright complications, equipment malfunctions, inadequate market forecasting and the need for more interdisciplinary data bases.

There are indications that these current problems will be resolved. One such indication was the shift in emphasis by OSIS in 1975 when, convinced that technological progress had outdistanced the development of the underlying discipline of information science, it decided to no longer support specific information services. Instead, it and its successor, DIS&T, concentrate on developing insights into, and understanding of, the fundamentals of human communication and information exchange. DIS&T's broader objective is to contribute toward systematically improving methods of acquiring, retrieving, transferring and using information in the solution of the world's problems.

Another important trend is the continuing technological progress in the computer and communications fields, and the resulting drop in per unit storage costs, said to be falling as much as 50% per year, compounded.[7] Other trends include intensified resource sharing (coupled data bases, common formats, cooperative abstracting, networking, etc.), improved computer programs, the development of new data bases, including both specialized subsets and multidisciplinary bases and increasing numbers of regional and national data base search centers. International cooperation is already commonplace, and a worldwide network of machine-readable data base search centers seems inevitable.

STRUCTURE OF THE INDUSTRY

In very general terms, the organizations involved with machine-readable bibliographic data bases can be divided into three categories:

- Producers, who actually produce the bibliographic files and make them available on magnetic tape.

- Distributors, brokers or vendors who subscribe to the data bases of several different publishers, process them and make them available for searching either off-line or on-line, as a service to institutions or corporations that do not themselves have the facilities or desire to do so.

- Users, the individuals who have need for the information held in the data bases.

In practice, however, the lines of distinction become very blurred, and the competitive situation is confused, if not chaotic. Some of the firms providing communications services to data base processors offer data base services of their own. Some data base producers market their wares both to academic and special libraries (users) and to commercial vendors who themselves market to academic and special libraries. Conversely, some libraries and not-for-profit information centers simultaneously buy data base services from commercial vendors and compete with the same vendors for user customers.

The federal government sells, buys and distributes data bases and data base services, both to and from — and sometimes in competition with — elements of the private sector, both commercial and nonprofit. Commercial and not-for-profit organizations commonly compete for federal grants and research contracts, the proceeds or results of which may be used by any one of the parties involved to try to steal a march on any of the others. Some data base producers also offer data base services in competition with some of their own customers, and of course certain data base services compete with other products — such as print versions of the same material — offered by the same producer.

The pricing picture, complicated as it is by a variety of missions, objectives, sponsorship, subsidies, discounts and expectations, is equally confused, and subject to frequent changes. For the commercial enterprises, profits are hard to attain, and both the initial and sustained costs involved are high. Despite all this turbulence (which is common in any emerging industry), it is still useful to consider the data base industry as consisting basically of producers, distributors and users.

COMMERCIAL AND NOT-FOR-PROFIT PRODUCERS

Data base producers (and distributors) initially concentrated on serving and developing the scientific and technical market. More recently, general interest, economic and legal data bases have grown rapidly, but they are still very much in the minority. Of the 71 million data base records accessible in 1977, 29 million were scientific or technical and another 23 million were medical or biological (also scientific/technical); together they comprise 75% of the total. There were also about 7.5 million "mixed" records with some scientific or technical content, and only 11.5 million records that were totally non-scientific, nearly all of them in U.S. data bases.[8] Within the scientific-technical market, the progressively narrower specialization of researchers, and the growing need for more interdisciplinary searches seem to have divided the base producers into two rational and mutually supportive segments: the traditional professional societies and commercial companies.

Examples of the former, or nonprofit, type of data base producer include the American Chemical Society, the American Institute of Physics and its constituent societies, the American Society for Metals, Engineering Index Inc., the Institute of Textile Technology, the American Psychological Association, The Institution of Electrical Engineers, based in Britain, and the American Geological Institute. Various universities, centers and federal agencies also produce data bases.

Examples of the commercial sources of data bases are Predicasts, Inc., the Institute for Scientific Information, Data Courier, Inc., Xerox, The New York Times Co., Informatics, Dow Jones and Nexus Corp.

Neither of these lists is comprehensive, of course: the Williams and Rouse directory alone lists more than 360 machine-readable data bases, many of them the sole such product of a particular institution.[9] In fact, at least one observer has complained that machine-readable, bibliographic data bases are proliferating faster than they can be "metabolized" by the information community.

On the other hand, the road to data base publishing carries two-way traffic. A number of both print and magnetic tape services have collapsed, or been withdrawn after a short trial period. Notable examples include *Geophysical Abstracts,* the IEEE REFLECS file, *Basic Journal Abstracts* (chemistry), the CITE tapes of Engineering Index, MATRIX, and Macmillan's PANDEX and TRANSDEX data bases. (TRANSDEX is now being produced again, this time by Bell & Howell.)

Although each data base is unique in many ways, those discussed here are fairly characteristic of bibliographic data bases in general.

National Technical Information Service

The National Technical Information Service (NTIS) of the U.S. Department of Commerce publishes what is probably the best known machine-readable, bibliographic data base generated by the federal government. NTIS acts as a central clearinghouse for scientific, engineering and other technical documents generated under federally funded research contracts or activities, including those conducted by other government agencies.

Considering that the federal government sponsors perhaps two thirds of all the research conducted in this country, it is hardly surprising that the NTIS collection, which covers research from 1964 to work recently completed, is extremely broad, eclectic and uneven. Topics run the gamut from astrophysics to zymology, and there is even a smattering of material on "soft" sciences, e.g. sociology and linguistics. More than 1 million abstracts are now in the collection, which is growing at a rate of some 200 entries per day.[10]

Full-text copies of most of the cited documents are available from NTIS in either print or microfiche; the standard price is $3.50 for the first 25 or fewer pages, plus 50 cents for each additional increment of 25 pages or fewer. Thus, an article of 65 pages would cost $4.50, in either print or microfiche. (NTIS is easily the largest publisher of microfiche in the country, generating millions of them every year.) The underlying data base of citations and abstracts is available for on-line searching via interactive terminals connected to any of the nation's prime on-line retrieval systems: DIALOG, operated by Lockheed; ORBIT, operated by System Development Corp. (SDC), or the enhanced STAIRS system operated by Bibliographic Retrieval Services, Inc.

Purchased from any of these vendors, searching is paid for on an hourly basis; resulting citations and abstracts, when printed off-line, are charged for separately. Purchased directly from NTIS, however, the charge is $100 per search, including up to 100 citations and abstracts. (This fee reflects NTIS's insistence that it is legally obligated to recover all costs, although others argue that the act establishing the agency imposes no such rigid obligation.)

In addition, NTIS prepares "published searches" on selected subjects of wide interest. Conducted by the NTIS staff, these searches result in bibliographies of NTIS reports that should meet the needs of a number of researchers, who otherwise would have to conduct and pay for individual searches. NTIS currently offers more than 1000 of these published searches in dozens of subject categories. Each search is updated at least annually, and perhaps quarterly, depending upon the intensity with which new work is reported in that category. NTIS also conducts and sells "companion searches" to its own, using the files and data bases of Engineering Index (see below).

Published searches cost $28 each, and if, after examining one, a customer finds it wide of the mark, he or she may return the published search for a full refund, and may order a custom NTIS search tailored to his or her specific interests. Finally, NTIS operates the Journal Article Copying Service (JACS) which is licensed to provide reprints (from any of 16 "fill sources" — libraries and information service companies) or to copy and sell material from publishers who together put out more than 5000 learned journals. JACS also handles copyright fees for these publications, and for about 500 other journals that it copies under an agreement with the Copyright Clearance Center, through which such fees are normally channeled. Most JACS reprints cost $6.50 each, although a few are more expensive.

Engineering Index

COMPENDEX is the machine-readable counterpart of *The Engineering Index Monthly*. The Engineering Index (Ei) staff regularly monitors more than 3600 publications from all over the world — about 100 were added to the list in 1977 alone — and prepares in-depth abstracts of significant articles, professional papers, symposia and the like, embracing all disciplines of engineering. The data base now contains a total of about 650,000 citations, and is updated monthly, with about 95,000 items being added each year.

Material is arranged in the file according to a controlled list of more than 12,000 subject headings and subheads, with abundant cross references. The data base can be searched according to these subject headings or according to a dozen other categories of information, such as author, title, journal CODEN entry date, or free-language terms. Ei licenses the COMPENDEX tapes (12 per year) for $6900 (plus $300 for the tape reels), and back issues (1969 to date) are available. Licensees are charged royalties in addition.

Ei differentiates between not-for-profit customers, such as libraries, and commercial operations that resell the material in COMPENDEX. The latter must pay a surcharge of $500 per year, in addition to the normal royalty arrangement. Late in 1977 Ei authorized NTIS to publish searches it conducts of the Ei data bases as well as joint searches of Ei and NTIS bases. Ei does not supply the search and retrieval software necessary to utilize its data base, and does not supply full-text copies of the abstracted material.

Chemical Abstracts

Chemical Abstracts Service (CAS) monitors some 14,000 scientific and technical periodicals from at least 150 countries, as well as pertinent books, reports, dissertations, conference proceedings and the like. To capture important peripheral work, CAS includes in its purview journals and papers from such fields as metallurgy, biology and the earth sciences. The thrust of this activity is well stated in a CAS publication:

> To be selected for coverage in [*Chemical Abstracts*], a paper or patent must meet two criteria: it must be relevant to chemistry or chemical engineering, and it must contain new information. CAS defines [these] broadly to include all studies of elemental sub-atomic particles, elements, compounds, and other substances, their occurrence, composition, preparation, structure and properties, their reactions and changes of state and the laws that govern these, and those procedures usually classed as unit operations and unit processes and the design and construction of apparatus for them.[11]

Chemical Abstracts Condensates (CA Con) is the machine-readable version of *Chemical Abstracts,* a printed bibliographic tool that has been published by CAS since 1907. The data base of some 2.5 million citations is updated weekly. CAS expects to add more than 400,000 new abstracts to the base during 1978.

CAS is phasing out its former leasing arrangements and converting customers of all its data bases to licensees. Chemical Abstracts Condensates is now offered for $4000 per year, plus a "handling fee," which replaces the former add-on charges for such ancillary costs as postage, handling and the reels of magnetic tape that record the data base contents in machine-readable form. The handling charge for CA Con to a U.S. user is $347 per year. A Canadian user pays $749 per year, and users elsewhere are charged a handling fee of $1056 per year.

CAS does not provide supporting computer software nor copies to the cited publications. Commercial vendors or information centers must also pay a user fee of four cents per citation retrieved when searching the CAS tapes.

CAS also publishes 12 other machine-readable, bibliographic data bases. They are:

• Food and Agricultural Chemistry, issued biweekly, for an annual fee of $1600 plus a U.S. handling fee of $176.

• Chemical Industry Notes, updated weekly, for $2500 per year plus a U.S. handling charge of $347.

• Energy, updated every two weeks, for $2400 per year and a handling fee of $176 to U.S., $376 to Canadian users.

• Chemical-Biological Activities, issued biweekly, for $2900 per year plus a handling charge of $176 to U.S. users.

• Polymer Science & Technology, issued biweekly, for $2850 per year plus a U.S. handling charge of $176.

• Chemical Titles, a biweekly, at $1300 per year plus a domestic handling charge of $176.

• Materials, issued biweekly, for $4800 plus a handling fee to U.S. subscribers of $176.

• Patent Concordance, a semiannual, for $400 per year plus a $17 handling charge in the U.S.

• CAS Source Index (CASSI), updated quarterly, for a first-year fee of $2500 plus a $115 handling charge, and a subsequent annual fee of $1250 plus an annual handling charge of $29 in the U.S.

• Ecology and Environment, issued biweekly, for $2500 a year plus $176 handling fee.

• CASIA (CA Subject Index Alert), updated biweekly, for an annual fee of $4000 plus a U.S. handling charge of $176 per year. CASIA is a controlled-language derivative of *Chemical Abstracts.*

• CASEARCH, the newest CAS data base, at $8000 per year plus an annual domestic handling fee of $347. CASEARCH is a combination of CASIA and CA Con and, like them, is updated biweekly.

Machine-readable back files are available at the same price as the current file in all cases.

CASSI is especially noteworthy, as it affords users a machine-readable guide to the physical location of full-text copies of some 45,000 periodicals, conference proceedings and other documents that have been abstracted by CAS. Roughly 400 libraries in various parts of the world are mentioned, as well as sales agents and publishers from whom material can be obtained. The Source Index also indicates whether the library lends original journals or provides photocopies.

INSPEC

INSPEC (International Information Service for the Physics and Engineering Communities) is a department of The Institution of Electrical Engineers. This London-based organization publishes abstract journals and compiles several machine-readable, bibliographic data bases. The largest, ironically, deals not with electronic technology, but with physics.

Physics Abstracts is updated twice a month, while the other data bases, Electrical & Electronics Abstracts and Computer & Control Abstracts — both published jointly with the Institute of Electrical and Electronic Engineers of the U.S. — are issued monthly. These files, dubbed A, B and C, respectively, contain citations and extensive abstracts. They are made available under the INSPEC I name, either separately or as a package that essentially combines all three into a single data base.

The Physics (A) file leases for $5250 per year, the Electrical & Electronic (B) file for $4900 per year, and the Computer and Control (C) file for $3900 per year. In each case, subscribers are also charged a fee of $740 which covers the cost of the magnetic tape reels, postage and handling. Subscribers interested in all three INSPEC I files may lease them as a package for $7000 per year, plus a single handling fee of $740.

INSPEC II is a related data base, containing only the title, author and bibliographic references of each entry in the main files, but omitting the abstracts and indexes. INSPEC II, which covers all three files, costs $5250 per year plus the $740 fee.

As of early 1978, the INSPEC data bases contained more than a million entries, and during 1978 INSPEC expects to add a total of more than 160,000 new items; roughly in the ratio of eight items for the physics file to 3.5 items in the electrical and electronics file to two items in the computer and control file. Approximately 130,000 of these entries will represent articles drawn from more than 2300 journals; some 25,000 will describe conference papers; perhaps 1500 items will be drawn from theses, research reports, dissertations and the like, and some 300 will report new scholarly books.

Lockheed, SDC and BRS in the U.S., CAN/OLE in Canada, and ESA Frascati in Europe are licensed to provide on-line searches of the INSPEC data bases. In addition, INSPEC itself offers SDI services to patrons via the London headquarters, and the IEE library provides on-line searches for a fee. Obtaining full-text copies of any cited publications of particular interest is the responsibility of the individual searcher.

Institute for Scientific Information

The gap between finding the citation of a useful or intriguing paper and finding a copy of the paper itself is characteristic of both manual and computer-based bibliographic searches, of course. The gap can widen into a chasm when the citation refers to one of the many obscure, foreign and very narrowly specialized journals that are anything but widely available. While NTIS offers a partial solution for its particular clientele, its delivery of hard-copy documents is notoriously slow.

One effective solution is that of the Institute for Scientific Information. ISI has for some years been the leading commercial publisher of scientific and technical bibliographic information, generating a series of citation and contents indexes and related bibliographic services. One key to its success is the Original Article Tear Sheet (OATS) service, which provides either actual tear sheets or photocopies of articles cited in the data base. The Institute provided more than 100,000 of these during 1977.[12]

ISI subscribes to several thousand "core" scientific and technical journals and abstract journals, and indexes their entire contents, except for such incidental elements as advertising. When a researcher finds an ISI citation of interest, ISI can provide a full-text copy of the underlying document, getting the OATS copy in the mail the day the order arrives. ISI pays a royalty to the copyright owner of any article it photocopies. Charges for the OATS service average about $3.50 domestic ($4.50 foreign) for a typical 10-page article.

ISI has extended this concept to the electronic arena. Patrons who search ISI data bases on-line can command the computer to print or display the list of ISI citations at the user's terminal. When he or she has made the selection, the searcher can place a hard-copy order electronically, and the computer records it. Each night, ISI remotely commands the computer to print out the contents of these "electronic mailboxes," and gets the ordered OATS copies into the next day's mail. (The National Technical Information Service and the Educational Resources Information Center have similar arrangements to expedite sales and delivery of their myriad publications.)

That OATS is a valuable time-saver is evidenced by the increasing number of corporations that are switching to the OATS service as their primary source of full-text copies. Rather than have researchers or librarians spend time trying to find cited materials in the company or cooperating libraries and then photocopy them, these companies order OATS copies as a routine matter. Substantial customers, such as IBM's Technical Information Retrieval Center, acquire hundreds of OATS documents every week and find the service superior in terms of delivery time and economics to ferreting out full-text copies on their own.

ISI's machine-readable data bases are citation, as contrasted with A&I, files. Two of the bases, SCISEARCH and SOCIAL SCISEARCH, are updated weekly on magnetic tapes (although the commercial vendors who make these bases available on-line update the on-line bases monthly). SCISEARCH is a large data base (over 470,000 items added in 1977) that indexes every article appearing in about 3700 core publications in 26 fields, including biochemistry, botany, dental and drug research, genetics, virology, pharmacology and surgery. The taped source data and the citation data each lease for $10,000 per year, and both are available for $20,000 per year (a complete data base). This data base is made available on-line by Lockheed Corp.

ISI's SOCIAL SCISEARCH is a companion data base that alerts users to about 120,000 articles each year. These citations are drawn from more than 1500 journals covering such subjects as anthropology, geography, psychiatry, political science, sociology, history and urban planning. In tape format, the total data base leases for $10,000 per year, with the source and the citation tapes available separately for $5000 each per year. Supplemental royalties are imposed on commercial subscribers under certain circumstances. Lockheed currently makes the SOCIAL SCISEARCH data base available for on-line searching, and both BRS and SDC have it under consideration.

The Index Chemicus Registry System is another ISI data base available on magnetic tape, although it is not available on-line. Index Chemicus concentrates on articles that report new chemical compounds or reactions — about 12,000 articles, discussing perhaps 153,000 new compounds, per year. It can be searched by molecular formula, use profiles and Wiswesser Line Notation (for chemical structures), among other elements. The data base is updated monthly and leases for $9500 per year, with back files also available for $9500 per year.

New York Times Information Bank

The New York Times Information Bank (NYTIB) takes an entirely different approach to the problem of helping its customers obtain full-text copies of material abstracted in the data base. More than half of the NYTIB entries are drawn from *The New York Times* itself, and full-text versions of these can be obtained on microfiche. Users are on their own when it comes to tracking down copies of articles abstracted from the 70 other publications monitored by the NYTIB staff. These publications are widely available, however, since they are primarily major general and business magazines and newspapers ranging from *Advertising Age* to *Women's Wear Daily,* plus a few outstanding British papers.

The NYTIB data base already totals well over 1.5 million items, and new abstracts are added at a rate of some 20,000 per month, largely from *The New York Times* itself and from the four "top priority" outside publications — *Business Week, The Los Angeles Times, The Wall Street Journal* and *The Washington Post.* Most articles are abstracted and in the data base within four days of their publication. (Summaries of major *Times* stories go into the computer the day they appear.) The data base can be accessed either directly, via the telephone system, or via the Telenet communications network, which serves a growing number of cities in the U.S. and Canada.

NYTIB has waged a long and convoluted struggle with the problem of determining the proper fee structure. A succession of fee arrangements has been announced and then superseded. As of March 1, 1978, however, the access fee for subscribers was $90 per hour, plus 30 cents per "deferred print" abstract, plus mailing charges. Terminals, modems, printers, training, communications costs, hardware maintenance, microfiche and fiche equipment are all additional.

The number of subscribers to NYTIB is growing at a healthy rate, from 14 in 1973 to upwards of 600 in the first quarter of 1978. Most of the NYTIB subscribers are businesses and government agencies, but a substantial number are public libraries that accommodate individuals wanting to make a one-time search of the information bank. However, NYTIB itself also "retails" access to the data base to walk-in trade. Individual customers pay a fee of $50 per search, plus $1.00 per retrieved item (citation and abstract). Individuals can also browse around in NYTIB by proxy, simply by ordering a search through one of the various NYTIB subscribers who provide commercial searches — Editec in Chicago, Information Clearing House in New York City and a number of others. NYTIB's European customers are accommodated via the Telenet packet-switching telecommunications network.

The New York Times Co. has made a multi-million dollar investment in NYTIB, which has produced substantial losses each year. It did so again in 1977, producing a loss of $900,000.[13] This is a clear demonstration of the fact that launching a machine-readable data base is an expensive undertaking, and one that requires a major long-term commitment and sustained support.

The New York Times Information Services, Inc., which runs NYTIB, also makes available a series of major collections of related NYTIB abstracts on selected topics. The first of these, on "The Changing Character of Work," contains some 1500 NYTIB abstracts, the latest dated about a week prior to publication. The two-volume, looseleaf set of 13 chapters costs $250. The second effort is a set of three volumes devoted to foreign in-

```
  2 OF    2 NYT/JNL 1972- 2- 7    :   25: 1 4/WGT 17/LIN
  38-72- 1                   PHO/ILS       34428/IDN
United Farm Workers Organizing Com, farm labor orgn, has sent
reprs to Fla's citrus belt in move designed to improve working
conditions for indigent and migrant field hands; during last 6
mos, group of reprs led by M Chavez, cousin of C Chavez, has
led campaign to spur workers' active participation in movement
which seeks to establish bargaining machinery for field hands;
Chavez contends private talks with citrus producers have been
fruitful, and that accord is imminent with major producer;
union's Fla campaign held major test of its ability to appeal
to farm laborers outside Mex-Amer rank-and-file it has
successfully organized in Calif, since it must demonstrate that
it can win support from black workers who constitute
approximately 55% of labor force in state's citrus indus;
obstacles to organizing farm labor in Fla are held formidable,
since regional antipathy of growers to labor unions is
reinforced by tradition and mkt squeeze on profits; Chavez
illus with Fla farm workers
                  *** END OF DISPLAY ***
```

Suppose you have an interest in the field of agricultural labor and wish to scan a wide variety of items on that subject. To instruct the Information Bank to retrieve them for you, you would type:
Agriculture and **Labor**

This would bring out a substantial amount of material—news stories, feature articles, editorials, letters, etc.—unrestricted by date, type of material or the journal in which it appeared. Much of this material, by the nature of the subject, will involve migratory agricultural labor.

To expand the scope of the search to include all types of migratory labor, you would replace agriculture and labor with the single term:
Migratory Labor

Then, to further expand the search and look at the whole, broad topic of labor, you would key in only that single word:
Labor

Now, going back to the original search on "agriculture and labor," you can narrow its scope by pro-gressively adding descriptors and linking them by means of the "and," 'or" or "not" commands. You can also substitute descriptors that are intrinsically more specific. For example:
Labor and **Citrus** and **California** or **Texas**

Thus, you would retrieve only material dealing with labor activity in the citrus groves of these two states.

To be even more specific, you might frame the search this way:
United Farm Workers and **Citrus** not **California** or **Texas** or **Arizona**

By focusing on a single union and purposely excluding major western citrus-growing states, you would find out about the Farm Worker's organizing activities in other states, notably Florida (but not confined to Florida).

Finally, to be extremely precise, you might ask the computer for a search on:
Manuel Chavez and **Florida** and **Citrus** and **Coca Cola Company**
A search this precise would bring you only abstracts relating to the negotiations between Cesar Chavez's cousin, Manuel, and Coca Cola. Another method of refinement is possible with the use of modifiers. For example, if you wanted to view a photograph of Chavez's organizers or citrus workers, you would type in the modifier, "PHO" plus the descriptors for Chavez and Citrus and you would receive the abstract shown at right and any others that were accompanied by photos.

To see the photos, you go to your own New York Times Information Bank microfiche files or to roll microfilm files of The Times.

HOW A SEARCH is broadened or narrowed using the New York Times Information Bank (Copyright vestment opportunities and industrial development in the Middle East, the Far East and Latin America. The set costs $750, but the individual studies are also available at $300 each. An interested customer could not save money by simply rerunning the underlying searches, because the printed compendia are carefully organized and "highly edited" before they are printed.

Dow Jones News Retrieval Service

The fact that two of the outside publications abstracted by NYTIB – *Barron's* and *The Wall Street Journal* – are Dow Jones properties is especially significant in light of the fact that Dow Jones is itself a publisher of machine-readable data bases. Initially called NEWS/RECALL, the data base and its associated on-line access service was a joint venture of Dow Jones and Bunker Ramo, a company well established as a source of instant stock market quotations. Subscribers to the Bunker Ramo stock service could (and can) call up NEWS/RECALL on the same terminal. In 1977, however, Dow Jones introduced another service, called NEWS RETRIEVAL SERVICE (NRS), which affords access to the data base directly to any interested party, via the Tymshare network.

Although Dow Jones recently added conventional stock market quotations to the data base, the heart of NRS consists of material that has appeared in *Barron's, The Wall Street Journal* and on the Dow Jones News Service ("broad tape"). Subscribers to NRS need not concern themselves with tracking down the full text of at least the shorter articles cited; they can call up the full text right on their terminals. Users first scan the article headlines on their terminals, then call up either the full text or long (up to 1000 words), comprehensive abstracts of the original article. Access fee is $50 per month plus $40 per connect hour, which *includes* the Tymnet charge.

Subscribers to NRS receive extremely current information – literally up-to-the-minute – but they also have ready access to machine-readable back files covering material that has appeared in the preceding 90 days, any of which can be called up on the terminal just like current entries. Still older material can be had on microfiche from Dow Jones Microfiche Services. To protect its position as the prime source of instant business information, Dow Jones requires the New York Times Information Bank not to put Dow Jones material on-line until 30 days after it is first published. In May 1978, there were more than 150 subscribers to NRS and new ones were being signed up at the rate of almost one per day.

Meanwhile, Bunker Ramo continues to offer the Dow Jones data base, under the name NEWS/RECALL, to brokerage houses (which constitute about 98% of present subscribers), banks and other customers in the financial community. Bunker Ramo offers its customers access to NEWS/RECALL at the 1200 baud (120 characters/minute) speed of their CRT stock quotation terminals. (Top speed of NRS is 300 baud.) Early in 1978, Bunker Ramo was serving some 200 locations which together had about 3000 terminals, and the company expects "vigorous growth" in the number of its customers.[14]

There are three versions of NEWS/RECALL. RECALL I provides subscribers with up-to-the-minute Dow Jones news along with material that appeared in Dow Jones papers during the previous several days. RECALL II consists of Dow Jones back files going 90 days into the past, and RECALL III is a combination of the other two versions. Bunker Ramo specialists are also prepared to provide a subscriber with on-line access to his own corporate data center, a communications system linking terminals at scattered company locations, and the capability of utilizing other machine-readable data bases.

Legal Data Bases

Several data bases providing legal citations and court decisions are among the most rapidly growing of data base applications. The efficiency of the computer in this type of search is very attractive compared to the drudgery and expense of having law clerks perform the searches manually.

The leading supplier of legal research data bases is Mead Data Central, a division of Mead Corp. The development of its data base and associated hardware involved an estimated $20 million investment, but a recent report estimates that despite its high price tag for the user, LEXIS has not made money for its producer.[15]

LEXIS includes the full text storage and citation of the U.S. Code and all U.S. court decisions; regulations and rulings of most major regulatory agencies, such as the IRS, FTC and SEC; and appeals court decisions of many major states. Over time, the laws of all the states are being added.

The National Institute of Law Enforcement and Criminal Justice of the U.S. Justice Department produces a law enforcement and criminal justice data base called NCJRS (National Criminal Justice Reference System). Aspen Systems Corp. produces and distributes System 50 — State Statute File, a base of full-text statutes for all 50 states. West Publishing Co., an old-line legal publisher, is another major supplier of legal data bases.

Overall, legal data bases are utilized by several hundred subscribers, but the high cost has restricted use to the larger law firms and company legal departments. Law firms and legal research operations spent about $11 million on electronic data bases in 1977, and the amount is increasing about 20% annually.[16]

SIMILARITIES AMONG PRODUCERS

This brief sampling of the wares and *modus operandi* of representative data base producers indicates not only the scope and variations to be encountered, but also the fundamental similarities among them. There are both not-for-profit and profit-seeking organizations actively involved in generating and marketing machine-readable, bibliographic data bases.

Content tends to be objective, discipline-oriented material drawn from printed documents — periodicals, monographs, conference proceedings, dissertations, reports of government and foundation-sponsored research, and the like. This material is indexed and usually abstracted, then "captured" in machine-readable form — typically on magnetic tape — and made available to others. Usually, the data base producer does not provide the search and retrieval software required to process the tapes. For the most part, users are on their own when it comes to obtaining full-text copies of cited articles of particular interest.

Most data base producers offer to license or lease organizations interested in using (or selling access to) their data bases. Some use a combination of compensation schemes. For instance, the Engineering Index Inc. (Ei) makes magnetic tape versions of its Computerized Engineering Index (COMPENDEX) available on either a lease or a license arrangement. Most COMPENDEX tape users choose to be lessees — primarily corporations, government organizations and specialized institutions — who use the tapes entirely in-house for their own purposes. Others have elected instead to become licensees, so that they are free to repackage the contents of the tapes and make the material available to anyone for a fee. Among the typical licensees are Lockheed, SDC, the New England Research Application Center and the Canada Institute for Scientific and Technical Information.

Data base producers may or may not require or pressure those using their machine-readable data bases to subscribe as well to the associated printed material, or to acquire from the data base publisher full-text copies of the pertinent cited documents. The tape reels themselves, on which the data are recorded, are characteristically charged for separately. Some producers distribute their data bases directly to interested organizations, but an increasing number of them are making the bases available through one or more of the major commercial vendors. Some continue to use both modes of distribution simultaneously.

FOOTNOTES

1. Martha Williams, "Data Base and Online Statistics," *Bulletin of the American Society for Information Science,* December 1977.

2. *Bowker Annual of Library and Book Trade Information* 1971 and 1977 (New York: R.R. Bowker Co.).

3. Donald King, "Statistical Indicators of Scientific and Technical Communications, 1960-1980," National Technical Information Service, 1976.

4. *Chronicle of Higher Education,* September 19, 1977, p. 2.

5. *Advanced Technology/Libraries,* November 1976.

6. Martha E. Williams and Sandra Rouse, "Computer-Readable Bibliographic Data Bases" (Washington, D.C.: American Society for Information Science, October 1976; updated April 1977 and April 1978).

7. Davis McCarn, "Trends in Information," *Information Utilities,* American Society for Information Science, 1974.

8. Martha Williams, "Data Base and Online Statistics," op cit.

9. Williams and Rouse, "Computer-Readable Bibliographic Data Bases," op cit.

10. Personal communication, May 1978.

11. "CAS Today," Chemical Abstract Service, 1974.

12. "Information Center Profile, Institute for Scientific Information," *Information Hotline,* March 1977.

13. *Annual Report,* New York Times Co. (New York, 1977), p. 5.

14. Personal communication, May 17, 1978.

15. *The Computerized Data Base Market* (New York: Frost & Sullivan, 1977).

16. Ibid.

IV
Bibliographic Data Base Distributors

by Roger Christian

The dramatic upsurge in use of machine-readable data bases since the early 1970s is in large measure due to the development of intermediaries for distributing the information contained in those data bases. Before discussing these intermediaries, it is necessary, for perspective, to review the development of the communications links for digital traffic upon which they depend. That done, one can go on to examine the on-line commercial distributors, the information centers performing off-line searches, the "third-tier retailers" and the somewhat chaotic competitive situation among all these participants.

MODERN COMMUNICATIONS LINKS

Modern communications links are at the heart of the astonishing reductions in the cost of moving machine-readable data from one point to another. Until 1970, all communications between a computer facility and remote users had to be conducted over the telephone network, which — having been designed for voice (one form of analog) rather than data (one form of digital) communications, and being committed to technologies 30 to 50 years old — leaves much to be desired. The only "options" available were leased-line linkage or dial-up arrangements, either of which left one at the tender mercies of the telephone system.

Two approaches to the problem of improving data communications were, and are, being taken. The first is to adapt the existing telephone plant to better accommodate data traffic, and the second is to augment the phone system with specialized communications networks designed and operated specifically for digital data transmission.

With respect to the former, AT&T has developed and installed various specialized pieces of equipment, phone lines "conditioned" to reduce their noise and interference, error-detection procedures, new pricing policies and the like to make the telephone system more attractive for computer communications. Coupled with the sophisticated facilities, software (programs) and operating procedures provided by companies offering computer services for hire, these phone system innovations have greatly improved matters.

Reprinted from *The Electronic Library: Bibliographic Data Bases, 1978-79* (White Plains, NY: Knowledge Industry Publications, Inc., 1978).

Perhaps the prime example of developments along this line is Tymshare, Inc., a commercial service company that serves principal cities throughout the U.S. and Canada and, via trans-Atlantic cable, most of Europe and Scandinavia. The company's Tymnet is a distributed network; that is, data go directly from point to point, without having to be routed through a central computer. Approximately 180 computers, including what Tymshare calls "foreign" installations — those belonging to clients, such as the National Library of Medicine — are connected to the network, and seven or eight more are added every month.

Tymnet, which has been operating since 1970, was the prototype of three or four "value-added networks" that were once expected to blanket the country. (These networks either establish their own communication links or lease communication lines from the established telephone and telegraph companies and "dedicate" them to providing data transmission services on a commercial basis.) The Tymnet web already includes more than 100,000 miles of such leased lines. The number of U.S. and Canadian cities from which data bases anywhere can be reached with a local phone call has grown from 60 in 1975 to 135 in 1978.

Tymnet's cost impact has been dramatic, partly because users have only to dial a local number (or the number of the nearest input "node," or computer location) in order to contact any computer or data base available on the entire network. Moreover, once connected to the system, a user can switch quickly from one service or data base to another — a kind of electronic browsing. Tymnet charges, which were about $10 per hour in 1975, have since fallen to roughly $4.50 per hour, as compared with $30 per hour for direct distance dialing. When the NLM's MEDLINE computers were connected to Tymnet, user dial-up costs plunged from $24 per hour to only $5 per hour, and have since declined further.

Meanwhile, in a policy reversal in 1971, the Federal Communications Commission began deliberately encouraging the development of alternatives to the telephone/telegraph facilities for the distribution of digital data. For some years, companies with heavy data traffic — railroads, pipeline operators, airlines, etc. — have operated private communications systems to avoid the high cost, error rate, noise levels and connection delays associated with the phone system.

These private systems commonly make use of such space age technologies as microwave radio transmission, time-division multiplexing, computer-controlled circuit switching, and automatic "store and forward" message switching — technologies proven by the Advanced Research Projects Agency and by years of successful utilization for communication and control in the space program. With FCC licensing of such companies as Microwave Communications Inc., Datran and others, work got underway on installing the initial links of entirely new transmission networks intended ultimately to span the country, bringing the vastly improved speeds, accuracy, costs and reliability of such technologies to the nation at large. Some important links of these specialized data carriers are now in operation, and are demonstrating great promise.

In 1970, Datran's vice president of administration estimated that when the system planned by his company was fully operational, customers using microwave data transmission would enjoy communications rates about half of those then being charged by "Ma Bell" for comparable service. Several years later one of the hopeful new "value-added networks," Telenet, posted prices about one-fourth as high as those of Tymshare itself. A meaningful plunge in communication costs seemed assured.

To no one's surprise, AT&T, finally responding to the enormous market that was developing for digital data transmission, fought back with great vigor, vast resources and not a little imagination. Battered by such AT&T ploys as "hi-lo" (density route) tariffs, Digital Data Service, data-under-voice technology, and the accommodation of customer-owned interfacing equipment, tiny Datran was soon on the ropes, despite a game and determined battle. The knock-out blow was landed not by the Bell System but by the economy of the mid-1970s, and it took the form of tight money. Datran's ambitious scheme was enormously expensive — close to $100 million was invested in the first few legs of what was to become a nationwide system. Moreover, usable portions of the physical network had to be in place before any revenue could flow, so Datran's cash flow was virtually all in one direction — out. Consequently, when money got tight throughout the economy and the big lenders refused to lend more, it was all over. Datran initiated bankruptcy proceedings in 1976.

Fortunately for users, MCI and Telenet, a "packet switching" network, survived, and their low fees for telecommunications service have forced AT&T to develop its own packet switching service. (Packet switching networks accommodate messages of a fixed maximum length — the packet size. Longer messages must be broken into packets before they can be sent. Such networks use phone lines to provide very fast, efficient and reliable service, i.e., they add value to the service they buy from the phone company and sell to their customers.) Moreover, four other independent entities, RCA, Western Union, American Satellite Corp. and Satellite Business Systems (SBS), have jumped into the fray. All four firms hope to prosper by using communications satellites instead of noisy land lines to serve their customers. The RCA and Western Electric systems are already in operation. Unless the telephone companies succeed in defeating, or at least encysting, these upstarts (and SBS is backed by Comsat, Aetna Insurance and IBM), the fast drop in data communications cost inaugurated by Tymshare seems likely to continue for a while.

The existence of Tymshare's distributed, nationwide network dedicated to data transmission had an important second contribution to make, quite apart from slashing data communication costs. The network was seized upon as a data vehicle by two commercial companies — Lockheed and System Development Corp. — which were determined to meet the pivotal need for a more efficient and more effective way to market machine-readable data bases. (The third such firm, Bibliographic Retrieval Services [BRS], which was launched several years later, chose Telenet as its only communications link.)

Each of these companies brought to bear on the problem substantial systems expertise, computer facilities, marketing experience and general economies of scale. Through licensing, leasing and other arrangements, each has acquired a number of data bases and makes them available on a fee basis to customers all over the country. Each user is therefore able to "go shopping," as it were, for the information needed, in a central "store" that inventories a selection of data bases produced by various organizations, none of which could independently make its wares known or available to so large and dispersed a market.

THE MAJOR DISTRIBUTORS

Prior to 1977, when BRS began operations, there were only two major commercial vendors of machine-readable, bibliographic data bases in the on-line mode: System Development Corp. (SDC) and Lockheed Information Systems (LIS), both based in California. Both serve their customers via either the Tymnet or the Telenet communication system. Accordingly, a subscriber anywhere in the country needs only a telephone, an acoustic coupler and a terminal to access any of the various data banks maintained by the three major distributors.

Lockheed Information Systems

Lockheed makes its stable of data bases available to subscribers via both the Tymshare and the Telenet communication networks, each net being serviced by a separate LIS computer. Lockheed has had an interactive command language for information retrieval since the mid-1960s. It started working with files from the National Aeronautics and Space Administration in 1966, then handled the Atomic Energy Commission's Nuclear Science Abstracts in 1969-70. Called DIALOG, the Lockheed system today is used to provide customers with on-line access to about 70 different data bases (additional offerings are announced from time to time). Subjects covered include engineering, geology, education, electronics, agriculture, physics, chemistry, psychology, social sciences, computers and control, business, patents, federally sponsored research, vocational and technical instruction, management, exceptional children, and many more. Both retrospective and current awareness searches are provided.

SDC Search Service

System Development Corp., which receives most of its revenues from Defense Department contracts, got an early start in information retrieval when it provided access to the MEDLARS data base in 1969-70 and to the ERIC (Educational Resources Information Center) data base in 1971, both under the auspices of the Department of Health, Education & Welfare. Today SDC's Search Service provides on-line access to at least 35 distinct data bases and, like its rival, Lockheed, the company regularly announces the addition of one or more new ones. All are searched via a proprietary computer retrieval system called ORBIT. A number of the data bases SDC currently offers are also in Lockheed's repertoire, but SDC offers several important ones exclusively. Among them are files on pollution, telecommunications, geosciences, life sciences, ecology and petroleum, as well as the extensive files in the LIBCON file prepared by Information Dynamics Corp.

Bibliographic Retrieval Services

Bibliographic Retrieval Services, based in Scotia, NY, is the newest on-line vendor of multiple data bases, having opened for business in January 1977. The company firmly

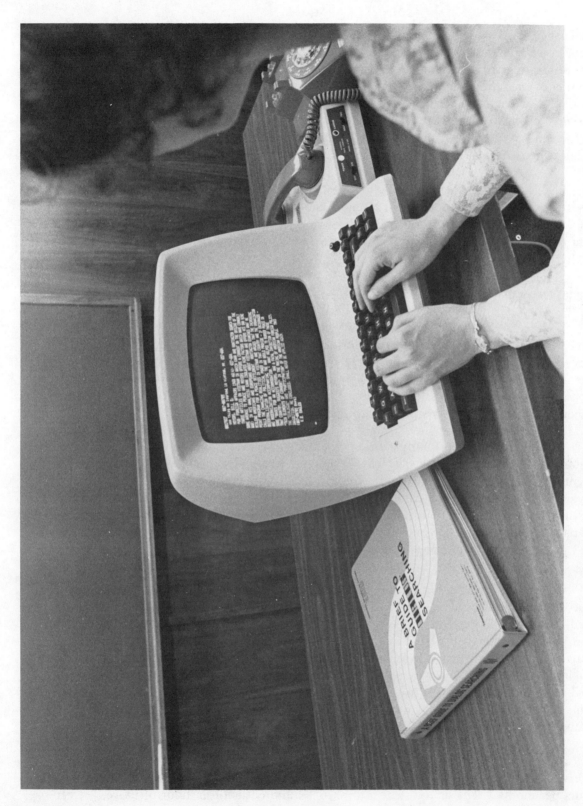

USING A VDT for on-line searching. (Courtesy Lockheed Information Systems.)

established itself by announcing a fee structure that could slash the search costs of heavy users by as much as 60%, and by launching an intensive series of regional training and education programs for users. (The firm trained about 600 searchers during its first six months of operation.) Initially, BRS confined itself to offering on-line access to the hand-ful of data bases most popular with academic libraries, covering agriculture, biology, business, chemistry, computer science, management education, engineering, medicine, physics and psychology, among others. An advisory committee of customers helps BRS decide when and which additional data bases should be added.

Each of these characteristics — low cost, frequent local training sessions, and data bases chosen to appeal to scholars, teachers and academic researchers — are especially attractive to academic institutions, which quickly became BRS's forte. The MEDLARS data base alone, which no other distributor offers, attracted some 50 medical institutions as charter members.

User Charges and Service

User fee schedules today are on the whole lower but far more complex than they were before BRS entered the market. Formerly, both Lockheed and the SDC Search Service charged patrons a flat hourly rate for each data base they accessed, regardless of the customer's annual search volume. Patrons who did not use the service in any given month did not pay for it. BRS introduced the notion of precommitted use and volume discounts, and the industry's pricing structure changed in response.

BRS charges a given hourly rate, on a sliding scale depending on monthly search volume, irrespective of which data base or bases a customer uses. The BRS hourly fee begins at $25 and drops in increments to $13. Added to this is a pro rata share of the royalties BRS must pay the data base. The medical data base MEDLARS is an exception, costing $10 per connect hour regardless of usage. BRS also offers large volume customers prepaid annual subscriptions at rates from $1500 to $6000, and has a group member plan that provides service to groups or consortia at significant discounts.

Lockheed's fee structure is also based on computer connect time, i.e., the length of time during which the user's terminal is in communication with the computer. At Lock-heed, however, this cost can range anywhere from $35 to $150 an hour, depending on the data base being searched. (Most searches require no more than 10 to 15 minutes of actual connect time.) From these basic fees, Lockheed, too, offers various discounts, ranging from $5 to $15 per connect hour, as the customer's volume of usage increases. Lockheed's connect-time fee structure includes three distinct modes — a standard service plan, a minimum-guarantee plan and a group discount plan — each with its own quantity discounts.

SDC Search Service, too, has a different rate structure for each of the data bases it offers, but a single quantity-discount scheme applies to all of them, based on "billable hours per month." The discounts, based on one-hundredths of an hour of usage, get pro-gressively more attractive as access time increases.

Further complicating things is the fact that both Lockheed and SDC incorporate into their fees the royalties levied by certain data base publishers, whereas BRS charges for them separately. Here, too, compensation plans vary widely, from royalties based on connect time to a percentage of gross on-line revenues, to upfront payments for the use of the data base tapes — with or without a fee per citation retrieved — and even including a royalty based on a percentage of the individual user's connect-hour rate. Normally, these major vendors also invoice their customers for Tymnet and Telenet (which also have volume discounts) communication charges. If the networks carry out their contemplated plan to market their services directly, it could introduce another element of turbulence into the cost picture.

To this maze of fees and discounts must be added two more complexities. The first is the cost — usually about 10 cents per item — of getting a hard-copy printout of the pertinent citations and their accompanying abstracts. The second is the cost of communications between the vendor's computer facility and the user's terminal. Here again, there is currently a certain untidiness that complicates comparisons between the true cost of using one vendor and that of another. Lockheed charges its customers $5 per hour for Telenet communications and $8 per hour for Tymnet; SDC charges $8 per hour for either one; and BRS, which is accessible only via Telenet, charges either $3, $4 or $6.40 per hour, depending on the traffic density and communication speed of the "node" the user has chosen.

Notice too that none of this discussion of fees touches upon the end user's subsequent cost (and perhaps frustration) of tracking down and acquiring full-text copies of the most promising cited material.

Contributions of Distributors

By acquiring magnetic tape recordings of the bibliographic data bases of a number of different publishers, and placing the data in random-access memory, vendors perform a valuable service, quite aside from their "shopping center" function. With the data base on disks or in core memory, the system can access any particular citation or reference directly and instantly, instead of serially examining every record in the data base until a particular entry is found, as is necessary when searching a reel of tape.

More important, the vendors make available the search and retrieval software, or programming, with which to make use of the data base. On-line, interactive searching naturally requires far more sophisticated software than off-line, serial searching. The vendors also serve an important editing and quality control function, eliminating nonessential elements from the data base.

Finally, of course, the major vendors make key marketing and economic contributions. By making an entire collection of disparate data bases centrally and conveniently available to potential users all over the country, the vendors are able to market and distribute data base services more efficiently and more economically than individual publishers could. Subscribing organizations gain access to many data bases without heavy initial investment, and researchers can successively examine several promising collections from a single terminal, switching from one to another at will. By monitoring the volume and nature of usage that each data base attracts, the vendors also gain important insights into the relative value of existing data base services and the likely demand for new ones.

A Burgeoning Market

There seems to be little doubt that the advent of multiple data base services by commercial vendors has had a significant impact on the popularity of machine-readable bibliographic searches. The convenience, speed, assured comprehensiveness and versatility of computer-aided literature searches have been appreciated from the outset by many people who could not afford to take advantage of them. Now, because of more attractive pricing and other benefits offered by the vendors, far more researchers can afford, and are willing to try, these services.

One measure of this burgeoning popularity is the well-informed estimates by Martha Williams of the University of Illinois that there were some 300,000 on-line retrospective data base searches conducted in 1973, perhaps 700,000 in 1974, more than 1 million in 1975, about 1.2 million in 1976, and over 2 million in 1977. On-line search volume continues to grow vigorously, and some authorities predict that in 1980 there will be more than 4 million on-line searches in the U.S., plus 2.8 million in Europe.[1]

Another measure is the total number of subscribers to the principal on-line data base vendors. In 1975 this number was probably less than 1000. By 1978, the number has probably at least tripled. Firm data are not available, both because the vendors consider the exact numbers proprietary, and because many institutions patronize two or more vendors. The resulting overlap would make a mere aggregate number deceptive even if it could be isolated. Even rough estimates of search activity and trends indicate, however, that on-line services are here to stay and are very rapidly gaining converts.[2] For example, at least 400 academic libraries now offer on-line searching, whereas only a few dozen did so a mere three years ago.

THE INFORMATION CENTERS: OFF-LINE SEARCHING

While the on-line distribution services are growing rapidly, a valuable role in disseminating the contents of data bases still falls to a string of regional information centers established more than a decade ago with federal assistance. The two principal agencies involved were the National Science Foundation (NSF) and the National Aeronautics and Space Administration (NASA). NSF is interested in encouraging and facilitating the dissemination and use of scientific and technical information in the public interest. This is done primarily through the academic community. NASA has similar responsibilities for encouraging technological transfer from the nation's space program to the private sector — commercial and industrial enterprises.

As one means of achieving these objectives, each agency chose, in the 1960s, to establish a series of independent, not-for-profit information centers, each affiliated with a major university. The NSF-sponsored search centers were at Ohio State, Lehigh and

Stanford Universities; the universities of California (Los Angeles), Georgia and Pittsburgh; and the IIT Research Institute (IITRI) in Illinois.

The NASA outlets, called Regional Dissemination Centers (RDCs) are also associated with important campuses in key geographic locations: The universities of Connecticut, Pittsburgh, New Mexico and Southern California; Indiana University; and Research Triangle Park (a facility serving Duke University, the University of North Carolina and North Carolina State University). The *raison d'être* of these RDCs is to disseminate technical information to business so that ultimately it will be applied to meeting the needs and desires of the public at large. Accordingly, they function as not-for-profit transfer points for a considerable body of technology other than that developed, and made available, by NASA itself.

Some of this additional information comes, like NASA's, from the federal government; particularly the Department of Defense, the Department of Energy and various national laboratories. Other sources are private, including a number of organizations that used NSF funds initially to place their data bases on computer tapes. For example, the New England Research Application Center (NERAC) at the University of Connecticut (Storrs), one of the most successful RDCs, has 35 data bases available on its in-house computer; the following examples illustrate the scope and variety of these data bases:

Abstracted Business Information (Inform)
Agricola (CAIN)
Biological Previews (BIOSIS)
Chemical Abstracts Condensates (CA Con)
Computer and Controls Abstracts (Inspec)
Engineering Index (Ei)
ERDA Energy Information File
Food Science and Technology Abstracts (FSTA)
Health Effects of Environmental Pollutants (HEEP)
Institute of Paper Chemistry (IPC)
International Aerospace Abstracts (NASA)
Mechanical Engineering Information (ISMEC)
Metals Abstracts (ASM)
Rubber and Plastics Research Abstracts (RAPRA)
Resources in Education (ERIC)
Searchable Physics Information Notices (SPIN)
World Aluminum Abstracts (WAA)

NERAC's objective is to have 40 data bases on its computer by the end of 1978. Moreover, "When a user's request cannot be satisfactorily answered with these in-house files, graduate students are available for manual searching in the large University library."[2] In addition, there is a full-time specialist in Washington, DC, to track down facts not in any data base and three full-time people concerned with full-text document delivery.

NERAC, which offers both retrospective and SDI searching in what it calls a "fast batch" mode, has a staff of 12 search strategy and profile specialists who combine training in information retrieval with graduate expertise in a technical discipline. They customarily search multiple data bases — as many as seem appropriate and promising — in the course of rating their patrons' needs. With the volume of searching it does annually (close to 1 million SDI searches plus 75,000 retrospective searches in 1977), NERAC finds that having a library of data bases in its own computer permits it to serve patrons at much lower cost than it would incur by using the on-line services of a commercial data base vendor.[3] It can also get search results from, say, 10 data bases on the specialist's desk overnight (unless chemical data bases are involved, in which case the turnaround time can be as much as two days). This is much faster service than can normally be obtained from an on-line search plus off-line printout plus time in the mails.

The key to NERAC's success is its resident computer, which is run around the clock, exclusively for conducting client searches. One result is that the heavier the search volume, the cheaper each search becomes. Client companies that fully participate in the subscription program (NERAC does not do one-time searches) can have an average search cost of $15 or even less. This combination of expert assistance, fast results and low cost are reflected in NERAC's very high renewal rate (more than 85% of clients stay with the program year after year) and its vigorous growth rate, which ranges between 50% and 75% per year.

Originally, owing largely to the technology available in the mid- to late-1960s, NERAC and the other subsidized information centers provided only off-line searches. Now, though, all of NERAC's sister RDCs are offering on-line, interactive searches, via Lockheed for the most part. The search centers initially funded by NSF have more or less atrophied since NSF subsidies were withdrawn. Those at Georgia and IITRI are still in operation, but the former concentrates on serving the university community, and the latter has shifted its emphasis away from data base searching, although it still maintains a few files.

THIRD-TIER RETAILERS

As is characteristic of burgeoning young industries, machine-readable bibliographic data base services are not developing in a monolithic, tidy way. Experimentation, combinations, segmentation and other departures from the mainstream abound, and this is as true of vendors as of producers.

A case in point is Editec, Inc., a Chicago-based company that calls itself "the electric library." Editec is fundamentally a computer-aided, information-on-demand service that responds to specific requests for information, including the generation of custom bibliographies. The company's researchers have access to about 80 on-line data bases, including all those offered by Lockheed, SDC, the New York Times Information Bank and several others — a combined hoard totaling 40 to 50 million bibliographic records. Editec provides individual searches to walk-in or phone-in clients for a fee, but heavy users can save money by prepaying for a certain number of searches per year, on a subscription basis. Full-text copies of cited documents are also provided, in either print or microfiche. Currently, the company conducts anywhere from 50 to 100 on-line searches per month.

It also has an in-house computer that is used for a growing volume of custom indexing work.

Like Editec, Information Clearing House (ICH) in New York City "retails" the New York Times Information Bank, as well as more than 100 other data bases distributed by BRS, Dow Jones, Lockheed and System Development Corp. Essentially, ICH is bringing electronic data base searching to bear on its long-established information-on-demand service called FIND/SVP. The company reports a 1400% growth since 1972 in its volume of on-line searching. In 1977, the firm's on-line searchers served about 3000 clients, mostly business and industrial companies.

Similar information-on-demand services, or information brokerage companies, are springing up all over the country. Most of them routinely utilize computer-based bibliographic searching in the course of digging out the facts their clients need. While the on-demand operations range from individual free-lance libraries operating out of the nearest phone booth to substantial organizations with dozens of employees, they are all in the business of finding facts fast, for a fee, and almost all of their clients are business people.

Among the better-known information-on-demand services, in addition to Editec and ICH already mentioned, are Information for Business (New York City), Information Access (Dewitt, NY), Warner-Eddison Associates (Lexington, MA), Information Resources (Toronto), Searchline (Chicago), Information Specialists (Cleveland), Inquiry (Buffalo), Library Reports and Research Service (Westminster, CO), Documentation Associates (Los Angeles) and Information Unlimited (Berkeley, CA). Business Data Analysts (Boston) is a relative newcomer with big ambitions. On the other hand, there have been casualties among the on-demand fact firms, just as there have been in other aspects of the information industry. Folded tents include those of Information Source (Los Angeles), Mills Inc. (Bethesda, MD) and Output Systems (Washington, DC).

Charging fees that seem to cluster around $15 to $30 per hour, but run as high as $50 per hour plus expenses — including, of course, the expense of appropriate computer-based searching — the successful information-on-demand services have been able to survive and grow even when they faced heavily subsidized, or even free, competition from nearby libraries offering computer searching. They perceive the advantages they offer as including speedier response, top quality searching, personalized service and, in some cases, full-text document delivery.

Several libraries have also plunged into the facts-for-a-fee arena. A notable success is the INFORM service of the Minneapolis Public Library, which has grown rapidly since it was started in 1974. INFORM was initially an acronym for *IN*formation *FOR M*innesota, but the service has attracted and served clients from many other locations in the U.S. and as far away as South Africa and Australia. INFORM charges $25 per hour — ostensibly just enough to recover the cost of providing the service — plus 10 cents per page for photocopies and 50 cents per page for microfilm copies of cited material.

Similar fee-based services are offered by the Rochester (NY) Regional Research Library

Council, the Dallas Public Library, the Worcester (MA) Area Cooperating Libraries and a number of other public entities. In addition many, if not most, of the substantial academic libraries that offer computer-based bibliographic searching for on-campus patrons will also accommodate businesses and private individuals — usually for fees higher than those paid by the campus community.

There is also a smattering of other computer-search "retailers," such as the Chemical Data Center (Columbus, OH) and Calspan (Buffalo, NY). Another prominent example is the World Trade Information Center, in the lobby of Manhattan's immense World Trade Center. The Center charges individuals about $25 for a computer search of either the New York Times Information Bank or any of Lockheed's on-line data bases. The price includes up to 10 abstracts from NYTIB or up to 20 from Lockheed; the Center also provides full-text copies of available documents for an additional service charge.

Predictably, some of the experiments with data base distribution have failed. One example was the rather short-lived arrangement between National Technical Information Service (NTIS) and the McGraw-Hill Book Co.'s business and technical bookstore in mid-town Manhattan. The experiment, which lasted about half a year, died of neglect on May 1, 1975. In addition to selling NTIS reports, newsletters and "wide interest" bibliographies, McGraw-Hill offered walk-in, mail and phone-order customers on-line access to the NTIS data bank, via a Lockheed DIALOG terminal right in the bookstore. In addition, McGraw-Hill could immediately order from NTIS full-text copies of any research reports requested. Customers paid the same prices for searching, printed material and other services provided by McGraw-Hill as were then being charged by NTIS itself: $100 per search.

While McGraw-Hill was officially the first retail, and certainly the largest commercial, access point to the NTIS machine-readable data base, the company painfully realized, after a few months in operation, that it had a local competitor offering much cheaper access to the same data base. Patrons of any of the cooperating libraries that constitute the METRO library group — of which the New York Public Library is one — were welcome to use the on-line search facilities of the Columbia Teachers College Library (CTCL). The charge there was at the rate of $35 per hour for on-line access through Lockheed's DIALOG, plus $10 per hour for the Tymnet communications link and a $5 surcharge imposed by the library. Clearly, McGraw-Hill, which under the NTIS agreement could not lower its prices, was at a distinct disadvantage with any user aware of the CTCL alternative.

Also in the mid-1970s a similar situation was encountered in connection with the New York Times Information Bank. One early and constant direct subscriber is the Chase Manhattan Bank, which had NYTIB permission to resell to other banks material it drew from the Times data base. Meanwhile, another NYTIB subscriber, the Brooklyn (NY) Public Library, with more than 50 branches, accommodated at no charge anyone interested in searching the NYTIB via the library's on-line terminal. Among the heaviest users of Brooklyn Public's service were at least three prospects that NYTIB would rather have served directly: Chemical Bank (a major Chase competitor), *New York* magazine and Information Clearing House (which later made arrangements to provide service to its own customers).

CHAOTIC COMPETITION

This chaotic competitive situation is disturbingly pervasive. Data base producers that market their wares directly, as well as through vendors, are competing with their own most important customers. Further, the data base distributors — particularly libraries — that pass the service benefits through to individual users at no charge, or on a cost-recovery basis, compete with their own suppliers. They also have a major price advantage over commercial "retail" outlets. Moreover, to the extent that machine-readable data bases are substitutes for the same information in print media, many data base producers are even competing with themselves. Everyone, of course, is competing for the same limited supply of money available for bibliographic search of whatever kind.

In no quarter does this peculiar competitive scramble generate more heat than in the clash between private enterprise and the federal government or government-subsidized services. A striking example of the impact of such competition was afforded by the announcement in 1975 by the National Library of Medicine (NLM) that starting in March that year, NLM would itself provide all patrons direct access to its MEDLINE and other data base services. Until then, while NLM had made its bases available to hospitals and research organizations, SDC had provided paid access to these bases to such important users as the 118 members of the Pharmaceutical Manufacturers Association.

Thanks to a hefty subsidy, NLM was then charging only $8 per connect hour for a MEDLINE search, not nearly enough to cover its total costs. Even after NLM's $15 per hour (prime time) rate went into effect in June 1975, NLM's direct charges were decisively attractive, compared to the $100 per hour ($55 per hour to PMA members) then levied by SDC. MEDLINE, moreover, was (and remains) far and away the most intensively used on-line data base in the world, being accessed well over 300,000 times per year by a body of patrons that was then growing at a dramatic rate. One estimate is that the loss of its MEDLINE revenues cost SDC more than $250,000 in annual billings.

SDC responded by suing the government — twice. In the first place, the company argued, the MEDLARS tapes are records, and therefore should be made available under the Freedom of Information Act (FOIA) for the mere cost of reproducing the tapes — perhaps $500 — rather than for the $50,000 fee NLM set for the tapes. In the second place, contended SDC, the government had breached its contract with the company by providing MEDLINE service to commercial customers (as contrasted with hospitals and medical schools), and therefore should pay SDC $4 million.

In court, SDC lost — twice. The court ruled that MEDLARS tapes, since they are bibliographic, are not records within the meaning of the FOIA. Later, another court dismissed SDC's other lawsuit out of hand with a blistering opinion that underlined the ambiguity, inconsistency and looseness of the contract. (Further, SDC's lamentations contrast with the fact that newcomer BRS not only pays full price for the NLM tapes, but manages to find a significant number of on-line customers for them.)

While this clash drew considerable attention, it is far from being the only instance of the government pre-empting a market segment that private industry would prefer to serve in the hope of turning a profit. One example that has drawn considerable fire is the data base of the U.S. Department of Energy (DOE). Initially, DOE made its data available only to government users, but it has since opened the door to government contractors. Few observers would be surprised if the DOE base, which includes Nuclear Science Abstracts, were ultimately thrown open to all comers — at heavily subsidized prices. Among other examples of government competition with private enterprise is the Journal Article Copying Service of NTIS and the Government Printing Office's rapidly growing "free" micropublishing activities, which threaten a number of commercial micropublishers.

Profit-oriented companies, whose taxes support the subsidies that lure away what might otherwise be customers, regularly attack these government "intrusions." The Information Industry Association stares with alarm. In the imitative hyperbole of its president, Paul Zurkowski: "From SUNY [State University of New York] on Lake Erie to NLM in Bethesda and from the Research Triangle in North Carolina to the Golden Triangle in Pittsburgh, an iron curtain, forged out of free information, is descending across the competitive marketplace of ideas."[4]

No doubt, direct competition from federal agencies, and from libraries and other institutions enjoying government grants and subsidies, *is* "unfair" to commercial enterprise. On the other hand, a very substantial investment of public money was necessary to bring machine-readable bibliographic data bases into existence in the first place, and federal contracts paid for development of the search and retrieval software required. Moreover, virtually all of the underlying technology is based on federally sponsored R&D or its "fallout," and, of course, the federal government is the largest single generator of the research data that finds its way into the literature to which data bases are a key.

In addition, the federal government is easily the largest single customer for data base services, including those provided by commercial data base producers and vendors. Finally, the federal government, and particularly the National Science Foundation, has long been the prime source of funding for research and experimental projects directed at developing and improving data base services. Private companies not only benefit from the resulting increased strength, diversity and viability of the industry, but often capture the study contracts as well. One appropriate example is the 1975 SDC survey of data base users, a study that was funded by a $98,000 NSF grant. Similarly, SDC's chief competitor, Lockheed, captured the NSF contract to study the prospects and impact of providing on-line services via public libraries in the three-year "DIALIB" project.

FOOTNOTES

1. Martha Williams, "Computer-Readable Data Bases," *ALA Yearbook, 1978* (Washington, DC: American Library Association, 1978).

2. Pauline Atherton and Roger Christian, *Librarians and Online Services* (White Plains, NY: Knowledge Industry Publications, Inc., 1977).

3. *Advanced Technology/Libraries,* April 1975, p. 1.

4. Daniel U. Wilde and B. Snodgrass, "The Value of Searching Multiple Data Bases," in *The Value of Information* collected papers of ASIS midyear meeting. Syracuse University, May 1977.

5. Daniel U. Wilde, "A Comparison of Costs Between On-Line and Fast-Batch Searching," paper presented at American Society for Information Science Annual Meeting, Boston, MA, October 29, 1975. Available from New England Research Application Center, Storrs, CT.

V

Bibliographic Data Bases in the Library: Start-up Considerations

by Pauline Atherton and Roger Christian

In this era of escalating costs and increasing competition for the scarce funds available, libraries, particularly academic and public libraries, have often found it difficult to win approval and money for new projects and services. Provision of on-line bibliographic retrieval systems is subject to these pressures, and in addition faces several other obstacles. Among them is the fact that the need for on-line services is not readily recognized and accepted by some administrators, given the shortage of funds. Moreover, while the relatively substantial cost of providing such services is highly visible, the cost of *not* providing them is not. Besides, the cost effectiveness of such services is not easily demonstrated.

THE PRELIMINARY PROPOSAL AND STUDY

Once library officials perceive the desirability of offering on-line bibliographic retrieval services, it behooves them to carefully document the need for and benefits of such services. Someone must delineate the scope and prospects of the services at the particular library or organization involved; prepare estimates of the volume and costs that can be realistically anticipated; estimate both the positive and the negative impacts that such services are likely to have on the library and the community it serves; and, in general, demonstrate that the idea has been carefully investigated and analyzed. The result should be a persuasive, written proposal for top management consideration.

One acceptable approach, which has the added merit of increasing library staff's interest in, and commitment to, on-line reference services, is for the library director to appoint a study group, or at least an individual, to investigate existing on-line systems and services in comparable libraries.* While the output of such a study is commonly an

---

*The University of Rochester (NY) followed this plan.

Reprinted from *Librarians and Online Services* (White Plains, NY: Knowledge Industry Publications, Inc., 1977).

extensive memorandum or report to the library director, it could just as well take the form — or perhaps the additional form — of an oral report to some administrative meeting of appropriate library officials and staff.

Either way, such a report would probably include a general description of the current state of the art and trends in the field, perhaps some discussion of its historical development and potential, and commentary specific to the library involved on such matters as these:

- The implications and applicability of lessons learned at other institutions.

- The kinds of services and modes of operation that seem most appropriate to the clientele serviced by this library.

- The service vendors and specific data bases that are most likely to appeal to the library's clientele, and that most closely parallel its collections and the interests of the population it serves.

- The competitive factors to be considered if more than one potential vendor offers appropriate data bases and services.

- The impact that a decision to provide such services might have on the staff, work load, responsibilities — particularly at the reference desk — schedules, attitudes and morale of the library staff.

- The possible need to bolster document delivery services in some way.

- The adaptability of key members of the current staff to training in the provision of on-line services.

- Some notion of the nature, locations and volume of demand for such services among the library's clientele.

- Some informed conjecture about the likely cost effectiveness of such services.

- At least a rough forecast of the initial costs that would be involved.

Such costs vary considerably, as witness estimates drawn up in proposals prepared for the University of Nebraska, in Lincoln, and for Northwestern University. (See Tables V-1 and V-2.) The University of Nebraska proposal calls for a single teletype-compatible terminal to be moved as needed between two libraries on the campus, and affording access only to the family of data bases offered by Lockheed Information System. The Northwestern University proposal envisions access to the data bases covered by System Development Corporation as well as by Lockheed (and, subsequently, to the New York Times Information Bank) via a relatively sophisticated video terminal in each of two library facilities.

Table V-1: On-line Start-up, University of Nebraska — Lincoln Libraries

1. Start-up Costs (January 1 — June 30, 1976)

Texas Instruments 735 portable printer terminal	$ 720
Training by Lockheed personnel (est.)	900
Supplies (paper, etc.)	100
Printing of service brochures and forms	100
Communications during start-up	100
User manuals	20
Computer time for training additional operators	300
Total start-up costs:	$2,240

2. Continuing Costs (yr)

Terminal $120/month	$1,440
Supplies and maintenance	250
Yearly cost	$1,690

Table V-2: On-line Start-up, Northwestern University Library Computer Assisted Information Services

Estimated Costs for 1975-76

Training (one-time costs)

Lockheed and SDC training seminars (Fees and transportation to Palo Alto, CA for 2 seminars for 2 people)	$1,000

Staff training for 12 staff members
$45 — Average cost per hour of computer time
$10 — TYMSHARE cost per hour

$55 — Total cost per hour

12 staff members x 2 hours/staff members x $55/hour	$1,320

Equipment costs

Telephone line in Reference Department	$ 50/yr.
Telephone line in Technological — Institute Library	$ 50/yr.
Terminal costs	
2 terminals x $140/month rental x 12 months/year	$3,360/yr.
Subtotal	$5,780

Staff and professional time costs

Professional time

3500 searches/year x 1/2 hour/search x $6.00/hour	$10,500/yr.

Staff time

3500 searches/year x $.64/search	$ 2,240/yr
Total	$18,520

For such an internal report to the library director to be used as the basis for a formal proposal, it would have to be elaborated upon. Supporting data should include an estimate of the number of searches that are likely to be generated on such a system during the first year; estimates of the necessary professional and support staff required to provide the forecast level of service; a tentative budget; an outline of plans for promoting and marketing the service; a plan for training the staff; a proposed organization; plans for recovering at least some of the costs of providing the search service; and a firm recommendation for action.

Normally, such proposals also include a timetable for implementing the services, if the proposals are approved. It is also a good idea for the library director to have at least a mental timetable for reassessing the situation, and for possibly preparing a second and stronger proposal, in the event the initial one is rejected.

Such administrative considerations as the detailed financial and promotional aspects of providing on-line services, and establishing service procedures and administrative controls, require substantial attention. In addition to these, however, library administrators bent on successfully inaugurating on-line bibliographic reference services must give intensive consideration to at least six other key elements:

- Establishing the mission of the service

- Market analysis

- Resource analysis and selection

- Organization

- Providing physical facilities

- Personnel selection and training

ESTABLISHING THE MISSION

Establishing a credible and achievable mission for on-line services at a particular library may be more complex than it might seem at first blush. It is easy to make a ringing statement about bridging the gap between the ever-increasing needs for bibliographic information to support teaching, research and the like, and the exponential rise — almost the explosion — in the volume of pertinent literature. But such a pronouncement may not be enough; and in fact it *should* not be enough.

A serious statement of mission should address itself to such matters as just who will be served, and in what order of priority. The parent organization typically makes this abundantly clear to corporate and other special libraries, most of which will not do on-line searches for outsiders. Thus, the Charles River Associates library in Cambridge accommodates only staff members of that consulting firm. However, the issue of who will be served can generate considerable discussion in an academic or public library — particularly where the imposition of user fees represents a distinct innovation.

Many academic libraries — Stanford and Northwestern among them — establish a policy of serving only the institution's faculty, staff and students. Others, including the University of California, will also serve faculties, scholars and students of other institutions, often on a time-available basis. Still others, like Dartmouth, agree to accommodate requests from commercial organizations. Some tax-supported institutions such as the University of Nebraska restrict their clientele to businesses within the host state or community.

The statement of mission should also specify whether the on-line reference services to be provided will be restricted to retrospective searches, current awareness or SDI searches, or both.

The mode of operation, at least initially, should also be spelled out. Will the reference desk or circulation department of the library function only as a well-informed referral node, sending interested patrons to other libraries that are equipped to actually conduct on-line searches? Or will the library function as an intermediary, offering patrons professional help in compiling interest profiles or discrete search statements and then, on the patron's behalf, getting the on-line searches performed at an affiliated institution with appropriate facilities? Or will the library staff itself provide personalized computer-based search services at its own facilities?

Another aspect of establishing the mission for on-line services is to set some specific — and, ideally, measurable — goals and objectives of service. Chief among these in some libraries, of course, will be simply establishing, for the first time, literature searching services of any kind. Another goal might be to serve a greater number of users. A third might be to improve services through access to additional sources of information, or faster turnaround time, or greater precision in the citations retrieved. A related goal might be greater user satisfaction as a result of the speed, versatility, comprehensiveness, convenience and other benefits of on-line searching.

Internal objectives might include greater staff productivity, or a reduction in the staff time needed for literature searching, or perhaps an absolute reduction in reference staff. Other valid objectives might include cost effectiveness of the literature searching services and perhaps more intensive use of the library's collections.

Another aspect of establishing the mission of the on-line services is to come to terms with the issue of cost recovery. Some libraries, particularly those within research-oriented corporations, have no cost recovery goals. They simply absorb the full cost of on-line search services within the unit's budget. Others, including Xerox, Bell Labs and Exxon, transfer all or portions of the cost to the budgets of the company departments or specific projects making the search requests.

Most academic and the few public libraries that offer on-line search services, however, have felt compelled to recover at least the identifiable, direct cost of providing a computer-based search. This includes the computer connect time, the communications cost and the cost of off-line printing of the retrieved citations. A few libraries endeavor to recover all their costs, including professional and staff time and general overhead, especially with respect to searches performed for outsiders — those not immediately connected with the sponsoring institution.

It is also conceivable that the library may establish the goal of making a profit. Currently, this is seldom done, but it does occur in situations where, for example, a strong academic library prices its on-line services to outside commercial organizations at a level that will yield a profit sufficient to permit the library to offer on-line search services to students at a significant discount. UCLA is one example of this practice.

MARKET ANALYSIS

A second major element to be considered during the start-up phase is that of market analysis. That is, just what user groups within the clientele normally served by the library have an articulated or potential use for on-line services, and which data bases have the most to offer them? Each identifiable user group, or potential user group, within the community served should be described in terms of its size, specific location or locations, and other pertinent characteristics, including particularly its ability to pay. In an academic community, these resources might consist of department budgets, grants, contracts, research funds and the like. Patrons of a public library might have to rely on personal funds, reimbursement from an employer or money from fellowships and grants.

To the extent possible, the need of each identified potential user group for bibliographic services should be quantified, and from this some estimate should be made of the demand on the part of each group for on-line search services. Ideally, the magnitude of the demand for each specific data base should be estimated. As might be expected, public libraries find the demand for on-line bibliographic reference services more elastic than do academic libraries. However, both find it highly sensitive to price, particularly when fees are instituted after an initial period of free service.

This phenomenon, and other intangibles such as the novelty appeal of newly instituted on-line services, the countervailing reluctance of many people to try anything new, and the resistance of traditionalists to the whole notion of paying for any kind of library service, must be taken into account in analyzing the potential market for on-line services and in forecasting levels of demand.

With these data in hand, the library is prepared to select the user community, or communities, that it will serve initially. Often, another strategic decision presents itself at this time. The relative attraction of serving a single, high-potential user group, at relatively low cost with one or two data bases, must be weighed against the lure of offering a wide spectrum of data bases, at higher risk, in the hopes of appealing to a larger number of users and user groups. Market segmentation and analysis may help provide some answers.

RESOURCE ANALYSIS AND SELECTION

The third major start-up activity is resource analysis and selection. As of this writing, libraries have little real choice in the matter of who will supply telecommunication services associated with on-line bibliographic searches. However, they can all choose from among at least three nationwide retrieval system vendors of multiple data bases, and a growing number of organizations that offer access to only one or a few data bases. In addition, each library must evaluate individual data bases in light of its own clientele and its own collections.

Choosing a Vendor

While a number of information centers and commercial organizations offer on-line retrieval services on a more or less localized basis, the three major vendors of on-line retrieval services are Lockheed Information Systems, System Development Corp. and Bibliographic Retrieval Services.

The costs of acquiring, processing and updating machine-readable data bases, and of providing on-line retrieval services, do not vary greatly from one vendor to the next. In a competitive market, their prices do not vary that much either. Hence, the evaluation and selection of a retrieval service vendor should turn on an assessment of the relative match between that vendor's offerings, services and modus operandi on the one hand, and the needs and desires of the library on the other.

The pivotal question, of course, is whether or not a vendor offers the particular data base or mix of data bases that will meet the needs of the user groups that the library intends to serve. While on-line access to several of the more popular data bases can be had through any of the principal vendors, other important files are uniquely available only from one.

Among the other factors to be taken into account when evaluating vendors of on-line retrieval services are the vendor's reputation and performance record; its reliability and speed of response; and the level of accessibility, cooperation and support available from the vendor's specialists.

Among the technical features of a retrieval service to be considered are:

- Availability of natural language commands.

- Ease of logging in and logging off.

- Type of search available – author, title, key word, organization name or source, etc.

- Speed and cost of communications options (300 or 1200 baud).

- Ease of access to search free text in record.

- Degree of logic offered – e.g., to what extent a key word may be searched in a certain context or in relation to other terms.

- Ability to store a search for future use (as in SDI profiles).

- Times that the service is available; printing/display options.

Still another key consideration in evaluating data base vendors is the package of support services offered to users. These commonly include a limited number of free demonstrations, formal training courses and workshops for library personnel, and instruction manuals. In addition, vendors usually provide guidebooks to assist searchers in preparing SDI profiles and retrospective search strategies and some sort of newsletter designed to keep users informed about search tips and short cuts, changes in indexing practices, the availability of new data bases or new searchable data elements, and suggestions on how best to take advantage of the peculiarities of the particular system or data base.

Printed search aids such as dictionaries, thesauri and vocabulary lists, and handy reminder cards summarizing important procedures and commands, are also commonly provided. So is a telephone "hotline," with which searchers can request immediate help with any equipment or search problem encountered in the course of an ongoing search.

Costs and Features

All of these are important considerations in choosing which vendors to use, but there is one more: comparative costs. The cost of a retrieval service is not the most important criterion in selecting one, but it is a long way from being an incidental matter. While prices on the average may not differ greatly, it is not unusual to discover that particular search features make it measurably cheaper to search data base X on system A, whereas system B is much the better and cheaper way to search data base Y. Accordingly, the person responsible for evaluating and selecting retrieval services must become familiar with the various fee structures and the basis for the charges associated with each candidate.

Integral to the selection of an on-line service is an analysis of the uses to which the service will be put. The library must ask itself whether its patrons will be primarily interested in current awareness searching, with SDI profiles being maintained for periodic searching, or in retrospective searches, e.g., to compile detailed bibliographies, answer specific questions or identify research trends that are of concern. A related question is whether the patrons will want to take advantage of full-text document delivery, as offered in the NTIS data base, or in that of Current Contents from the Institute for Scientific Information of Philadelphia. In these cases, once having identified a relevant citation, the user can instruct the computer to transmit a request for the document itself.

Selecting Data Bases

Evaluating and selecting the specific data bases that would be most useful to the library's clientele involves considering another "laundry list" of important variables. Among the chief concerns are the scope, content and currency of the data bases themselves. Depending on the source documents utilized, some data bases are discipline-oriented (Psychological Abstracts), others are problem-oriented (ENVIRON), still others are mission-oriented (AGRICOLA), and a number include various combinations of these categories.

The type of source material covered may include not only articles from learned journals, but books, government reports, monographs, theses, newspaper and magazine articles, patents, and in the case of the Smithsonian Science Information Exchange, statements of the current status of ongoing research projects. A separate question is whether the source material is covered at the primary level or only at the secondary level, that is, via an indexing and abstracting service.

Another factor is the time span and timeliness of the coverage. Where clientele interest is high, data base publishers and vendors are inclined to broaden the data base's coverage by adding older, as well as newer, material. Where this has not been done, comprehensive retrospective literature searches may have to overflow from the on-line search to manual investigation of older literature in the more traditional print media.

The timeliness of the material in a particular data base may reflect an unconscionable lag between the time a journal article or report appears in print and the time when its citation data finds its way into the computer memory. At the other extreme, some material may be available in machine-readable form *before* it appears in print. This could be the case where, as is increasingly common, a computer tape is used to produce the hard-copy journal.

The completeness of the data base's coverage might also be questioned in certain circumstances. The fact that a particular journal is listed as being "covered" by a data base publisher or vendor does not necessarily mean that every issue of the journal is covered, nor that each issue is covered in its entirety.

The indexing and coding practices used to generate the data base constitute another subject of inquiry. Dependence on a controlled thesaurus of hierarchical vocabulary terms has important implications for the utility of the data base and for the search strategies that are brought to bear upon it. The number and kinds of access points, and the specific data elements that can be used as searchable and printable fields, are other important considerations. Does the data base include abstracts, or citations only? If abstracts are included, can they be searched as well as displayed? Can they be printed?

Another factor worth considering is the degree of overlap with other data bases that might be accessed, and the general consonance of the data base, not only with the anticipated concerns and interests of the library's clientele, but with the library's own collections. For the most part, patrons are in hot pursuit not of citations but of documents. Hence, a data base strongly oriented to subjects and materials only meagerly represented in the library's resources can generate a great deal of turbulence with respect to acquisition, collection development and interlibrary borrowing.

The relationship between the data base and the corresponding printed index should also be investigated. While there may be a one-to-one correspondence between the two media, the machine-readable data base could also be merely a subset of the hard-copy version, or conversely, more inclusive or more accessible than the counterpart printed index.

Other matters worth probing are what vocabulary aids or search aids might be available on-line to facilitate use of the data base, the total number of citations included, and the rate and frequency with which the data base was being updated. Finally, one should weigh the cost of searching the data base and of printing out a reasonable number of retrieved citations compared with the cost of manually searching that service.

ORGANIZATION OF SERVICE AND STAFF

The fourth key matter to be deliberated and decided during the start-up phase of a program to inaugurate on-line search services is that of organizing and locating the service. While not all libraries will be in a position to seriously consider more than one option, those that are should carefully weigh the feasibility and relative merits of each possibility. For example, the library could choose to provide all on-line services from a single, centralized location. MIT does this — interestingly, after several years of using dispersed search locations. Alternatively, a given library may elect to follow the lead of the University of California at Berkeley, and conduct searches from two or more decentralized locations, each of which might specialize in providing access to a particular kind of data base (medical here, social sciences there, hard sciences somewhere else, etc.). Another possibility is to conduct on-line services from the central headquarters facility, while using satellite locations to screen and refer patrons.

Some libraries in unusual circumstances might even want to consider other options, such as having information service librarians go to particular patrons and negotiate search questions in the office or laboratory of the clients they serve. For instance, Edith Dalton serves a consortium of special, academic and public libraries called the Worcester (MA) Area Cooperating Libraries by taking her 13 pound TI 735 terminal to whichever institution the search patron is associated with. To a large extent, decisions of this kind will dictate the most logical physical location for support and clerical staff as well as for the computer terminals, search aids and other facilities.

Another organizational matter to be decided is that of assigning specific responsibility for monitoring and managing the library's on-line services. Commonly, this assignment falls to a special coordinator, whose qualifications and duties are addressed more specifically below.

The final organizational element is that of deciding, in light of the anticipated level of demand for on-line services, how many professional-level personnel will be required and what size clerical staff will be necessary to support them. Coupled with these decisions are those related to the specific qualifications, duties and responsibilities of each member of the on-line services group, and of course their professional and organizational relationships, including supervision, coordination and possible lines of succession.

In some libraries, the anticipated work load emanating from such services will dictate that the people providing them will only be required to spend a certain percentage of their total work time in this connection.* In all libraries offering on-line services, however, some organizational provision should be made for competent and dependable back-up staff, particularly for the active information service librarians.

---

*University of California at San Diego, Cornell University, and University of Toronto, Robarts Library, to name a few.

One logical commonplace way of achieving this is to make sure that the on-line services coordinator keeps his or her searching skills up to date in a disciplined way. In larger organizations, one or more assistant coordinators should do the same.

PROVIDING PHYSICAL FACILITIES

The next undertaking to be addressed is that of arranging the physical facilities necessary to support the provision of on-line bibliographic search services. Some — especially public — libraries have chosen, at least initially, to place the library's computer terminal near the main desk or in some other highly visible location, in hope of catching the interest of library patrons who are there on other business. The San Mateo County and the San Jose (CA) public libraries are among those who chose this course. It is now generally conceded, however, that it is better to locate the terminal and associated computer search facilities in a reasonably private spot — ideally, in a separate room, as is done, for example, at the Dallas and Philadelphia public libraries. Often, the on-line services are located within the reference department of the library — where they can be more easily integrated with other reference facilities. Moreover, the entire reference staff can be more actively involved in providing and supporting the on-line services — and vice versa. James Bement of Xerox's Technical Information Center in Rochester says its terminal, at the reference desk, gets heavy use for "quick and dirty stuff" such as checking citations that can be done faster and more conveniently that way than by turning to the printed services.

Communications and Space

Fortunately, no elaborate site preparation is necessary. Even when the library elects to use relatively sophisticated video terminals, the installation typically consists of no more than unpacking the terminal, plugging it into a grounded electrical convenience outlet, and connecting it, via a black box called a modem (for modulator-demodulator), to a telephone line. It is best if this line is dedicated exclusively to provision of on-line services.

Aside from the terminal itself, the telephone link to the computer and, where desired, a compact output printer, all that is really required is a modicum of furniture and amenities that will create a productive work environment. Obviously, the site must also provide the information services librarian with ready access to the necessary manuals, thesauri and other search aids.

While any specific library may have to accommodate certain compromises, the services location chosen should be convenient to the reference staff and the reference collections, and reasonably accessible to patrons who might be interested in investigating what the service has to offer them. It should be out of the way enough to avoid interference from established traffic patterns or other activities of the library. Redwood City (CA) Public Library located its terminal in the main reference/reading room, but noise complaints from patrons soon forced installation of an acoustical cover. Naturally, the location chosen should be conducive to the interviews and other activities associated with preparing and evaluating searches.

The room or space dedicated to the on-line services should be adequate to allow a search specialist and one or two users to work freely at and around the terminal in some semblance of comfort, free of outside interruptions and with a modicum of confidentiality. If possible, perhaps by rearranging a few pieces of furniture, there should be enough room around the terminal to accommodate small groups for demonstration purposes. There should also be room for files or shelves to accommodate related records, bibliographic search aids, and printed reference materials.

Work tables are generally better than desks, both because they afford the librarian and the user more leg room, and because the ample work surface is less likely to get cluttered up with the paper and other impedimenta that tend to accumulate on the desk tops. Sara D. Knapp of the State University of New York at Albany also notes that "while promoting joint collaboration, the table preserves a comfortable distance for those who find too much physical closeness distracting."[1] If a portable terminal is contemplated, a cart to facilitate its movement would be in order, and some librarians seem to be partial to a small rack to display the promotional brochures and other literature associated with the on-line services.

A few chairs that aren't too comfortable, lamps as necessary, ashtrays and other accessories, if appropriate, and the necessary manuals, retrieval aids, materials and supplies complete the picture. The matter of decorative touches we leave to the discrimination of the individual librarians and the tender mercies of the available budget.

Necessary utilities include a grounded (three pronged) 220 volt electrical outlet for each terminal and a separate telephone line and number for each terminal's communications. In addition, it is advisable but not necessary to install a separate telephone line and number dedicated to communications between the library and its on-line user clientele and suppliers. This way, the institution and maintenance of on-line services will not be dependent on availability of regular telephone circuits. Lighting, heating, air conditioning and ventilation levels at the on-line services location should be adequate, but need not be any different from those provided elsewhere in the active areas of the library.

Another consideration not to be overlooked is the security of the on-line services area. Thefts do occur; in fact, the MEDLINE terminal at the University of Kentucky's medical library has been stolen twice. Elements to consider include at least the security of the terminal itself from theft, tampering and unauthorized use; the security of the telephone communication lines; control of the integrity or privacy of manuals, supplies and other printed materials, including records and service files; and protection of the location itself from the hazards of fire, vandalism and the like.

Signs pointing the way to the on-line site, and listings in various directories and handbooks, will help potential users to find the service.

The Computer Terminal

In terms of physical facilities, the most critical item is the computer terminal. While an exhaustive treatment of terminal features is beyond the purview of this report, a serious comparative study of what is available is certainly in order. The possibilities range from relatively pokey teletype terminals — which many libraries consider unacceptably noisy — to sleek, silent video terminals, some of them incorporating a full-fledged programmable mini or microcomputer. Optional features are available with most equipment to help adapt it to the special needs of each particular library.

Library managers totally new to the mysteries of terminal selection, and ignorant of the wide scope of choice available, generally seek outside advice. This can come from the institution's computer or data processing staff, from the supplier of the on-line retrieval services they have selected, from representatives of the manufacturers of the terminals themselves, or from experienced people in libraries that have already been providing on-line services for some time.[2] While these sources can provide insights, it is important not to impute to them more expertise, or broader familiarity with what's on the market, than they can really bring to the question. Moreover, once a particular terminal is decided upon, library managers are likely to want further expert advice on such matters as the intricacies and implications of leasing arrangements and maintenance contracts.

At minimum, those responsible for selecting a terminal will want to consider such factors as:

• Speed of operation (and printing speed, if printout facilities are required).

• Operating noise levels.

• Ease of operation.

• The readability of the display screen presentation, in the case of video terminals.

• The number and variety of command keys.

• The actual portability, if a portable terminal is desired.

• Any ancillary equipment required to make the terminal compatible with the communication lines and the computer facilities of the data base processer.

• Reliability.

• The comprehensiveness, responsiveness and cost of repair and service arrangements.

• The relative attractions of rental, leasing and outright purchase.

• The terminal's ability to accommodate new data base suppliers that the library may want to consider.

• Cost.

Other materials needed at the search site include:

- Handbooks, thesauri, and other manuals for the data bases and retrieval systems in question.

- Forms for logging in search requests, user profiles, search results, charges and other administrative details.

- Printout paper, ribbons, miscellaneous supplies.

- Promotional materials such as brochures, newsletters or price lists that will explain the on-line services to potential patrons.

PERSONNEL SELECTION AND TRAINING

The sixth major start-up consideration is the selection and training of the library personnel who will be providing the on-line services. Every member of the library staff should receive at least a general orientation to the new on-line services, the physical location in which they are provided, their relationship to the more conventional reference services provided by the library, and their contribution to the library's overall mission.

Ideally, every professional member of the reference department staff should be trained to interview patrons and to conduct on-line reference searches. In the best of all possible worlds, at least one of the information services librarians will hold a degree in each of the subject disciplines covered by the data bases being offered.

As a practical matter, of course, most libraries will have to make do with the human resources that are already aboard. Until the next generation of librarians finds its way into the profession, libraries will have to develop internally a cadre of information services librarians, starting with staff members who, in all probability, have never before switched on a computer terminal.

Fortunately, the task is not as formidable as it might seem. Except for the very rare library that can justify maintaining its own computer facilities to process data bases, the provision of on-line reference services is essentially a turnkey operation. The necessary equipment and facilities, programs, systems analysis and design, the generation or acquisition of data bases, the communications links and all ancillary services are the concern of specialized outside vendors. These firms merely contract with the libraries to provide interactive on-line access to bibliographic data bases for a fee.

Accordingly, just as a driver is not required to understand internal combustion engines in order to operate the family car, an information services librarian does not have to master the intricacies of systems analysis, computer programming and telecommunications in order to operate the terminal and competently search remote data bases. Communicating by telephone is certainly a familiar activity, and the keyboard of the computer terminal is very similar to that of a conventional typewriter. Further, the skills, insights and activities involved in providing computer-based reference services build upon the knowledge and skills that have long been in the repertoire of reference librarians.

Learning about data bases is very much along the lines of collection development. The structure, format and other characteristics of the data bases echo those of the corresponding printed indexing and abstracting services. Moreover, compiling a unique bibliography for an individual does not differ fundamentally from compiling one for a group with identical interests. Thus, viewed merely as a tool for enhancing, augmenting and extending the traditional activities of reference librarians, the computer terminal loses much of its mystique.

That said, however, relatively intensive initial training is nevertheless required, as is an ongoing effort on the part of information services librarians to stay abreast of new developments and to maintain their proficiency in searching. Deft use of the terminal itself is a relatively minor factor in the overall efficiency and effectiveness of an on-line search. As Ann Ross, manager of the Business Library at G.D. Searle put it in an interview, "The difficulty with training is not memorizing buttons but showing people how on-line services fit in with their other tools."

Much more important than terminal proficiency are the librarian's interviewing and negotiating skills and the ability to devise an intelligent search strategy in response to a particular challenge. This being the case, candidates for training as information services librarians should be selected on the basis of their personality and intellectual power as well as their reference or subject matter backgrounds. Among the many attributes that searchers should possess, only a few seem to be more pertinent to on-line searching than to conventional research librarianship. Particularly important is the ability to relate to and communicate well with other specialists. Searchers should also have a strong service orientation, for they should see themselves as *advocates* of clientele needing information, not as keepers of the keys to the terminal.

Interest in the field is critical. Some librarians have found these new services vaguely threatening, and in the words of Kris Brooks of Oregon State University, "have deselected themselves as search consultants." Others are uneasy in what is called the "machine interface," particularly where a typing or spelling error might be evident to a library patron that they are serving. Some dislike the pressure and unforgiving nature of the terminal, or simply resent using it. "I didn't go to library school to sit and type all day," one snapped. Other librarians lack the energy or inclination to undertake intensive retraining. Finally, some simply prefer the easy familiarity of traditional bibliographic tools to the structured ritual and intellectual demands of providing individualized reference service.

Types of Training

To say that training is required to convert a reference librarian into an accomplished information services librarian is not to say that the training has to be formal. In fact, results of the survey by Wanger et al indicate that, being avid readers almost by reflex, about half the librarians then functioning as on-line searchers simply collected various instruction manuals and whatever other literature came to hand, and curled up to teach themselves how to become information services librarians.

Among those lacking formal training, most librarians seem to have simply read the available literature and then practiced with the computer terminal until they felt confident enough to tackle their first search for a patron; others have been tutored by colleagues who had been formally trained or had gained experience elsewhere. A number have taken advantage of the MEDLEARN program made available by the National Library of Medicine. Still other on-line searchers have had formal training during their professional education in a library school, as many courses now have incorporated hands-on training and experience with on-line services (e.g., those at Syracuse University, University of California at Berkeley, Drexel University, UCLA).

The most popular source of formal training with on-line retrieval systems is, not surprisingly, the vendors of such retrieval systems. The basic training courses offered by the on-line retrieval service vendors concentrate on manipulating the system itself; that is, logging on and off, submitting search and output commands, responding to system messages and the like. Normally, there is only limited discussion of the peculiarities of particular data bases and of the best ways of exploiting them in the course of a search.

This omission works to the disadvantage of librarians in public and academic libraries. Unlike their counterparts in special libraries (especially corporate libraries), these librarians have less experience in doing reference searching for individual patrons, and less exposure to the indexing and abstracting tools of a particular discipline.

Nevertheless, the cost of the training from Lockheed, SDC and BRS is relatively low, the quality of instruction is high, and both competitive forces and the rapid growth in the number of academic libraries accessing these systems is likely to result in at least selected sections being expanded and more fully oriented to the needs of academic and public libraries.

In addition, the newsletters published by the principal on-line retrieval service vendors include valuable tips and techniques which make useful training aids. Also, the companies make available various instruction manuals and guidebooks.

Finally, a growing number of library schools offer short extension courses in on-line searching (in addition to the longer courses, at the schools mentioned earlier). Among those with workshops open to outsiders are the Universities of Arizona, Denver, Illinois and Toronto, as well as Simmons College (Boston) and Rosary College (River Forest, IL).

While one can master the data bases and operating principles by diligent study, one can only become a proficient on-line searcher by being on-line. Learning to search data bases effectively can only be done through individual practice, on-line, at the computer terminal. A typical, well-prepared reference librarian will probably require at least several hours of live connect time, practicing and interacting with the computer, exploring new possibilities, and refining skills and techniques, before the first search for a patron can be realistically attempted.

While a new searcher's learning curve rises very steeply at first, and then tends to flatten out, it can be expected to continue to rise throughout the first year. A number of studies confirm that experienced searchers are able to complete an on-line search considerably faster than a neophyte. Randolph Hock noted, for example, that between a new searcher's first and second month on the job at the University of Pennsylvania in Philadelphia, the average search time dropped by 11 minutes.[3]

Where feasible, new searchers can also learn a great deal by observing more experienced searchers working at the terminal. Opinion is divided on the question whether or not it is better for a new information services librarian to fully master one data base before trying to learn about others, but there is clearly merit in learning to use only one on-line retrieval system at a time. Subsequent ones can then be mastered much more quickly.

The value of advanced training, or refresher sessions, is also well established. "You can't learn it just once," cautions Xerox's Jim Bement. "I've been to three Predicast meetings on how to use their data base, and I go to SDC and Lockheed updates at least once a year. I always learn something new and useful. Searcher training is ongoing, and it must be. You learn when you *need* to know something. Manuals and first-time courses overload the newcomer. You need annual updates; you learn because your needs grow with experience." He's certainly not alone in that observation. Turning again to the Wanger survey: 96% of the searchers who had had some advanced training reported that they considered it to be useful, while 81% of those who had *not* had the benefit of such training were convinced that it would be useful.[4]

The major vendors of on-line retrieval services offer well-thought-out advanced courses of this kind, but a number of libraries are precluded from taking advantage of them, both because of the steep tuition fees and the associated transportation and accommodation expenses involved, and because of the internal disruption that would result from the absence of the search specialist attending the sessions. The gist of the information imparted in these advanced workshops will probably find its way into print, and therefore be more conveniently available to all who could benefit from it.

Meanwhile, most information service librarians will have to keep themselves up to date by diligently reading vendors' newsletters and announcements, literature distributed by any groups or consortia with which their library may be affiliated, publications of the various professional societies serving the field, and such relevant publications as *Online Magazine, On-Line Review,* and *Messages from MARS.* Within budget limitations, attendance at seminars, workshops, symposia and conferences can also help information services librarians refine and hone their skills.

Interviewing Technique

One aspect of training that may get overlooked in the preoccupation with terminals and data bases is the need to prepare information services librarians for the pre-search interviews with patrons. Here, as with reference librarians who refer patrons to printed sources, the problem is to transform the patron's information need into a question that can be answered by one or more specific sources. The key difference is that with computer-based searches, the user delegates the actual search to the librarian.

Hence, the pre-search interview must describe the nature of the search services and the data bases available, elicit information about the patron's needs, and cast those needs into search statements using the vocabulary of the relevant data bases.

This process calls for sophisticated interviewing skills on the part of the information services librarian. It is not enough for the librarian to have familiarity with the service itself and with the data bases offered; he or she also needs a manner that encourages efficient communication between patron and specialist. Thus, training should deal with techniques for conducting the interview, and with the effects of such nonverbal behavior as eye contact, tone of voice, etc.

The technique of using video tapes or audio tapes to record and later analyze the interview process is being used more and more. Workshops at the Universities of Toronto, Denver, Pittsburgh and Washington, as well as at Syracuse and Drexel Universities, have concentrated on this aspect of on-line services. Tables V-3 and V-4 reproduce forms used by the author for observation and analysis. Not all events occur during the interview, but some are regarded as essential to the success of the search.

Table V-3: Checklist for Observing Events in Pre-Search Interview (Atherton)

DESCRIPTIVE

UD   User Description

_____   a — Experience with computer searches
_____   b — Manual search techniques and experiences

SD   System Description

_____   a — Search service
_____   b — Search procedures

DBS Data Base Selection

_____   a — Discussion of choices
_____   b — Choice made by information specialist

TA   Tutorial Activity

Requested by user		Offered by information specialist	
_____	System	_____	System
_____	Data base	_____	Data base
_____	Search strategy	_____	Search strategy

NEGOTIATION & CONSTRUCTION

CR   Clarification of Request

_____
_____
_____

a — Offered by user
b — Requested by information specialist
c — Agreement on narrative statement of request (may be
  prepared before interview and revised)

RN   Request Negotiation

_____

_____

_____
_____

a — User *discusses* subject area terminology and
  literature relevant to his/her research
b — Information specialist *discusses* retrieval system terminology,
  vocabulary, indexing practices
c — Requirements to be imposed on output (date, language, etc.)
d — Broader or narrower search?

VC   Vocabulary Construction for Search

_____
_____
_____

_____

_____

_____

_____

a — Discuss free text search vs. controlled
b — Terms *offered* or rejected by user (prompted or volunteered)
c — Terms *selected* or rejected by information specialist (with or
  without user agreement?)
d — Vocabulary aids consulted
e — BT, NT, RT, synonyms, etc. reviewed
f — Accepted or rejected terms (by either user or information
  specialist)
g — Terms to be excluded

SS   Search Strategy Formulation

_____
_____
_____
_____
_____

a — Logic formation *discussed* (and, or, not) broader or narrower
b — Concepts arranged in categories
c — Strategies *formed* (with or without user agreement)
d — Fields for searching decided
e — Output formats and limits (no. of references) decided

OTHER ACTIVITIES

DA   Diverting Activity

_____

interruptions, conversation

OA   Other Activities

_____
_____
_____
_____
_____

administrative (name, address, billing arrangements)
explanation of costs
arrangements for on-line session
arrangements for post-search interview
user's use of output

Table V-4: Checklist for Observing Interpersonal Communication During Pre-Search Interview (Atherton)

INFORMATION SPECIALIST	USER
Positive Occurrences	

INFORMATION SPECIALIST	USER
Initially, used open questions	Freely stated information need
*Encouraged discussion Answered questions in understandable way Thoughtful pauses before answering	Asked questions freely
Summarized or paraphrased request	Appeared confident in skill of information specialist
Listened to user *Gave full attention Remained objective about subject of request	Listened to information specialist *Gave full attention
Appeared comfortable and relaxed	Appeared comfortable and relaxed

Negative Occurrences

INFORMATION SPECIALIST	USER
Initially, used closed questions	Had to be prompted to give information
	Changed topic often
	Showed indecision about choices
*Interrupted or talked-over often Gave command or directives, expecting compliance Attempted to demonstrate superior knowledge	*Frequently interrupted or talked-over Objected to suggested strategies Exhibited insufficient knowledge about subject
*Placed user on defensive	*Placed information specialist on defensive
*Gave erratic attention	
Reacted subjectively to request	
Exhibited uneasiness	Exhibited uneasiness
Appeared competitive Appeared submissive Ended interview prematurely Seemed annoyed	Appeared competitive Appeared submissive Terminated interview prematurely Seemed annoyed

Training for Non-searchers

Also important in the start-up of on-line services is training for those not actually conducting searches. A brief orientation for professional librarians not actually engaged in searching can help them understand its role and deal with patrons' requests for information. Training for clerical staff who will be engaged in related tasks, such as manning the information desk, scheduling appointments or handling billing, may also be advisable.

CONCLUSION

This chapter has tried to give the flavor of the many administrative and professional considerations required to launch on-line reference services. Once the initial decision has been made, the library administrator is faced with the need to establish the mission of the service, analyze the potential user market, allocate needed resources, provide organization and physical facilities, and train the specialists who will carry on the service.

In a period of enormous pressure on library budgets, the financial aspects of on-line services quickly come to the fore. Almost no institution can afford to completely subsidize searches for its patrons, and the various ways of charging are complex and controversial.

FOOTNOTES

1. Sara D. Knapp, "The Reference Interview in the Computer Based Setting," *RQ,* summer 1978.

2. A useful discussion of terminal selection considerations, by expert Mark S. Radwin, appeared in the January and April 1977 issues of *ONLINE Magazine* ("Choosing A Terminal," Parts I & II).

3. R.E. Hock, "Providing Access to Externally Available Bibliographic Data Bases in an Academic Library," *College & Research Libraries,* 30 (May 1975).

4. Judith Wanger, Carlos A. Cuadra and M. Fishburn, *Impact of On-Line Retrieval Services: A Survey of Users 1974-1975* (Santa Monica, CA: System Development Corp., 1976).

Part II

Technologies and Applications

VI

Minicomputers and Their Uses

by Audrey M. Grosch

In the late 1960s minicomputers first attracted the eye of some information systems practitioners concentrating on developing library automation systems. As far as can be determined, simultaneous interest was taking place in the U.S., Great Britain, Canada and Australia as libraries moved into the 1970s. Some of the pioneer institutions that employed minicomputers were the University of Minnesota, Oxford's Bodleian Library, the University of British Columbia and the University of Sydney.

However, the early use of minicomputers by libraries was constrained by both hardware and software limitations. Although some hardware limitations were removed by 1972, when Digital Equipment Corp. introduced its PDP 11/40 model minicomputer, software was still a major problem. For example, there still existed no operating systems to allow online real-time use.

Libraries developing online applications in the conventional large computer environment have very sophisticated aids at their disposal which make it possible to move immediately into the design, coding, debugging, testing and installation of a system. Operating systems with file management and peripheral equipment servicing routines exist for these systems in a tested and serviceable form. A variety of higher level programming languages are available that can speed program creation. Software which assists a programmer in testing and debugging programs is also available. But in the minicomputer development era of the early 1970s, software was well behind hardware development. Software of the type and quality found in conventional computers was either nonexistent or too primitive to permit actual development of the interrelated applications found in many library data management activities — activities which demand fast response and quick handling of large numbers of transactions. For example, a circulation system must interact with a cataloging system to obtain bibliographic data, but it must also give rapid response to a charge even though dozens of charges may occur each minute.

Today, on the threshold of the 1980s, this picture has changed. In the minicomputer field, and the very rapidly developing microcomputer area, both hardware and software

Reprinted from *Minicomputers in Libraries, 1979-80* (White Plains, NY: Knowledge Industry Publications, Inc., 1979).

have matured to the point where library applications can be developed practically and economically using readily available hardware and system software products from a variety of manufacturers in the U.S., Europe, Japan and Great Britian. In some cases these foreign products equal or surpass U.S. manufactured equipment, e.g., Facom and Okitac in Japan and Siemens in West Germany.

To gain some idea of the use of small scale computers in libraries, i.e., micro, mini and midicomputers, a questionnaire was sent to subscribers of *Advanced Technology/ Libraries* newsletter as well as libraries known to have interest in such systems. Questionnaire returns were predominantly from domestic libraries, with scattered foreign responses. Although the results cannot be considered as a complete picture of small scale computer use, particularly as new systems are being installed almost daily, the questionnaire does provide the basis for discerning some trends in the application of minicomputers. This chapter highlights the findings from the questionnaire.

Few librarians who answered the questionnaire on behalf of their libraries sent any system documentation. Therefore, the questionnaire responses produced general information about the system's hardware and software environment and the applications performed. It may be helpful to point out that the questionnaire was structured to determine: how the system was developed, i.e., whether it was a commercial, turn-key or in-house system; whether the system operates independently as a stand-alone system or as a front-end computer sharing processing tasks with another or host computers; whether system documentation existed; and whether the library would be willing to consider arrangements with another library interested in its software for replication (unless the software was a commercial proprietary product).

The remaining sections of this chapter address commercially developed systems, both North American and foreign, and then examine some significant work in non-commercial developments. Omission of a system does not imply that the system was of lesser significance but merely that insufficient information was available. Some systems may not even have been reported at all.

TRENDS IN COMMERCIALLY DEVELOPED SYSTEMS

United States and Canadian Firms

Initial minicomputer installations, for the most part, have been concentrated in the area of circulation control. Particular emphasis by commercial system vendors is very apparent here. These basic circulation systems capture data online using optical character recognition (OCR) or bar codes scanned by a hand-held reading device called an optical wand reader. File updating is also performed online for these transactions. Patron or staff inquiry of these systems is usually through an author/title search key or a numeric identity number if the book is in hand. This inquiry is performed by using a visual display terminal with an attached keyboard.

Major commercial vendors of these systems are CL Systems, Inc., DataPhase Systems,

Inc., Systems Control, Universal Library Systems, Ltd., Geac Canada Limited, and Gaylord Bros. Although the Gaylord system uses a minicomputer, it is actually a front-end processor to a host computer at Gaylord which is shared by Gaylord system users. The other systems use a variety of minicomputers alone or in network configurations for very large multi-library systems. An example of this latter type of system is the North Suburban Libraries system near Chicago. In this case, CL Systems, Inc. LIBS 100 installations in individual libraries are connected to and communicating with LIBS 100 systems at other libraries.

It is not the objective here to recommend any single system. Such a choice depends upon many factors which each library itself must consider. However, certain trends in the field of commercially available systems are apparent. Among them are:

• Competition is increasing, with the expectation that in the short term at least, even more firms will enter the field, particularly with new applications for libraries of different types.

• Present firms will build stronger customer bases, permitting them to gain experience in many different operating environments, and making their systems constantly more efficient in serving their users' needs.

• The latest commercially available technology is being used in these systems, but at the same time they are being built to facilitate later expansion for other functions.

• Program reliability and customer response, particularly with the larger companies, are improving.

• New functions, such as cataloging data entry and direct online user catalog searching, have been or are being added by most of the commercial vendors, thus easing the task of keeping the circulation/catalog data base current with library holdings.

• Connections with other bibliographic systems, although still primarily accomplished by processing magnetic tape data from another system, are moving in the direction of direct, online computer-to-computer interaction.

• As the power of minicomputers rapidly increases, the available mass storage and main memory capacities have grown to the point that many libraries, funds permitting, can now have fully online catalogs and in-process files.

• Foreign firms, particularly Canadian, are now attempting to enter the U.S. market. If their efforts are successful and their systems can be supported in the field to compete with U.S. companies, foreign suppliers may be expected to offer some exciting new technology. On this point alone, investigating foreign systems is important for the future.

As an example of the competitive situation, five years ago CL Systems, Inc., then called CLSI, was the only marketer of a workable and successful minicomputer-based stand-alone circulation control system, which in several installations also performed film booking and acquisitions. But since 1976, DataPhase Systems, Inc. has provided systems to Dallas County (Texas) Community College District, Wichita (Kansas) Public Library, Tacoma (Washington) Public Library, Houston (Texas) Public Library, and Oral Roberts University, Tulsa, Oklahoma, among others. Meanwhile, CL Systems, Inc. grew from its initial system installation at the Cleveland (Ohio) Public Library to over 100 installed systems at the end of 1977 and over 200 by the end of 1978.

Each of these companies is introducing devices representing the latest technology into its systems. For example, DataPhase was the first to offer a choice between OCR and bar-encoded labels for book and borrower identification numbers. In late 1977, CL Systems, Inc. introduced a touch screen visual terminal as a device for the public to make inquiries. This terminal, manufactured by Information Dialogs, Inc., one of several terminals currently offered with touch screen capability, allows users to make their choice of displayed alternatives for input by merely touching the appropriate spot on the screen. This affords a whole new approach to access to a computer system for a general public having varying social, psychological or intellectual acceptance of computerized systems.

Another matter of importance in these commercial systems is their move to more flexible record formats. Initially, CL Systems, Inc.'s LIBS 100 used a short, fixed length bibliographic description for each title. Anticipated for introduction in early 1979 is a full Library of Congress MARC record capability which will be offered as a part of their applications software. Obviously, this will enhance their system's functional capabilities, particularly in academic or research libraries which require in-house systems capable of storing and accessing full cataloging records.

One of the latest commercial entries into the U.S. library market is a system offered by Informatics, Inc.'s Library Information Services Group to support L.C. MARC cataloging. It is aptly named Mini-MARC. Full L.C. MARC cataloging records are stored in the floppy diskette attached to a Computer Automation LSI-220 processor packaged into a desk-sized work station. A Hazeltine Co. visual terminal is used to search the MARC catalog record file by main entry, title and L.C. card number. Retrieved records can be modified in any way desired by the user and, with the addition of a special program package, catalog card sets may be printed out on an optional printer. Also, magnetic tape may be substituted for floppy diskettes output. The L.C. MARC data base resides intact on floppy diskettes much like a set of phonograph records in their dust jackets and is updated by weekly mailings of MARC on this medium. The appropriate diskette is chosen by scanning an author/title index which gives the correct diskette for a range of L.C. card numbers.

Moreover, Mini-MARC has as another option full telecommunication capabilities with linkages to systems such as CL Systems' LIBS 100 circulation system, Baker & Taylor's BATAB acquisition systems and soon OCLC's cataloging network. Informatics intends to offer future application packages that will permit this presently single function system to grow as its users may require.

Other Firms

Outside of the United States and Canada several innovative commercial systems are being developed and installed in libraries or information centers.

The CAIRS (Computer Assisted Information Retrieval Systems) retrieval package, offered in Great Britain, was developed for the Leatherhead Food Research Association by Libra Information Systems, Ltd. This turn-key system includes a choice of hardware appropriate to the size of the installation and all software necessary to begin actual use of the system by a library. One installation outside of Leatherhead has been made in the corporate library of The Streetley Co. in Nottinghamshire. CAIRS offers the following functions in each of its five versions: data entry, inverted file subject searching, author searching, accession number location, document or file searching, two library acquisition list outputs and complete file listings, key word index listings, SDI processing, serial character string searching and full record editing/updating.

Searching in this system employs Boolean logic and can be qualified by date. The system also provides for an online thesaurus of terms and implementation of some automatic indexing of documents.

The smallest version of CAIRS is 1A which utilizes floppy diskette storage and a microprocessor in a single, one location installation. This system stores an index to over 2000 items. The largest version is CAIRS 5C which will contain 700,000 bibliographic records and uses a large minicomputer and removable media disk drives in a multi-terminal application.

This system appears to be well designed and affordable for automation of bibliographic retrieval functions for special libraries having patents, reports, reprints, in-house documents or records to access. No such comparable commercially available system is being offered by a U.S. vendor, although the CAIRS system employs Texas Instruments micro- and minicomputers in its respective versions.

Another British system, ADLIB, is designed with the special library and information center in mind. It is being offered both as a turn-key hardware/software product or as a time-sharing service by Lipman Management Resources, Ltd. Thus, very small to large diversified libraries can utilize this system in whichever of these manners would be most cost effective for their file sizes and transaction volumes. ADLIB comes from: an ADaptive management system for special Libraries and Information Bureaux.

ADLIB can store full or partial bibliographic records for monograph, report, preprint, serial or audio-visual materials. Searching is by Boolean operators, i.e., and, or, not, linking keywords or by interrogation of simple rotated string subject indexes. Selective dissemination of information (SDI) and retrospective searching are both accommodated in this system. Online thesaurus maintenance and the ability to accept British MARC format bibliographic data are features of the system that lend appreciably to its utility for a variety of libraries. Circulation control is also handled by the system via data entry from visual terminals. Output can be generated on the line printer or on magnetic tape for COM processing for micrographic catalogs. The hardware system supporting ADLIB is a PRIME 300 central processor with a minimum of 128K (128,000) bytes of memory, with peripheral equipment chosen appropriately to the size of the system.

A final commercial system which was discovered through the questionnaire was the VUBIS system, a joint development of the Free University of Brussels and Interactive Systems, N.V.S.A., also in Brussels. This system employs Digital Equipment Corp. PDP 11 minicomputers and can be arranged to support up to 1.4 million titles. The software supporting this system is the MUMPS (Massachusetts General Hospital Utility Multi-Programming System) operating system, data management system and application programming language. The language version is that supported by Digital Equipment Corp. (The DataPhase Systems, Inc. system previously discussed also employs MUMPS but with a version supplied by Medical Information Technology, Inc.)

VUBIS is an interactive cataloging input and public catalog inquiry system which is being planned to also include a circulation control subsystem. Acquisitions and serials check-in are expected to be implemented in 1979. This system has several features which make it quite unique and responsive to the environment of its first installation.

A prime feature is multiple language interaction. At the Free University a user may inquire in French, Flemish or English. In a university which has a French- and Flemish-speaking clientele separated into essentially two user groups, this affords each language user equivalent access to the system. Interactive Systems is planning on marketing the system to other European countries and is prepared to handle German and other European language versions.

The second unique feature of this system is the manner in which subject searching and access is provided. In this scheme, keywords are assigned within the Universal Decimal Classification (UDC) scheme so that one may search by keyword tied to appropriate UDC numbers which are then employed to locate the item on the shelves. One may also search directly by UDC, starting with a general number and receiving keywords associated with this number and moving through more specific related numbers, narrowing the search in this manner. This is an appropriate technique for libraries using the UDC classification but one which would apply only to very few libraries in the U.S. or Canada that do not use either L.C. or versions of the Dewey classification.

NON-COMMERCIAL SYSTEMS IN THE U.S. AND CANADA

Not surprisingly, most libraries having minicomputer systems acquired their software from commercial vendors. But some libraries have systems which were not supplied by outside vendors on a turn-key basis. These libraries either developed their own systems in-house using their own staff or contracted with outside software or systems engineering firms.

Again, the tendency in this area is initially to develop a system concentrating on a specific application such as circulation and then move to incorporate further applications. Libraries which have invested considerable effort and expense in software for a large-scale shared computer have tended to acquire minicomputers to provide front-end local processing capability to remove some of the host computer central load and improve responsiveness at the library end.

An example of this kind of minicomputer installation is at the Hennepin County (Minn.) Library (HCL). HCL employs a Digital Equipment PDP 11/34 with 96K words of memory to perform online cataloging data entry and serve as a remote job entry station for its link to the Hennepin County IBM 370/168 computer. But Hennepin County is planning on extending minicomputer usage to support public catalog access and circulation.

Another example of the front-end type of configuration is the medical library network serials management system PHILSOM III, developed by the Washington University School of Medicine Library. PHILSOM III is designed to employ a PDP 11 computer at each site for local holdings file maintenance. This is an alternative to remote batch job entry or mailing of sets of punched cards to update local holdings files on the central system. Also, a PDP 11 serves as a terminal communication handler for the network coordinator's terminal for the basic data file, which is maintained centrally for all network member libraries.

University of Minnesota's MILS

The first U.S. development effort using a stand-alone minicomputer as a host system designed for library applications was funded at the University of Minnesota Bio-Medical Library in 1972 by a three-year National Library of Medicine grant. After a continuation grant, the effort is now totally funded by the University of Minnesota through state funds. This system is simply called Minicomputer Library System (MILS), an acronym following in the tradition of the Minnesota Union List of Serials (MULS).

MILS began in the early minicomputer era when no vendor software was available and few hardware systems afforded the necessary features to permit easy use. MILS thus developed independently of Digital Equipment Corp.'s operating systems. MILS can be used with any PDP 11/34 or larger PDP 11 series minicomputer. In its Bio-Medical Library installation at Minnesota, it uses a large PDP 11/40 configuration. In its new St. Paul Campus installation, a PDP 11/60 system was installed in late November 1978.

MILS software employs multi-purpose program routines. Figure VI-1 provides a simplified diagram of MILS software organization.

System operations handle functions such as input/output procedures, data conversions and service of interrupts, which are messages generated by users at terminals connected to the system. Applications are defined by the procedures software which direct the other portions of the system to execute the tasks required to build a user application. Terminal management involves video display and character printer devices for communication, security and main memory allocation. The interface routines set parameters to process data between its internal and external coded forms. Preparation of data

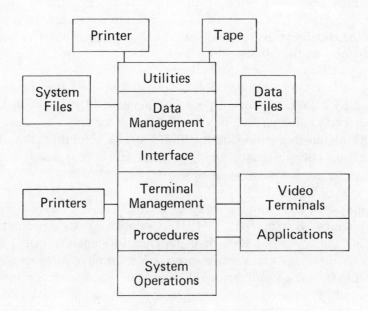

Figure VI-1: MILS Software Organization.

for file input or output is controlled via the data management module. Special purpose activities such as file regeneration, magnetic tape conversion and printed record outputs are handled via the utility module. These modules are organized operationally into a system component and a library component.

By 1978, after six years, all of the system component modules and some of the library modules are operational in the Bio-Medical Library system. On the library application side, components for monograph cataloging, data entry, editing and conversion are operating together with an online searching capability by author, title and various numeric coded fields. The Bio-Medical Library has a record conversion in progress for monograph titles which started by using magnetic tapes of selected L.C. MARC records for works identified as MARC titles. Acquisitions/accounting and a user online cataloging inquiry application are being designed in the Bio-Medical Library system.

At the new St. Paul campus installation, development of a serials management application is scheduled for 1979 and further systems programming work is also planned. The University of Minnesota Libraries plan further MILS installations as funds and staff permit, all using common software and applications tailored to the requirements of each individual user library. Ultimately, communication links will be created among each library's processor, creating a local University of Minnesota Libraries network system.

Since 1977, the Lister Hill Center for Bio-Medical Communications has been developing a full functioning online library management system using Data General minicomputers and the MUMPS software system. Its system design, however, unlike MILS, is even more generalized and less dependent upon the present hardware. Thus, versions could be more easily created for different minicomputers than with MILS, although MILS can accommodate any configuration based on a PDP 11/34 or larger PDP11 computer.

MILS was designed to take maximum advantage of the DEC PDP 11 series hardware and assembly language during a time when limited memory made such an approach imperative. At the National Library of Medicine (NLM), a system for acquisitions and an interface to NLM online files are operational. Circulation and several other applications were being programmed in late 1978. This work is also being performed to meet the needs of the U.S. Army library, which has contracted for this system as its basic supporting system.

Both of the above institutions should bear watching as they are trying to achieve modular, flexible systems able to be replicated within their own institutions and have gained considerable support. Yet both of these systems use very different design and programming approaches.

Other Non-Commercial Systems

Another longtime user of minicomputers is the University of Pittsburgh, which uses a PDP 11/10 and an 11/34 along with a DEC System 10 shared large-scale computer for acquisitions, accounting, payroll, circulation and some online searching and complete in-process file control. Book form catalog production processing is also handled via this system. Similarly, the University of California at Berkeley General Library has used Datapoint minicomputers for online cataloging and data entry for approximately four years.

Although many systems in the U.S. and Canada depend upon Digital Equipment Corp. and Data General Corp. hardware, many other manufacturers are also represented. For example, Hewlett-Packard Series 3000 minicomputers are employed in the circulation system designed and installed at Virginia Polytechnic Institute and State University. One decided attraction of this system is its data base management facilities provided through a package called IMAGE and its associated retrieval/inquiry facility, QUERY. A powerful programming language called SPL also makes this a very attractive machine host for online library applications. Another Hewlett-Packard user is the Claremont College (Calif.) Honnold Library, which has a reputation as one of the pioneering users of data processing in its library. Also industrial libraries such as Allied Chemical Corp. and a school system in Fairfax County, Virginia use Hewlett-Packard systems for their library support. In Canada, the International Development Research Centre Library has developed a multi-function system around a Hewlett-Packard 3000 which supports acquisitions, payroll, cataloging, serials check-in and claiming and full author, subject, title Boolean searching. This system will be offered to developing countries' governments and is in use by at least one other Canadian agency, the Sport Information Resource Centre, Ottawa.

The City of Cerritos (Calif.) Public Library, through a system development contract with Tamas Associates, has installed a custom designed system run on a General Automation 440-DS minicomputer programmed in commercial FORTRAN. The National Library of Canada uses equipment from IV Phase Systems, Ltd. (its full model name is the 7009-M System IV/90) with five magnetic tape units and 14 terminals for Canadian MARC file data entry and file building. Later processing is done from these magnetic tapes on a large IBM system.

FOREIGN DESIGNED NON-COMMERCIAL SYSTEMS

Of interest to special libraries and information centers which must produce abstract bulletins or published indexes from relatively large bibliographic data bases, the STATUS II system developed by the United Kingdom Atomic Energy Authority is used there and at the BNF Metals Technology Centre's Grove Laboratories in Wantage, England. The STATUS II replaces a system which requires a shared, large scale computer operating in batch mode for searching and file processing.

STATUS II runs on a Prime 300 minicomputer under the PRIMOS operating system at BNF. FORTRAN programming language is used to implement STATUS II. Originally, the software at Harwell was implemented by an IBM 360 and a Digital Equipment Corp. PDP 11/45 minicomputer. Only two man months' effort was needed to transfer the software over to the Prime 300, indicating how readily the software lent itself to another hardware system.

In this system a user is provided a searching capability using Boolean operators and word proximity on both full text abstracts and bibliographic structured indexes. Thus, both free text and controlled vocabulary searching are supported. A structured thesaurus can be handled by the system to support the controlled vocabulary approach, as are macro, word truncation, synonym and homonym handling facilities. One may also search by values imbedded within text, a feature particularly useful for numeric data files. Full editing facilities exist which allow the user to add, delete, change or replace any elements of information defined in the files.

From this online system, BNF produces magnetic tapes of abstract text for computerized photocomposition by author, subject and other index products. Online, the system may be used for retrospective searching and entry of bibliographic data or production of current awareness output based on user interest profiles. A large retrospective file conversion project is also underway to move data from its former batch system called ASSASSIN.

In Switzerland, the Hauptbibliothek der Universität Zürich Irchel has installed a system supplied by Interdata, AG which is used for acquisitions, cataloging data entry and bibliographic file maintenance. It employs a minicomputer by Interdata built around an Intel 8080 model microprocessor. The software is named TEX 400 and the configuration is a single user terminal with two floppy diskette units which provide low cost direct access storage on removable media. It is a preprocessing system essentially for data entry. with the production then finished on another university computer system via batch processing.

Australian libraries were very early users of minicomputer technology. At the University of New South Wales Library, a Digital Equipment Corp. PDP 11/40 operating under the Bell Laboratories-developed UNIX operating system is used for the cataloging system. Five video terminals provide data entry to the system, with additional applications being planned over the next several years.

Another system for cataloging is in place at the Australian National University, which uses an Interdata 8/32. Its processor is equipped with a very large main memory and disk storage which will undoubtedly make its minicomputer able to add many other applications.

For those interested in an Australian system based on a Digital Equipment Corp. PDP 11/34 minicomputer using the RSTS/E operating system and implemented in FOR-TRAN IV, a cataloging system with book fund accounting and order writing is operational at La Trobe University Library. Both book and card form catalog production is supported via this system and some programs also run on another computer system. In development is an acquisitions capability, of which the book fund accounting and order writing routines will form a part. The system is also used to list and process gift materials. This system performs some functions as an independent processor, but also communicates with a DEC system 10/70 host computer.

An even earlier use of minicomputers for cataloging support, perhaps even the first, was that of the Bodleian Library in Oxford, England, using a DEC PDP 11/20 for the conversion of a 1.25 million title catalog. This system performs online data entry and editing prior to processing by a large shared computer.

Although only one system was reported from Japan through the questionnaire, there may well be quite a few similar systems throughout the Orient, which run on Japanese micro- and minicomputer models. The Gunma University Library in the city of Maebashi uses an Okitac-4500C minicomputer in a small single user configuration serving a library with 300,000 volumes and annual serials subscriptions of 6000 titles.

In contrast with most other systems, however, the Gunma installation shows a departure from the prevalent trend of online processing back to batch processing for acquisitions, accounting, cataloging and serials control functions. The single terminal is used for an online circulation system. Thus two jobs — one real time, the other batch — can be serviced at the same time in what is known as a multi-processing system.

CONCLUSION

This overview has attempted to highlight some of the information gleaned from the wealth of data found in the bibliography, as well as to provide some information about systems which exist but may not have been formally reported in scholarly and professional journals. It should generally serve to stimulate the interest of librarians and encourage them to look at systems which are moving libraries in new directions, toward greater responsiveness and improved manageability. Ideally, it will motivate librarians in dealing with new problems and provide the knowledge needed to contend with these problems.

VII

Computer Application: Integrated vs. Individual

by Audrey N. Grosch

Historically, most library systems have been conceived to perform the tasks associated with a single application. Usually that application has been defined in light of the particular library's most pressing need. This is in contrast to a logical process where possible applications are identified by looking at all library activities, which are mostly labor intensive. Much of this work revolves around the initial decision to make an acquisition, followed by that acquisition's repeated retrieval for patron use.

This is not to say that many libraries have not taken an integrated, broad view of their requirements. However, few libraries have actually proceeded to develop applications and install them with the detailed perspective needed to assure that each separate function can be linked with the others. Typical library applications in acquisitions, cataloging, serials, circulation or reference use common information, change the status of certain data fields and need to share data. But too often the recognition of this overlap comes about only after a number of applications have been already implemented.

SINGLE APPLICATION SYSTEMS

The basic premise of single application development is to define a set of procedures, both human and computer related, to achieve a desired result. Thus, libraries have developed procedures to fulfill the acquisitions, cataloging or other departmental responsibilities in a library. For example, the desired results from an acquisition system may be:

• To maintain an up-to-date record of the status of items under consideration for purchase, actually ordered or received but not yet available for public use.

• To maintain book fund accounting, detailed transaction records and produce summary accounting data for institution-wide accounting use.

• To produce purchase orders or issue payment authorizations and/or checks to vendors.

Reprinted from *Minicomputers in Libraries, 1979-80* (White Plains, NY: Knowledge Industry Publications, Inc., 1979).

• To monitor vendor performance in order fulfillment.

• To produce any transmittal documents needed to send the work to cataloging or to the requesting library unit.

• To monitor claim status and issue claims as deemed appropriate by guidelines set up within the computer system or by the librarian upon alert by the system.

• To issue lists of newly acquired works for distribution to library users.

To deliver these results, the acquisition system must provide certain data. Later, some of this data may be used and modified in the cataloging process, particularly if the bibliographic information is obtained from verified information such as L.C. MARC. Other information related to the price, shipping instructions or vendor is usually not required for the cataloging process. If the library uses a separate system for the cataloging process, there is the problem of transferring this information to that system in machine-readable form without rekeyboarding data, particularly if separate computer systems are involved. Unfortunately, with separately developed data files, the limits on the data required for each of the two systems may not be recognized until both systems have been installed.

Developing a single purpose system which has its own files defined solely for that application is the easiest way to quickly achieve a workable solution and deliver specific results for a given function in the library. This is the reason that circulation systems have been relatively easy to bring into operation when compared with other application areas. Since the data in a circulation system are usually subsets of full bibliographic data and requirements for circulation transaction recording are readily isolated, the desired result for circulation control is relatively easy to achieve. In this separate circulation system, each file usually contains brief bibliographic information sufficient for recall, overdue notice issue or identification of the item upon a user's request. In the ideal situation where such a separate circulation system is developed, its bibliographic data would be provided through processing machine-readable data from an automated cataloging system. Examples of such machine-readable catalog data may come from OCLC, a COM catalog or an outside commercial vendor. But if the library does not already use such outside sources, then the library must manually keyboard the precise information from its catalog record required for the circulation system.

One can see that although there are advantages to simplicity in using the single application accompanied by its specifically designed data files, there are problems which can cause difficulty in the integration of several systems each designed this way. These problems revolve around the following factors:

• Application programs are usually written so that they depend upon explicit data and file structures and thus are not independent of data, i.e., if the physical position of data in the file changes or requires alteration to accommodate a new field of information, then the programs which process this data must also be changed to enable them to locate the correct data in the file.

- Most frequently the organization of the file depends upon the primary method of processing used by the system, e.g., online interactive systems use some form of random organization while batch processing systems use sequential file structures.

- It is not always possible to design a system that will make full use of every bit of information that is available, e.g., the ISBN number included in a cataloging record may only later be recognized as a possible identification number for a book to be circulated on interlibrary loan.

- Although fixed length record and file structures are simpler to employ and might be advisable for a single application, they are inefficient in disk storage of bibliographic files. Thus, the use of fixed structures minimizes flexibility in altering the system without major file reorganization and reprogramming.

- On the one hand, there is a need to minimize redundant data due to the long record lengths commonly encountered in library systems. Yet where a fast online response is required, it may be necessary to maintain controlled redundancy of certain specific data elements.

In order to minimize these problems, one must first evaluate the needs of each library unit for data processing support and determine how these needs relate to each other. The data requirements and relationships of these applications must be determined at the time that general design is being done for each potential application, before actually procuring or developing any specific application. As an example of what this means, an acquisitions system will produce information that must be used at some point in an accounting procedure, a cataloging procedure, perhaps a circulation procedure and also perhaps a binding procedure. Every library application essentially depends upon information that may be generated by either a preceding or following application.

Once this is accomplished, there are two options to creating the system. The first of these is to acquire programs, packaged systems or network services for each application, with the interrelationship problems in mind. In this manner, for example, data from a network cataloging service could be readily transferred to a minicomputer based, in-house circulation system.

The second of these approaches is to view the development of all applications around the design of an integrated data base which enables data representation and file organization to be independent of application programs. This preserves flexibility to adjust applications once they are installed or to install new applications without adverse impact on existing applications. This second approach is discussed below.

INTEGRATED APPLICATION APPROACH

Applying computer systems to technical processing, bibliographic information retrieval or library management is a complex situation. Devising systems which handle many of these traditional library tasks in an integrated fashion is complicated further by the nature of the information with which library systems deal. Moreover, depending on use, some data base structures lend themselves more readily to specific methods of accessing or retrieving information. Thus, many trade-off design decisions characterize application development for libraries. In addition, some applications, such as recording circulation transactions and discharge, require very fast response times and ability to handle very large volumes of essentially short transactions. On the other hand, interactive data base searches or retrieving a record for a cataloger require adequate response times but with less frequency and longer transaction length.

Many libraries and librarians have taken the position that they cannot afford to develop any but the simplest of application support. Yet, perhaps more than any industry or government system, the library data processing problem is one that requires intimate involvement of librarians and many specialists from the data processing field before complex, integrated, multi-application systems can be developed.

Minicomputers have brought computing power to the individual library so that local library needs can be more economically and responsively handled. However, before this is possible on a larger scale, sufficiently capable programming must be available to the individual library.

Some of this software will undoubtedly come from commercial vendors who will be in a position to develop a standardized application which can be tailored to the needs of an individual library system. However, more complex functions such as online interactive cataloging, serials management or specialized systems for archival finding aids and collection management will require a substantial investment in custom development by the individual library.

This investment will vary according to the services, needs and mission of each library. Some libraries may be able to effectively obtain and modify software developed by other institutions, marry this software with commercially supplied systems and network services and achieve a degree of integration. As one possibility, the Sports Information Resource Centre, Canada, is using an online cataloging and retrieval system developed by the International Development Research Centre, also in Canada. It could conceivably add other bibliographic services via access to a system such as the UTLAS system or search services such as Lockheed, CAN/OLE or System Development Corp. But many large, sophisticated libraries and information services will require complex and highly integrated systems to meet their own special needs.

In the case of the University of Minnesota Libraries, the Wilson Library Cataloging Division and several other library units use OCLC, have developed programs in-house and maintain them for the Minnesota Union List of Serials (MULS) on an IBM 370 computer system, and since 1972 have been working on one of the earliest projects to create a dedicated, online minicomputer-based library system in the Bio-Medical Library. The plan is eventually to serve the library units through a series of minicomputer installations using the same system and applications software. The hardware configuration of these systems will vary but will all involve using a DEC PDP-11 series minicomputer. A series of dedicated minicomputer systems is the alternative to using a large conventional computer system. Clearly, to achieve this kind of system will require considerable time and investment.

Integrated system development requires a team of experienced data processing professionals working closely with librarians who know how to define the procedural and data needs of the library. Obviously, not every library in this situation can or should support its own in-house project staff because the management of such development activity also requires a special expertise not usually found within a library. The alternative is proper use of technical consultants to design a general system. This general design specification may be used to solicit the services of outside vendors who specialize in developing minicomputer programming or supplying packages of both hardware and software. In this way, the library is then in a position to determine if the vendor's technical approach is sound and if the cost of development is reasonable for the work proposed. The library is also responsible for judging the performance and standards developed to test the system for the results desired, and to see that the vendor receives the cooperation of the library staff which he needs to fulfill his obligation under the contract.

SUMMARY

Traditionally, libraries have designed systems to accomplish a single, specific task, such as acquisitions or cataloging. With increasing frequency, however, libraries are recognizing that there is overlap and the possibility of shared data in each of these systems, suggesting the design of a system which integrates these tasks from the very beginning, through the development of an integrated data base. If the system is so designed, a library may add or expand applications without the need for reprogramming or other adverse impact on the existing applications.

This integrated approach is not without its costs, however. Devising even single application programs is complex and multi-application systems are even more complicated. Some of the software is available from commercial vendors or may be obtained from other libraries or networks. On the other hand, a specialized system for archival finding aids or collection management may require substantial investment in custom development by the library.

A PDP 11 SERIES minicomputer, shown next to standard five-drawer file cabinets for size comparison. (Courtesy Digital Equipment Corp.)

HARDWARE FOR A MINICOMPUTER system: central processing unit, hard-copy printers, keyboards and CRT displays. (Courtesy Data General.)

VIII

Computer-Supported Catalogs

by S. Michael Malinconico and Paul J. Fasana

AUTOMATED CATALOG CARD SYSTEMS

The most effective uses of computing equipment in support of catalog maintenance have been the recent systems that print catalog cards on demand. The most successful of these systems has been the one developed by OCLC, the pre-eminent producer and distributor of catalog cards in the United States. In 1975 the Library of Congress' card sales, which had been showing a steady decrease since 1971 (the inauguration of OCLC services), dropped to 45 million cards; OCLC printed in excess of 52 million cards that year.[1]

Using a computer to produce catalog cards is clearly a gross under-utilization of its capabilities. Nonetheless, it is economically justified when used by a network like OCLC, which provides access to a prodigious store of bibliographic data for shared cataloging purposes. When used in this way, automation intrudes only minimally on the status quo. In a sense OCLC can be viewed as a replacement for the catalog card services its participants were using prior to implementation of the system. Catalog cards produced by computer can be just as easily integrated into an existing catalog as can overtyped LC cards. In fact, OCLC cards can be more easily used, as they come already overtyped with headings and call numbers and are presorted for filing.

Adopting computer-produced cards removes the need to consider divided catalogs, freezing existing catalogs or any other traumatic changes. Moreover, since the machine-made cards can be safely filed in a standard card catalog, a library may have the illusion that it can reverse the commitment to use a computerized system at any time. To all appearances, business can be carried on as usual.

This sense of security is generally false. Far-reaching administrative changes are usually effected along with the introduction of shared cataloging systems into catalog departments. Professional positions are often replaced with paraprofessional staff for copy cataloging; proof slip and depository card filing units, as well as card preparation units, are disbanded. Administrators gain an opportunity to exercise professional creativity without the need to worry about technical consequences with which they are not

Reprinted from *The Future of the Catalog: The Library's Choices* (White Plains, NY: Knowledge Industry Publications, Inc., 1979).

in general very comfortable. Computer-produced catalog cards offer a relatively simple way to introduce automation with seemingly little risk.

Catalog card production systems are a relatively straightforward computer application. A machine-readable cataloging record, like a catalog card, represents a unit record that can be reproduced under all of the headings specified by its entry elements. Thus, a unit record once created in machine-readable form can easily be used to print an entire card set. In addition, a computer can easily manipulate the text contained in that record to produce headed cards automatically. If the unit record is created with a call number, or one is added to it prior to card creation, the number can be made to appear on each card in the set. Since all of the data is entered only once, and automatically reproduced on each card, the possibility of transcription error is greatly reduced.

The LC MARC distribution service introduced the possibility of access to machine-readable records requiring only the addition of local call numbers. The extremely low price of LC MARC records virtually assured the success of automated card production systems. Though the price of MARC records has risen over the years, the cost of a single record obtained via the distribution service can still be reckoned at approximately 3.5 cents, whereas a single unheaded card obtained from LC was approximately 6.8 cents in 1977.[2]. In addition, cards can be produced from MARC on demand. A library can order precisely the cards needed; it need not pay for, and store, extraneous cards.

OCLC began by providing such a simple service, offering a batch-processing service in which catalog card sets were produced from LC MARC tapes.[3] The only variation permitted in the content of the record was the library's local call number. Nonetheless, OCLC provided, and continues to provide, great flexibility in formatting cards according to a user's unique specifications.

This process represents the simplest possible card production service. The library provides the processing center with an LC card number for the record desired, along with its own call number. The system then produces the requisite number of copies needed to complete a card set. The library can also introduce some simple refinements that permit cards to be produced for a number of catalogs in presorted order.

Such a system can be highly effective and economical, but it does have limitations. It does not permit alteration of the bibliographic content of a cataloging record or creation of a new record: it requires waiting for the desired MARC record to be issued by LC. In addition, there is no assurance that a record exists or when it will appear when a card request is submitted. These same limitations, of course, exist with the LC card distribution service. The only recourse a library has in that case is to prepare its own cards if it cannot wait for LC copy.

Shared Cataloging Systems

When a MARC record does not exist, the library can provide for the creation of a new record from which the desired cards can be generated. In an automated environment the contributed MARC record can be used just like an LC MARC record by any other user of the system. The chances are therefore greater that an existing record will be found when a card request is made to that system. Thus, the investment made in creating MARC records need not be justified completely by the increased efficiency in creating card sets. All system users have a share in the effort of creating machine-readable cataloging records, and all share in the benefits of their use.

Such a system is not practical if operated in a batch-processing mode. One might be quite willing to accept without prior inspection a record created by the Library of Congress, but one might not be so confident of the acceptability of cataloging created by all of the other participants in a cooperative system. Thus, in 1971 OCLC made the entire data base instantaneously accessible to all system participants.

In this way a library gains a number of important advantages. It can know immediately if: 1) a machine-readable cataloging record exists in the data base; 2) whether it is an LC MARC record; and 3) if not, whether it is acceptable. If the system permits modification of existing records, users can increase their reliance on contributed records. Many will be quite acceptable with only minor modifications.

The increased usability of contributed records is an important justification of the costs of an on-line system. Another is the resulting simplification of local procedures when a library can determine immediately whether or not a cataloging record exists in the data base; for example, there is no need to establish and maintain procedures to control materials while awaiting cataloging copy. If, in addition, the system provides flexible and efficient access to a large source data base for copy cataloging, a library can easily dispense with subscriptions to manual cataloging copy sources (e.g., LC proof slips) and with the need to maintain and search these files.

From the foregoing it should be apparent why an on-line system whose principal product is computer-printed catalog cards would be a successful venture. OCLC's success has been such that it has continuously attracted additional users, thereby decreasing the costs of the service; this in turn attracts an increased number of participants who contribute to the shared data base, serving to increase further the attractiveness of the service. In short, there has emerged a self-perpetuating cycle restrained only by the technical capacity of the system.

Card Creation Process

All modifications made by individual OCLC participants appear in an off-line file. Once this file has been made, card creation is a fairly straightforward process. The content designators in a MARC record provide computer programs with all the necessary data distinctions needed to format the text in a card image. Since all tracings are identified by specific content designators, the system can also create the required number of cards, each appropriately headed. Additional card sets can easily be created for a variety of catalogs.

For the sake of efficiency, most modern computer systems create a print image file before actually printing a lengthy report, providing the library with an opportunity to sort the printed report *after* it has been created. Thus, it is quite simple to produce cards sorted into batches intended for various catalogs, and further presorted for filing into each. The filing requirements of a card system are not particularly stringent, as cards are eventually placed into catalogs by human filers who can make any necessary final adjustments. In addition, only a relatively small number of cards are produced at a time, so minor filing errors are of no particular concern.

Depending on the sophistication of the system's card profiling facilities, particular entries can be selected for inclusion in different catalogs, or the format of the card can be varied for particular catalogs, producing a flexibility, not possible in a manual system, to custom tailor cards. Unlike a manual system, a computer can very easily rearrange and reorganize data in as many combinations as desired. Although a computer provides the ability to abbreviate records in those instances where the full bibliographic detail is both unnecessary or actually distracting, there is not much advantage in doing so with catalog cards. The full 3 x 5 inch catalog card must be used whether or not it is covered with print.

Printing catalog cards by computer has required solving some particularly complicated mechanical problems, such as the physical extension of a catalog card and the presence of a rod hole. Further complications are introduced when an entry requires overflow cards. Sufficient information must be carried over to a continuation card so that it can be related to its parent card. Formatting call numbers by computer also presents particularly tricky problems.

Each of these, though complicated, does not require any particular conceptual breakthroughs. They can all easily be solved. (OCLC, among others, has done so.) The problems are enumerated here merely to provide a sense of the effort required to produce a truly flexible card printing system.

Catalog Maintenance

Since a number of operations are eliminated when catalog cards are produced by computer — searching for cataloging copy, duplicating cards, overtyping headings and presorting cards for filing — such cards can generally be produced and entered into a catalog fairly quickly. OCLC usually delivers card sets within two weeks, frequently more quickly.

The content of computer-produced catalog cards is easily custom tailored for integration into an existing catalog. The benefits of such a facility can hardly be disputed. However, it should also be apparent that such a system cannot fully address the problems of maintaining a catalog. Ohmes and Jones note that an automated facility, such as OCLC, addresses only half — the simple, clerical half — of the cataloging process. The difficult, time-consuming part is not only totally ignored but actually made more troublesome by the efficiency with which the automated portion can be pursued.

> Catalog building consists of two phases: (1) the creation of cataloging copy representing the works being added to the collection; and (2) the integration of that copy into the existing catalog. Phase One simply involves the creation of a record; Phase Two determines whether or not the reader will be able to retrieve that record once it has been dropped below the rod among a million others.[4]

Ohmes and Jones compare computer processing to the manual procedures that would be required when an inconsistency is encountered between a new record to be added to a catalog, and an existing entry:

> When older copy is used for a work being added to the collection, obsolete entries on the card can be altered quickly and cheaply. A drop of correction fluid, a neatly typed correction, and the card is ready for

duplication. When the older form is embedded in the catalog, however, revision is tedious and costly. Conflict of a current LC entry with an earlier LC entry, for instance, may require the removal and revision of a partial set, a full set or multiple sets of cards from the catalog. *There is no inexpensive method for updating the card catalog.*[5] [Emphasis added.]

Obviously, a computer can have no effect on cards created and filed before implementation of the automated system. Unfortunately, it can have little control even over those cards it has created. Changes to the data-base records are easily made; however, mechanisms that would permit these changes to be reflected in a card catalog are at best cumbersome, complex and costly. To reprint cards automatically when a data-base change is made requires a method of identifying the cards to be replaced; i.e., the system would have to create a "before and after image" of the record. The cost of locating and withdrawing the revised cards would generally be nearly as great as filing them in the first place.

This problem is by no means infrequent, nor is it confined to errors committed when records are created. LC's own printed cards are subjected to close scrutiny and revision before they are filed. Nonetheless, 5% of all LC cards need to be modified and reprinted at least once in the first year following their original printing, 22% will require some alteration in a 10-year period and 42% will be modified at least once in a 30-year period.[6]

Thus, although a computerized system can provide invaluable assistance in *creating* cards to be filed into a manual catalog, it cannot begin to address questions associated with finding a more effective means of *maintaining* a catalog. A catalog card production system implies that the catalog is off-line. The system is best seen as a mechanized cataloging support facility whose principal objective is the maintenance of a resource data base.

An automated system can have no effect on the intrinsic limitations of a card catalog. The capacity of the computer to produce virtually limitless added entries cannot be utilized, as card catalogs cannot absorb the resulting increase in bulk. Of even more serious consequence is the restraining influence a large card catalog can exert on an automated system. A machine-readable data base can be quite simply and efficiently modified and reorganized, but one is generally reluctant to do so because of the difficulty inherent in reflecting these changes in the images of these records, which have already been inscribed on 3 x 5 inch cards. Thus card files, though an efficient and timely method of displaying additions to a machine-readable data base, literally force one to hold the capabilities of an automated system in check.

AUTOMATED BOOK FORM CATALOG SYSTEMS

One answer to these limitations is to select a display form for the cataloging data base which is periodically recreated. If previous displays can be unceremoniously discarded, they exert no inertia against data-base changes or reorganization. The traditional printed book catalog satisfies this requirement; when revised cumulations are issued, the entire weight of the past is discarded.

This section will discuss the creation of *book form* catalogs, both printed and in microform. The problems and advantages of producing book form catalogs are for the most part common to both versions. Although the medium chosen does exert an influence on many decisions regarding the content of a catalog, this influence is usually a secondary consideration. Any system that can produce a printed book catalog can with relatively trivial modification produce a computer output microform (COM) catalog. However, a system designed to produce a COM catalog cannot be readily modified to produce a printed catalog. The ease with which a microform catalog can be produced by a system designed to create a phototypeset printed book catalog has been demonstrated by The New York Public Library, which has produced both printed and microform catalogs with the same automated system.

Development

The first uses of computing machinery as a means of maintaining a catalog were intended to solve the problems of producing printed book catalogs. In 1951 *New Serial Titles* and the King County Library (Seattle, Wash.) developed the first effective mechanized systems for this purpose.[7] These systems used the punched card sorting devices that were actually forerunners of modern tabulating machines.[8] By today's standards this technique seems quite crude. It required that data be entered one line at a time onto punched cards. An IBM Tabulator was then used to sort and print the text.[9]

The Los Angeles County Public Library (LACPL), a sprawling system with 114 service outlets, had card catalogs in only 26 of its branches in 1952.[10] The situation was reaching crisis proportions when the LACPL learned of the King County experiment and decided to follow suit. The Los Angeles County project began with a pilot catalog of the system's juvenile holdings in August 1952. The first edition of the library's Children's Catalog was published before the end of that year.[11] It was decided that the children's catalog was to be a quick reference alphabetical tool, rather than a scholarly bibliographic instrument.[12] Much of the information contained on catalog cards, which is important to the cataloging department, was considered either unnecessary or confusing to the public.[13] Thus, book catalog entries were highly abbreviated, containing only author, title edition, publication date, number of volumes, short annotations and classification numbers.[14]

Having demonstrated the viability of the technique with a juvenile catalog, the LACPL began work immediately on an adult catalog. Preparation of the first edition, which contained 161,000 titles, required two years (1953-1955). The catalog was issued in 170 copies of 24 500-page volumes.[15] More than 1.6 million cards were needed to produce the full catalog of 161,000 titles. In a system as large as Los Angeles County's the technique, although somewhat cumbersome, proved viable. In 1958 LACPL determined that maintenance costs for a card catalog were 17 times greater than those for the book catalog, despite the awkwardness of the techniques used to produce and maintain it.[16]

Fortunately, modern computer systems have eliminated such cumbersome procedures. Today, the data that occupied 1.6 million cards in the original LACPL system can easily be contained with greater security on a single reel of magnetic tape. A number of such book catalog creation systems have been developed. Among them are the Harvard University Widener Library Shelf List, the Stanford University Undergraduate Library

Catalog, the University of California Union Catalog Supplement and the book catalogs of The New York Public Library. In addition, a number of systems were developed by commercial vendors such as Auto-Graphics, Inc. and Science Press.

The culmination of printed book catalog systems development came with the production of the University of California Union Catalog Supplement (UCUCS) and the catalogs of The New York Public Library. The UCUCS is significant because it represents the single largest catalog yet produced by automated means. When it was issued in 1972, the catalog contained some 2.6 million entries representing 798,000 titles.[17] Because of its massive size a rather unique approach was taken to its creation. The data base was collected without extensive editing or control.[18] The hope was that additional software could be developed later to edit and reconcile the data base automatically. Although resources were not available to undertake this step, the UCUCS data base remains a valuable source of retrospective machine-readable cataloging data.[19]

The most sophisticated of the automated book catalog systems implemented was that of The New York Public Library. This system features high quality automated typeset output, an integrated system for controlling the catalog's syndetic structure and a highly controlled data base. In 1972 the card catalogs of the NYPL Research Libraries were closed and continued with book catalogs produced by the automated system. At the same time the system was also used to maintain the entire catalog of the newly opened mid-Manhattan branch library. In 1973 the system was extended to provide a phased replacement for the card catalogs of the NYPL's 83 circulating branch libraries.

The NYPL system was also used in 1972 to produce printed book catalogs for the Hennepin County (Minn.) Public Library System. This venture is somewhat unique, as it represents the use of software developed by two institutions to satisfy the requirements of a third. Hennepin County began by implementing the system developed by the University of California Institute for Library Research to create and maintain a machine-readable cataloging data base. The product of this system was a data base in MARC-like format, which served as input to NYPL's authority control and book catalog production systems. Thus, Hennepin County was able to implement a sophisticated hybrid system with very little investment in system development.

In 1975 the NYPL system was enhanced to accommodate Hebrew data in vernacular form; in 1977 it was further extended to include Cyrillic data. NYPL, thus, became the first institution to develop automated facilities to process data in non-Roman scripts.

Advantages of Book Form Catalogs

The advantages of book form catalogs have been discussed quite extensively in professional literature. Maurice Tauber provides a particularly detailed analysis of the advantages and disadvantages of book catalogs.[20]

The principal advantages result from the fact that a book form catalog produced by computer represents a total, coherent entity. It represents both the bibliographic information of a catalog and its organization. Since there is no need to file individual catalog entries manually, maintenance costs are substantially reduced. Filing catalog cards in a library that maintains only a single catalog and acquires 15,000 titles annually can cost more than $6000 per year.

Book form catalogs are generally produced by first creating a master copy, which is then reproduced. The major costs of catalog creation are, thus, associated with production of the master copy. The incremental costs of additional copies of the catalog are usually quite low. This contrasts with the expense of maintenance and the space required for a card catalog, which render additional copies impractical. For example, a 100,000 title card catalog requires 470,000 cards, 470 card trays, or eight card cabinets, occupying a minimum of 33 square feet of floor space. The same catalog, typeset and printed, requires only 1.5 feet of shelf space. If produced in microform, such a catalog could easily be contained on 81 4 x 6 inch fiche and viewed with a fiche reader that occupies little more than 1.5 square feet of desk space. Thus, a book form catalog clearly provides an opportunity to place copies at locations where additional card catalogs would be totally impractical.

The possibility of a single catalog that can be reproduced in many copies permits maintenance of a single system-wide, union catalog in lieu of individual catalogs. Besides the savings, an added advantage is that individual branches of a library system can provide ready access not just to the holdings of their particular collections, but to the resources of the entire system. This was precisely the approach adopted by the Los Angeles County Public Library and The New York Public Library, among others, when they produced book catalogs.

Because of the nature of the display, a book form catalog can provide another advantage not feasible with any other medium. These catalogs present an entire page (or frame, if produced in microform) of entries to view, containing from 40 to 50 entries. A card catalog clearly permits only a single entry to be viewed at a time. A CRT display is also limited by the amount of information that can be displayed on a screen. Existing CRTs permit no more than 2000 characters (generally 24 lines of 80 characters each) to be displayed at any given time.

Finally, a book form catalog totally eliminates the need for catalog maintenance. Since the entire catalog display is recreated at periodic intervals, the whole catalog can be reorganized whenever it becomes necessary. The process of catalog reorganization is also greatly simplified, as any desired changes need only be made to individual unit records. Since the entire catalog will be reorganized by computer, the library need not be particularly concerned with the number of entries affected by maintenance activities.

Book Catalog Creation Process

To a large extent, the mechanical processes required to print catalog cards and those required to print book catalogs are similar. An automated system must be capable of reading an input file of MARC records from which it creates the descriptive records to be filed in each of the sequences specified by its entry elements. There are three major differences, however, between a card printing system and one intended to create a book catalog:

1. The precise filing of entries is much more important when producing a book catalog than when presorting catalog cards.
2. Entries must be formatted in a context defined by other entries that might appear on the same page.
3. Entries representing the catalog's syndetic structure must be included.

When a book form catalog is produced, the entire sequence of a large file, not simply a single week's output of printed cards, must be mechanically determined. When catalog cards are filed the opportunity always exists for *ad hoc* fine tuning by a human filer. This is simply not possible with a book catalog, short of printing a proof edition to be edited prior to publication. Thus, filing algorithms must be much more refined in a system intended to produce book catalogs.

The MARC record format was designed to accommodate the particular computer-compatible filing rules developed by John Rather of LC's Technical Processes Research office.[21] The Rather filing rules are a dogged attempt to obviate the need for any manual intervention in computer filing. The result is a set of rules whose guiding principle is "file as seen." The outcome is the possibility of the dispersion throughout the catalog of titles such as *Four Greek Plays* (under F), *IV Greek Tragedies* (under I), *4 Greek Comedies* (at the beginning of the alphabet), etc. The proposed solution to this problem is the creation of added entries with the numbers spelled out. However, a reader must be taught this additional rule before he can be dissuaded from believing that, having found *IV Satires,* he has found all of the "Four. . . ."

The MARC format makes very poor provision for filing information under any but simple title headings. There is no existing mechanism for associating filing information with name, subject or author/title headings. This is perhaps a consequence of a naive faith in computer-compatible filing rules and a format derived principally from a card image. Regardless of the cause, the MARC format presents a number of problems to a system intended to produce book form catalogs from a machine-readable data base. If satisfactory filing arrangement of MARC records is to be achieved, local provision must be made for it in the format.

Whatever the filing system, greater care must be taken in creating a MARC record to be used for book catalog production than when it is to be used to print cards. Since the arrangement of entries in a book catalog is determined by the contents of the entry elements in the record, the consequences of minor transcription errors are greatly magnified by the computer's totally unimaginative and literal approach to problems such as co-filing.

The problems of precise filing are much more complicated when entry elements are intended to be common to a group of records. Inconsistencies such as *Auden, W.H.; Auden, Wystan Hugh; Auden, Wystan Hugh, 1907-; Auden, Wystan Hugh, 1907-1973,* etc., wreak havoc when these records are sorted by machine to produce a book catalog. Also, the addition of a new record to the data base must have an explicit influence on the entire data base. For example, adding a record with a name heading with closed dates simultaneously alters all other occurrences of that heading with open dates. In addition, greater care must be exercised in ensuring the consistent use of all common access elements. For example, a simple error such as the distinction between the subject headings *Horse* and *Horses* can create wide dislocations in a book catalog. The *Library of Congress Subject Heading Guide,* 8th ed., lists 45 primary headings and 14 cross references that file between *Horse* and *Horses,* including *Horse Meat, Horse Radish, Horseflies,* and *Horsemint.*[22]

Once the problems of consistency and filing information have been solved, the mechanical process of creating a book catalog from a machine-readable data base proceeds much as it does for card creation. There will still, however, be important differences when generating the catalog display. Since any space saved on a printed page by abbreviating an entry can be used by other entries, thereby making the catalog more compact, there is a benefit to abbreviating some or all of the entries. In addition, since several entries are listed on a printed page, there is no need to repeat an entry element that is common to a sequence. For example, if several entries are to be arranged under a particular author or subject heading, it is undesirable to repeat that heading with each entry. The layout of the page can be used to indicate the arrangement. This permits substantial printing savings. More important, the display becomes less crowded and less distracting — hence, easier to scan.

Since a book catalog must represent a complete, self-contained catalog into which nothing can be inserted that is not contained in the machine-readable data base, there must be a provision to include the catalog's syndetic structure. Such information cannot be included as part of the bibliographic record, as it would need to be repeated with each occurrence of the heading to which it pertains. In addition, there is no provision in the MARC bibliographic record format for such information. This information can best be carried in an authority file of headings. The authority record for a heading can also serve as the vehicle for pertinent filing information.

The catalog's syndetic structure presents a major problem that must be addressed by an automated system. Since records may be added to, deleted from or altered in a machine-readable data base, there is a need for facilities to ensure the integrity of a catalog's structure, e.g., to prevent "blind references." Such assurances can be provided with greater certainty in an automated system than in a manual one. In addition to being more essential in an automated system, they are also more desirable, because the added flexibility of such a system permits the creation of separate catalogs containing only a subset of the data base.

Book Form Catalog Supplements

As it is impractical to produce a book form catalog with any great frequency, there is a problem in displaying recent additions to the cataloging data base, or changes in records already printed. The simplest solution is to produce card supplements to the cumulative catalog. This was the solution adopted in the 19th century to the problems of the timeliness of printed book catalogs.

But using supplementary card catalogs has proven impractical for a number of reasons, including requiring that an automated system be capable of producing both types of products. The investment required has precluded the development of such systems. Moreover, the advantages that justify the investments made in book catalog systems also serve to make card catalog supplements economically impractical. In addition, such a solution is still subject to all of the difficulties of maintaining synchronism between a machine-readable data base and its display analog in card form.

The most practical and popular solution is to produce supplements in book form. Unquestionably, these supplements should include all entries new to the data base. However, modifications to records previously printed can be treated in two ways: 1) ignore the modifications until the next cumulation is issued, or 2) print a revised entry in the first supplement following the modifications. The first option is simple and the least expensive, but it presents certain problems. For example, the library would not wish to wait for the publication of a new cumulation if a modification is made to correct a serious error, such as an incorrect call number or access element.

The second alternative also has drawbacks. Modifications to a record in a machine-readable data base are made to a single, unit record. Display in a book catalog will result in a number of entries generated from that unit record. If a modification affects all entries generated from the record, all entries should be redisplayed. However, if a modification affects only one, or some, of the entries, it seems quite wasteful to reprint all entries.

The choice depends to some extent on the sophistication of the system. For example, the data elements of a record can be divided into those which are considered critical and those which are not. If an element deemed critical is modified, then all entries in which it appears could be reprinted. This refinement is only possible if the cataloging department has available a display independent of the catalog, a display which shows the current condition of all records in the data base. Otherwise, there is the risk of repeated attempts to correct the same error, or the need to maintain an ancillary file of pending corrections.

Finally, just as with computer-printed cards, once an entry is printed in a book catalog a computer can have no effect on it. A supplementary correction will at least provide access to the correct information if the user or librarian consults it. When a revised cumulation is published, the correction will be completely absorbed into the catalog, leaving no trace of the error.

Supplements to a catalog can take many forms. The least expensive contain only entries not found in a basic cumulation or previous supplements. Such a scheme, though economical, forces the catalog user to consult a large number of supplements issued between cumulations. At the other extreme are cumulative supplements, containing *all* entries not found in a basic cumulation. This has the advantage of reducing the number of alphabets to be consulted to two. It has the disadvantage that each succeeding supplement must reproduce all of the entries contained in previous issues.

Between these two extremes are a variety of compromise schemes, e.g., issuing a number of independent supplements which are periodically collected into one or more cumulative supplements. Perhaps one of the most elaborate of such schemes is that used for the National Union Catalog (NUC). The NUC is issued in the form of monthly supplements, which are cumulated into quarterly supplements; the quarterlies are cumulated into annual editions, which in turn are combined into full cumulations every fifth year. Thus, a comprehensive search in the NUC covering the most recent decade requires consulting a maximum of 10 alphabets.

The cost of an annual cumulation with monthly cumulative supplements will be 2.67 times as much as a catalog produced according to the NUC publication schedule. The NUC system does, therefore, represent a very economical alternative, despite its clear disadvantages. In a larger sense, there are no savings; the costs are merely passed on to the users of the catalog.

Regardless of the schedule chosen, each supplement represents a subset of the cataloging data base; thus, control of the syndetic structure must be exercised within each supplement. It is not necessary to repeat the entire syndetic structure, even if controlled, which pertains to all entries in a supplement. Since a supplement will generally contain very few entries under each heading, the cross reference structure could overwhelm it. In addition, it is expensive to reproduce the structure in each issue.

The most effective solution is not to repeat in a supplement a reference that appears in a basic cumulation. Thus, supplements should only contain cross references that are new to the catalog and that refer to headings contained in the supplement.

The process of creating a book catalog from a machine-readable data base, the problems of repeating entries and cross references in supplements, and possible solutions, are discussed in detail in "The NYPL Automated Book Catalog Subsystem."[23]

The Role of Bibliographic Utilities

Since a book form catalog represents a snapshot of an entire data base, an intimate connection must be established and maintained between the automated system to maintain the data base and that used for production of the catalog. Periodic archive tapes from a bibliographic utility such as OCLC have been used successfully to produce book form catalogs. Generally, however, a duplicate data base must be maintained locally. There are two possible approaches to this.

First, the utility's data base can be used as a source of bibliographic information and as a facility for maintaining a particular library's records. That is, records are selected from the utility's data base and transferred only for the purposes of book catalog production. No facilities are provided to modify records selected for catalog production. Manipulation of records selected must be effected through data-base maintenance facilities provided by the bibliographic utility. The product of such data-base maintenance is received in the form of new archive tapes. The local system must then be capable of receiving such update records and of using them to replace records contained in the book catalog production data base.

Despite the apparent simplicity of such a scheme, there are significant operational problems involved. For example: a record might be selected from a bibliographic utility's data base and modified in accordance with a local library's requirements. These modifications, which might include addition of a local call number and location information, will all be reflected in the first archive tape received from the utility. They will, however, not be recorded in the on-line data-base record. Thus, if there is a need to make any further modifications to the record, the library must start again. All of the original modifications must be repeated before any additional modifications can be applied.

This process can be seriously complicated if the initial record was a contributed record that has in the interim been replaced by an LC MARC record. The complications can be even worse if the facility is attempting to create a union catalog from the archive tapes created for a number of users.

A second alternative, which eliminates many of the complications enumerated above, requires the development of a parallel data-base maintenance system. In this scenario an initial record is received on an archive tape. This record is transferred into a local data-base management facility where all further modifications are performed.

The local system can be considerably simpler than that maintained by a bibliographic utility. It need not, for example, make any provision for the large, comprehensive data base that a utility must maintain; nor does it need to provide the same kind of sophisticated access facilities, since it is dealing only with records for known items. If the local system is only required to maintain a catalog for a single institution, it does not have to address the complex problems of instantaneous data-base update.

Neither technique addresses the problems associated with maintaining a catalog's syndetic structure. This clearly will need to be accommodated by the local data-base system through implementation of an authority control system. The broader scope of the local system means increased complexity and cost.

A linked authority control system, i.e., one that permits global changes to be made to a local data base, is inconsistent with the intended simplicity of the first alternative. Thus, it would appear that if book form catalogs are to be derived from a data base maintained by a bibliographic utility, a parallel data-base maintenance system must be implemented. The problem can be addressed in other ways; for example, the Washington State Library Network has provided for a variety of simultaneous organizations within a bibliographic utility's data base.

On the surface, maintaining a parallel data-base management system for a local catalog seems unadvisable because of the loss of the economies of scale. However, the rapidly decreasing cost of computing devices (minicomputers in particular) and on-line storage may be nullifying many of the advantages normally expected from economy of scale.

Forms of Book Catalogs

Having decided to produce a book form catalog, the library faces a variety of choices regarding the nature of that catalog. A catalog produced from a machine-readable data base need not be an exact image of that data base, since much of the information contained in a bibliographic record is useful only to a minority of users — principally scholars and the library's professional staff. It is of no particular interest to the overwhelming majority of a library's patrons.

In an age when public catalogs had to be produced by making exact copies of unit bibliographic records, each record had to serve all possible purposes, e.g., the requirements of the collection development staff, the library's bibliographers, the cataloging staff and of course the library patron. But even with traditional catalogs, library staff maintain annotated records, such as the official shelflist, to which the public does not have access.

If an on-line system is available to the library's collection development, bibliography and cataloging staff, and if the system can be made available, albeit on a limited basis, to users with a pressing need for detailed bibliographic information, a public catalog that presents only limited bibliographic detail may be quite acceptable. Abbreviated entries can be provided in the public catalog, thereby making it more compact, less confusing to use and easier to browse.

Some argue that if elements of data are not included in the public catalog, the user who would have come upon them fortuitously will be deprived of this information because he or she would not suspect that it exists in a more complete catalog. The problem here is one of re-educating library users to the nature of a new catalog form. If a library user has found the particular item he is seeking, the abbreviated display has served his requirements. If, however, he has not, or suspects that he needs to make a more comprehensive search, he can be directed to the full catalog. A serious researcher should not find it too difficult to learn the difference between the abbreviated and full catalog. If the brief catalog maintains the fundamental principles of library catalogs espoused by Charles Cutter, then even a brief display will not conceal useful material.

After deciding on the fullness of the entries to be displayed, it is necessary to determine the organization of the book form catalog. Will it be in dictionary form or divided? The advantages to a dictionary catalog are:

1. It permits access to a library's total resources by whatever approach with only a single alphabet.
2. It brings together works by and about a particular subject.
3. It eliminates the need for a catalog user to make distinctions that are obvious to a librarian, but not intuitively obvious to patrons, such as that the General Motors Corporation annual report should be sought in the author not the subject catalog; whether to seek works *about works* in the subject or the author/title catalog; or where items entered under form headings should be sought.*
4. In a traditional card catalog it permits a certain degree of economy of space by eliminating the need for title-added entries when those titles are exact replicas of the subject, or for repeating an author of an autobiographical work as a subject entry, etc.

Among the advantages of a divided catalog are:

1. The filing arrangement in each catalog is simpler.
2. In a large research library, where approach to the collection by subject is infrequent, the resulting simplification of the author, title or author/title catalog is a significant asset.
3. In a system that permits multiple copies of the catalog, the most heavily used catalog segments can be reproduced in greater quantity.

The method chosen for division of a catalog can be a very significant factor determining its usability. A particularly simple and effective approach to the problem of which catalog should include name/subject entries or subject/title entries is to adopt as a principle that all works by and about a subject will be contained in a single catalog segment. Thus, works about Shakespeare's *Hamlet* should be found in the names catalog along with all other works by Shakespeare and the various editions of *Hamlet*. Likewise, works about the *Bible* or the *Song of Roland* should be found in the titles catalog along with the various editions and translations of these works. This has been the method of catalog division chosen by the Hennepin County Library and The New York Public Library.

Register/Index Catalogs

A catalog form made possible by automated systems, which is actually a response to the problems of cumulating large book form catalogs, is the register/index catalog.

---

*This particular problem has been eliminated by the *Anglo-American Cataloguing Rules, 2nd Edition* (AACR2).

This is a method of providing a very abbreviated display with ready access to full bibliographic data when needed. An entire catalog containing all entries is produced with very abbreviated entries. This catalog is considered to be the *index* to a full catalog. Each entry in the index contains a registration number, which provides access to a separate catalog segment arranged by that number and known as the *register,* which contains full bibliographic entries. The searcher performs an initial look-up in the index. If it provides sufficient information, the search ends there; if it does not, he or she must consult the register for more detailed information.

In the vast majority of cases, where brief information is sufficient, the searcher has the advantage of dealing with a display uncluttered by superfluous detail. But the principal advantage to this catalog form is simply economic. Both a catalog cumulation and all supplements can refer to a single register. The register can be simply produced by adding entries to the end of it, as the registration number has no intellectual value beyond serving as a location device. If in microfiche, new fiche are added to the end of the register; if in printed form, a new volume is added to the set.

Substantial economy can thus be achieved, because the full entry is produced only once. Since each unit record on average results in 4.71 catalog entries, it would take only a 22% reduction in the average length of each index entry to make the overall index/register catalog less expensive than a single catalog with full records under each entry. A more significant economic advantage is achieved, however, when considering periodic cumulation of the catalog. Only the catalog's index has to be cumulated, not its register. If a change has been made that affects data contained in the register, only that single entry needs to be redisplayed with a new registration number. Since there will no longer be any reference to the previous register entry, it becomes as inaccessible as if it had been physically removed.

The economic advantages can be easily computed, as demonstrated by a highly simplified example. Assuming that index entries are half the size of entries contained in a full catalog and that both the full catalog and the register/index catalog are produced as annual cumulations with monthly cumulative supplements, then the cumulative cost in five years of a register/index catalog is 38% lower than it is for a full catalog. However, if the average index entry can be shortened by only 25% the cumulative savings will be only 13%.

The savings are not particularly dramatic considering the amount of bibliographic detail that must be omitted. There are other possible solutions that lessen the problem of double look-up and can achieve even greater savings, among them reverting to the 19th century technique of providing an abbreviated entry under all but the main entry. If added entries are reduced by only 25%, such a technique can result in a 20% saving.

PRINTED BOOK CATALOGS

Thus far book catalogs have been treated as a generic form, with little consideration given to the particular display medium chosen. Although one generally tends to think of printed book catalogs, various other media are possible. The similarities among catalogs produced in various output forms are much greater than are the differences. (In all cases there is a static display, which must periodically be recreated.) Nonetheless, the choice of output medium does introduce differences. These differences will be treated in this section and the next.

A computer can be used to produce line-printer copy or phototypeset copy as the basis for an offset printed book catalog. Or, it can generate computer output microform (COM) by means of a COM recorder. The choice will generally be made on the basis of economics vs. the quality desired.

Direct-impact printing is a requisite first step in the production of all line-printer catalogs. Such a scheme is the simplest and most direct method of producing a catalog needed in only a single copy. (However, a catalog that is to be produced in a single copy can hardly justify the costs of an automated system.) Although multi-ply paper can produce six or more copies of a printed listing, the quality of the fourth and subsequent copies is generally so poor as to render this option unworthy of consideration.

The next choice is to produce a single, clean copy with a high speed line printer, then use it to produce additional copies by electrostatic reproduction (e.g., xerography). This technique, too, is only practical if a limited number of copies are required, since unit costs for such reproduction do not decrease as the number of copies increases.

Alternatively, the master copy can then be used to produce an arbitrary number of copies by offset printing. This technique requires high preparation costs for the first copy, which can only be underwritten if a large number of copies is required.

Typical costs for xerographic copies are $.038 each, while typical costs for offset printing depend on quantity. The cost of making the printing plate may be put at $1.82, while the cost of each copy can be around $.003 for printing book catalogs that run to thousands of pages. At a cost of $.003 per copy, offset printing will be more economical than xerographic copying when 50 or more copies per page are needed.

The highest quality printed output is that produced by photocomposition, i.e., automated typesetting. Variations in type style can be used to great advantage in a book catalog: boldface type can be used to highlight the filing elements appearing in catalog entries, thus making a page easier to scan; italic type can be chosen to indicate data elements to be given special consideration, or ignored, in particular circumstances; smaller type can be used to indicate the secondary importance of certain data; etc. Typography, therefore, affords an additional dimension to an information display, i.e., it can be used to convey information by implicit means. Any information which can be presented in an implicit manner can be absorbed at an intuitive level without elaborate mental processing; thus, such a display will be found easier to use.

Photocomposition devices can also represent a wide range of characters and character sets. The MARC character set developed by the Library of Congress contains 175 characters.[24] Many of these characters are diacritics superimposed on other characters. The MARC character set can only represent languages written in a Roman script or those that can be Romanized. If non-Roman scripts are to be included in a catalog, a device such as a phototypesetter, which can place an unlimited number of graphics with precision, is absolutely essential. Catalogs produced by photocomposition containing the full extended Roman character set, Hebrew and Cyrillic have been created by The New York Public Library.[25]

Phototypesetting is the most expensive of the printed alternatives. But some of the cost can be recovered in reduced printing charges, because by adjusting type size and spacing, phototypeset output can be made more compact than typewriter or line-printer copy, thus resulting in fewer pages to print. On a purely economic basis, phototypesetting costs tend to be balanced by lower page printing costs at about 150 copies.

Although printed book catalogs are less costly to maintain than card catalogs under certain conditions, the continuing need to reprint the entire catalog will generally make this form of catalog prohibitively expensive with the passage of time.

Regardless of the reproduction technique employed, the creation of a printed catalog by computer must include several steps:

1. Creation of individual entries from a unit record bibliographic data base;
2. Sequencing of those entries;
3. Direct printing of a master copy, or creation of a phototypesetting device driver file;
4. Creation of printing plates, or phototypeset copy (if the catalog is to be reproduced by offset printing);
5. Creation of multiple catalog copies; and
6. Binding of each copy.

This entire process can take several weeks. For example, The New York Public Library, despite the fact that it uses vendors for photocomposition and printing located less than one mile away, allows a minimum of four weeks for the production of its catalogs. Thus, printed catalogs simply cannot be completely current representations of a library's collections. A printed catalog like a card catalog represents a static, pre-coordinated display. This, along with the relatively high cost of printing and binding, are the two greatest disadvantages to catalogs in printed form. Thus, although in many respects printed book catalogs produced by automated means can represent a significant advance over card catalogs, they suffer from too many limitations to be considered a totally satisfactory alternative.

COM CATALOGS

Computer output microform is one of the means by which data manipulated by a computer can be rendered intelligible to a human. A computer deals with information in the form of individual characters, each represented as a unique configuration of electrical signals. Thus the same computer data base that can produce line printer or phototypeset output for a printed book catalog can be used to generate COM.

If only devices that produce monospace copy are considered, the system differences resulting from choice of display method disappear. Output used to drive a line printer can with little additional manipulation be used to drive a COM recorder. Any substantial data manipulation required to produce COM from line printer output will generally be performed by the COM vendor.

The entire catalog creation process will be identical for both a COM and a printed book catalog. That is, a system accepts as input a file of unit bibliographic records, explodes the requisite number of entries from each unit record, sequences the individual entries, formats the sequenced entries into pages, takes due account of the physical extension of a display page, and directs the output to an appropriate display device (a line printer, or a magnetic tape for COM output).

The more fundamental process — the creation and maintenance of a bibliographic data base — must precede, and is totally independent of, the form of catalog display chosen. This facility generally represents the single largest investment that must be made in an automated bibliographic system. It is the quality and sophistication of this system component that determine the quality and usefulness of the resulting catalog, not the display system.

The differences, if any, between catalogs produced in various physical forms are not the consequence of technical considerations. They are the result of economic factors. The extremely low cost of microform serves primarily to relax the constraints imposed on a bibliographic system by the display medium. Consider, for example, an arbitrary bibliographic listing, comprising 600 pages, to be printed on four-ply paper costing $26.10 per 1000 sheets. The cost of the paper for such a listing will be approximately $15.67. Typical costs for COM microfiche are $3.50 for a 207 frame master copy and $0.15 per copy for additional copies. Thus, 12 microfiche copies of this hypothetical listing will cost less than the blank paper needed for four printed copies.

The low cost of microform as a display medium can also be used to advantage in other ways. For example, the number of access points can be increased substantially while still achieving an increase in savings. COM also makes possible the recreation of the entire catalog at lower cost than other media would require. Frequent recreation of a catalog results in a self-refreshing display, which can represent data base activity in a timely manner.

The costs of microform are low enough that several vendors of microform catalogs have totally dispensed with supplements, and have begun simply providing periodic total cumulations. The advantage to such an approach is that the number of sources a user must consult is reduced from two to one. A disadvantage is that total cumulations cannot be created as frequently as supplements, even when produced in microform.

The restraining influence is provided not by the cost of the display medium, but by the cost of the computer processing required to create frequent catalog cumulations. For example, the printing and typesetting costs for 200 copies of a catalog containing 100,000 titles and growing at a rate of 10,000 titles per year, if created as a cumulation with cumulative supplements would be approximately $35,350. The cost of microfilm if this same catalog were produced as total cumulations each month would appear to be comparable, $35,200. But computer processing costs ($0.05 per title for a cumulation and $0.08 per title for a supplement) bring the cost of a printed catalog to approximately $48,700 (excluding binding). Complete monthly cumulations will cost nearly $90,000 more for computer processing than an annual cumulation with monthly supplements.

With more modest requirements it is economically feasible to cumulate this hypothetical catalog bi-monthly, and to dispense entirely with supplements. To produce such a catalog bi-monthly in microform would cost $48,000, almost exactly the cost of a printed catalog with monthly supplements. However, the printed catalog would also involve binding costs in excess of $16,000 annually, enough to pay for 200 microfiche readers in two years. Eliminating supplements might be viewed as reducing the timeliness of the COM catalog, but even a printed book form takes a month for production, compared to a week or less for even a large microform catalog. So the COM alternative is not much different in this respect from the printed version.

Typefonts and Character Sets

Aside from user acceptance, the principal disadvantage of COM as a medium for displaying bibliographic information has been the unavailability of the required character sets. This has not proven to be a major problem for the majority of libraries in the United States, which collect mainly English-language, U.S. trade imprints. Character set restrictions, however, pose a more serious problem for large research libraries. These collections generally contain materials in a wide variety of languages and scripts.

In recent years there have been a number of attempts, with varying degrees of success, to develop bibliographic character sets for COM recorders. Their availability varies with the nature of the particular COM recorder chosen. There are two basic types of COM recorders. The first, known as *alphanumeric* devices, are the most common. These have been developed to support normal commercial applications. They provide the Roman alphabet in upper and lower case, Arabic numbers and common punctuation. (The amount of punctuation can vary from device to device. For example, simple square brackets [ ] may or may not be available.) Despite its limitations, alphanumeric COM is readily available and is generally very low in cost. Master copies can usually be produced from approximately $.015 to $.02 per frame.

The second type of COM is known as *graphic quality* COM. Graphic COM devices are normally used to produce line drawings or other complex displays. This same class of COM recorders is also used to create output with the graphic quality of typeset copy. Graphic quality COM can provide virtually unlimited character sets and typefonts. The output is usually created with a photocomposition device fitted with special adapters that create highly reduced film output. This form of COM permits all of the advantages of typeset copy, including more compact display at costs more closely associated with microform than with printed copy.

It might appear odd to be concerned with limiting the size of a listing in microform. Although the cost of microform generally makes the size of a listing only a negligible concern, there are other considerations that still make a smaller size desirable. If the catalog is produced in microfiche, it is desirable to limit the number of fiche in order to simplify their refiling; if the catalog is produced in microfilm, it is desirable that it be contained entirely on a single reel, or cassette, of film. Several microfilm readers have been developed specifically for library catalog applications. These readers can be used most effectively if an entire catalog, or catalog segment, is permanently contained in a single machine. Hence, the library would want its catalog to fit on one reel of film to be mounted in such a reader. In addition, though the absolute cost of microform copies is low, substantial *relative savings* can still be achieved if the size of the catalog is reduced. This can become an important concern if the catalog is to be created in many copies.

Graphic quality COM is one method of obtaining an extended character set in microform. The full MARC character set has also been developed for devices that are essentially alphanumeric COM recorders. Since there have been relatively few experiments with such output, there is little definitive cost information available. The New York Public Library, which has been the single most active institution encouraging such developments with several vendors, has had extremely varied experiences. Prices have ranged as high as $.095 per frame, extremely high for COM. Several new COM recorders have begun to appear in the last several years, most notably the devices known as the COMP

80 series of phototypesetters developed by Information International, Inc. (III). Vendors utilizing this device offered COM with the full MARC character set in monospace fonts at reasonable prices: approximately $.030 to $.035 per frame.

Obviously, the most attractive and versatile form of COM is graphic quality COM. Although the cost of master copies will be approximately $.35 per frame, additional copies still will cost considerably less than $.001 per frame. Since a COM catalog will generally be produced in many copies, the effect of the cost of the master copy can be amortized. For example, a catalog of 100,000 titles produced in monospace COM with a commercial character set would require approximately 17,300 frames. If produced in 42X microfiche, the catalog requires 84 fiche per set. Thus, the cost of such a catalog in 100 copies is $1555. If the full MARC character set were to be used, the cost of the master copy can be as much as six times greater. However, the total cost of 100 copies of the catalog would be $2900. This represents an 86% greater cost — a substantial fractional increase, but not nearly as intimidating as a six-fold increase seemed to augur.

Likewise, the cost of phototypeset microform, despite a 100-fold greater cost per frame for the master copy, would be no more than that for full MARC character set alphanumeric COM. The reason is the greatly reduced number of frames. For example, experiments performed at NYPL have shown that the information contained on 2.6 frames of monospace output can be accommodated on a single frame of phototypeset output. The actual amount of reduction will, of course, depend on the details of the format used. Nonetheless, the figures given above are indicative of what might be expected.

Microform Readers

There are two basic types of microform: microfilm and microfiche. Microfilm is perhaps the more common form found in libraries. It is available in a variety of reduction ratios, the most common being 16 and 24X. Microfilm is available for use in the form of open reels and in cassettes or cartridges permitting easier loading. However, cassettes and cartridges occupy considerably more storage space than roll film, and they add approximately $2.00 to the cost of each reel of film.

The most frequent use of microfilm is for the preservation of documents such as back issues of newspapers, periodicals and other printed materials in danger of deterioration. Because of the need to reproduce faithfully the original image, source document microforms are frequently produced on 35mm roll microform of archival quality. This need to reproduce fine detail, along with the fact that source documents are often viewed for extended periods, dictates the use of 35mm film. For COM catalogs, these considerations do not apply; hence, film can be a smaller gauge and need not be of archival quality.

The second most common microform is microfiche, available in a variety of reduction ratios, the most common being 24 and 42X. Recently much higher reduction ratios have begun to gain popularity. Unfortunately, there is little standardization of microforms, particularly of microfiche. Microfiche are available in 16, 24, 34, 42, 48, 72 and 96X reduction ratios.

Microfiche are increasingly being used for source documents; however, because of the costs involved in "stripping-up" a master copy, they are most frequently used for original publication such as COM products. The principal advantage of microfiche is that they permit rapid access to a particular group of frames. There is no need to pass through a reel of film; one simply inserts the appropriate fiche into a reader and locates the desired frame. Microfiche do, however, present a greater control problem than does microfilm; users must handle many more physical pieces. The probability of losing a group of "pages" is therefore greater with fiche — a serious concern if the microform represents a document intended to be permanent. It is, however, not a serious concern for a microform catalog, which will be recreated periodically.

On the whole, in fact, a microform catalog shares few of the requirements that are traditionally associated with other library microforms. A COM catalog is the product of original publication; hence, greater control can be exercised over the quality of the original image and the typography appearing in the resulting display. A COM catalog is intended to be replaced with a completely revised edition periodically, so need not be produced on film of archival quality. A COM catalog is not intended for extended viewing; thus, the requirements for the quality of the image are far less stringent than they are for source document microforms.

It can also be expected that user resistance to such a form of display will be considerably milder than to its other applications. Nonetheless, since the time a user spends looking at a microform catalog display will be relatively brief, the ease with which it can be accessed will be a major concern. A user will not be pleased with a catalog that requires spending several minutes locating and loading a microform in order to view it for only a few seconds. Thus, microform readers intended to serve as a replacement for card catalogs must minimize the amount of time which a user perceives as not contributing directly to satisfying his own needs.

Microfiche — Advantages/Disadvantages

Microfiche provide the simplest and most direct access to a catalog in microform. They are generally produced with eye-readable dictionary captions across the top of each card, making it fairly simple to locate the correct fiche. Color coded captioned fiche can be used to distinguish segments of a divided catalog, or supplements to a catalog from its cumulation. In addition to a dictionary caption, microfiche are generally produced with an eye-readable, sequential number to facilitate refiling.

Microfiche prove most useful for a large catalog. However, large microfiche catalogs pose the greatest problems in maintaining their physical coherence. A catalog of 250,000 titles can require more than 200 fiche. If it is growing at a rate of 25,000 titles annually, supplements can comprise up to an additional 115 fiche. It is not difficult to imagine the potential confusion that will result during a day of heavy use if several copies of such a catalog are used in close proximity to one another.

Microfilm — Advantages/Disadvantages

The time required to thread and load roll microfilm makes this particularly unsuitable for a COM catalog. Cartridges and cassettes reduce this problem somewhat. Film cassettes and cartridges, however, generally hold only 100 feet of film. Even if two 8mm tracks are used on a 16mm film, and the image is reduced 42X, fewer than 12,000 frames can be contained in such a cartridge. This would only be sufficient for a catalog of fewer than 70,000 titles; supplements, if any, would require separate cartridges. As a consequence, users would have to cope with the inconvenience of selecting, loading and unloading numerous cartridges. Frequent mechanical problems can result if cartridges need to be loaded frequently into a reader. Although under particular circumstances a COM catalog in cartridges or cassettes can prove practical, this format does not represent a general solution to the problems of maintaining a catalog in microform.

In the last several years two vendors have developed microfilm readers specifically designed to serve as library COM catalogs — Auto-Graphics, Inc. and Information Design, Inc. Both readers use roll film on large capacity reels, which are permanently installed in the reader. Both provide an alphabetic index pointer synchronized with the passage of the film through the reader, permitting users to judge their position in the catalog during movement of the film at high speed. The manufacturers of these devices claim that up to 50,000 frames can be contained in their readers on 1000 foot reels of ultra-thin film. This is ample to contain a complete 250,000 title catalog; a larger catalog can probably be accommodated if it is formatted efficiently.

Relative Costs

The costs of creating film and fiche are about the same. The only real difference is introduced if cartridges or cassettes are used; the cost of loading film into a cartridge or cassette will add approximately $2.00 to each reel. The major difference between the two forms derives from the cost of the readers. Microfiche readers cost between $160 and $200. Microfilm readers are four to five times as much. While it can be assumed that savings can cover the cost of microfiche readers in one or two years, it is considerably more difficult to fund the initial capital outlay for a sufficient number of microfilm readers.

SUMMARY

This chapter has explored a number of computer-supported catalog forms, and has considered the advantages and disadvantages of each. Computer-produced catalog cards are the simplest catalog products to create with an automated system. Using a computer in this manner, however, represents a gross underutilization of data-processing technology. The nature of card catalogs can actually represent an inhibiting force on our ability to maintain a cataloging data base by automated means. Nonetheless, shared cataloging systems whose major tangible product is catalog cards have been found to be economically viable in practice. The major advantage of such systems is that catalog cards produced from a machine-readable data base can be interfiled into existing catalogs; thus, they imply little, if any, disruption. It is quite clear, however, that such systems do not address any of the major problems of maintaining a catalog. Catalog card systems can be considered to be *cataloging support* systems, but not *catalog alternatives.*

Printed book catalogs have been shown to be well-suited as a means of displaying the contents of a machine-readable data base. Although in many instances they are less expensive than card catalogs, and in general more useful than card catalogs, they are expensive to maintain. The high cost of production limits the ability of a printed catalog to reflect in a timely fashion a dynamically evolving data base. Nonetheless, it can display data base activity more readily than can a card catalog.

A more promising display medium for an automated catalog is one produced in microform by direct computer output — COM. The continuing costs of such a catalog are so low that innovative alternatives can easily be considered. However, despite the clear advantages of COM catalogs, they require substantial capital investments in microform reading equipment.

FOOTNOTES

1. Library of Congress, *Annual Report of the Librarian of Congress for the Fiscal Year Ending September 30, 1977* (Washington, D.C.: Library of Congress, 1978), A-12.
   Barbara Evans Markuson, "The Ohio College Library Center," *Library Technology Reports,* 12 (January 1976):22.

2. Library of Congress, loc. cit.

3. Markuson, op. cit., p. 13.

4. Frances Ohmes and J.F. Jones, "The Other Half of Cataloging," *Library Resources and Technical Services,* 17 (September 1973):321.

5. Ibid., p. 323.

6. *Conversion of Retrospective Catalog Records to Machine-Readable Form* (Washington, D.C.: Library of Congress, 1969), p. 145.

7. Jesse H. Shera, "The Book Catalog and the Scholar," *Library Resources and Technical Services,* 6 (Summer 1962):214.

8. Ibid.

9. Joseph Becker, "The Rich Heritage of Information Science," American Society for Information Science, *Bulletin,* 2 (March 1976):11.

10. William Spence Geller, "Duplicate Catalogs in Regional and Public Library Systems," *Library Quarterly,* 34 (January 1964):59.

11. Catherine MacQuarrie and Beryl L. Martin, "The Book Catalog of the Los Angeles County Public Library," *Library Resources and Technical Services,* 4 (1960):211.

12. Ibid., p. 210.

13. Ibid.

14. Ibid.

15. Ibid., p. 212.

16. Ibid., p. 225.

17. University of California, *Union Catalog of Monographs Collected by the Nine Campuses From 1963 Through 1967* (Berkeley, CA: Institute of Library Research, 1972), p. i.

18. Ibid., p. vi.

19. Ibid., p. iii.

20. Maurice F. Tauber and Hilda Feinberg, *Book Catalogs* (Metuchen, NJ: The Scarecrow Press, 1971).

21. John C. Rather, "Filing Arrangement in the Library of Congress Catalogs," *Library Resources and Technical Services,* 2 (Spring 1972):240-61.
   Library of Congress, MARC Development Office, *Books: A MARC Format,* 5th ed. (Washington, D.C.: Library of Congress, 1972).

22. Library of Congress, Subject Cataloging Division, *Library of Congress Subject Headings,* 8th ed. 2 Vols. (Washington, D.C.: Library of Congress, 1975).

23. S. Michael Malinconico and James A. Rizzolo, "The New York Public Library Automated Book Catalog Subsystem," *Journal of Library Automation,* 6 (March 1973):3-36.

24. Library of Congress, MARC Development Office, *Books: A MARC Format.*

25. S. Michael Malinconico, Walter R. Grutchfield and Erik J. Steiner, "Vernacular Scripts in the NYPL Automated Bibliographic Control System," *Journal of Library Automation,* 10 (September 1977): 205-225.

IX

Automated Circulation Systems

by Alice Harrison Bahr

INTRODUCTION AND OVERVIEW

According to Barbara Evans Markuson, circulation control will be "the major automation growth area during the next five years."[1] Full-capacity attendance at two December 1977 American Library Association institutes on "Automated Circulation Systems" (at both, an overflow of registrants was turned away) supports that prediction. In part, the growing interest may be attributed to technological advances which have increased competition and lowered costs.

The first full report on automated library circulation control systems appeared in the July and September issues of *Library Technology Reports* in 1975. When it was updated in May 1977, only one of the originally described systems was still available; and four new vendors had entered the market. By early 1979 the picture had changed again, and drastically. Not only had one vendor withdrawn from the marketplace, but three more had entered and even more stood on the sidelines, planning to enter at some future time.

Vendors with installed, operative systems and those awarded contract bids in 1978 were:

- Checkpoint/Plessey
- Cincinnati Electronics (CLASSIC)
- C L Systems, Inc.
- DataPhase
- Decicom Systems, Inc. (abandoned the market in 1979)
- Gaylord Bros., Inc.
- Systems Control, Inc. (SCICON)
- Universal Library Systems, Inc. (ULISYS)

---

[1] Barbara Evans Markuson, "Granting Amnesty and Other Aspects of Automated Circulation," *American Libraries*, April 1978, p. 205.

Reprinted from *Automated Library Circulation Systems, 1979-80* (White Plains, NY: Knowledge Industry Publications, Inc., 1979).

Planning to enter the market after successful system implementation are Knogo Corporation, in conjunction with the British firm Automated Library Systems, Ltd., and the University of Toronto Library Automation System, a network serving 46 Canadian libraries which is currently installing its system, referred to as CIRC, in the University of Toronto undergraduate library.

Other institutions with home-grown systems (systems designed by libraries around commercially available equipment) plan to enter the market at less specified times. For instance, the East Brunswick (N.J.) Public Library, whose on-line system was designed by city data processing staff, is presently accepting bids from vendors who may wish to market the system. Bucknell University (Lewisburg, Pa.) still uses an off-line system it developed (BLOCS I) which relies on punched cards for data input. However, BLOCS II, an on-line system which uses bar-coded labels to input data, is currently under development.* Honeywell, which supplies the system's computer, may market the system at some future time.

The increased market activity is good for libraries. Struggling for economic survival, vendors have become more responsive to the library's needs. As a consequence, newer systems are more flexible. One example of that flexibility is the trend either to sell software separately or to design it so that libraries may modify programs. Partly as a result of increased competition, optical character recognition (OCR) is now a standard option in many systems. Reserve book modules are available, as are a greater number of conversion methods.

The greatest boost to the competition responsible for the development of new features is a series of hardware innovations: the minicomputer, the microcomputer and the 1647 series of terminals from Epic Data. It's difficult to define terms like mini and microcomputer since their capabilities change almost daily. However, the mini was once what the microcomputer now is: a small machine dedicated to a single purpose, limited in the amount of storage and in the amount and kind of software that it can accommodate. Introduced in the early 1970s, the minicomputer made it possible for libraries to have stand-alone systems (systems relying on a computer housed in the library). Today, because of more sophisticated software, minis can store as much as four million bytes of core storage and some can support well over 30 on-line circulation terminals. The future may hold the same promise for microcomputers, currently dedicated to small off-line systems.

Initially, terms like mini and micro designated less capability. However, they also referred to size. For example, Bill Scholtz points out in the May 1977 issue of *Library Technology Reports* that in 1960 the IBM 1620 computer occupied a 20 x 30 foot room; by 1974, a machine capable of the same tasks occupied nine square feet and could be carried from room to room. In 1971, when the first one-chip central processing unit

---

* For a full description of BLOCS I, consult ERIC documents ED 09 46 97 and ED 09 46 98. For information on BLOCS I and II, contact Ms. Helena Rivoire, Chief of Technical Services at Bucknell University Library.

was revealed, it took up an area of about a sixth of an inch long and an eighth of an inch wide. "Yet this inert microprocessor had a calculating capacity almost equal to the room-size ENIAC – the first fully electronic computer, completed in 1946."[2] Today, the minis and micros do more than save space; they rival the capabilities of larger units.

The Epic Data terminals, model series 1647, have facilitated conversion for libraries relying on keypunched book cards for circulation. Terminals may be modified to reformat and transfer data from 80-column punch cards to an on-line disk storage medium.

Technological strides like these reduce costs, and reduced costs are a significant part of librarians' renewed interest in automated circulation control systems. Markuson indicates that in 1963 hardware alone for a proposed circulation control system for the Library of Congress was estimated at $1 million. Today, hardware and software could be supplied for one third that cost.[3] Ken Sheedy, vice president of Universal Library Systems, Inc., believes that the system installed at the Phoenix Public Library in 1977 for $350,000 could be installed today for approximately $220,000. A number of newly developed off-line and on-line microcomputer based absence systems designed for small libraries range in price from $10,000 to $30,000.

While increased competition and price reductions make a more attractive market, they do not minimize the complexity of the decision process. Only a dedicated examination of what competing systems offer, a thorough study of how those systems operate and a sure grasp of the library's future development, i.e., the uses to which a machine-readable data base will be put, assure a reasonable choice. To assist in that painstaking task, *Automated Library Circulation Systems* reviews present systems' capabilities, design and performance, defines key terms, outlines important selection questions and discusses implications of automated library circulation control systems. Based on independent research, evaluation of vendor-supplied information and informal user interviews, the study reaches the following conclusions:

- The trend away from punched book cards and embossed IDs to on-line minicomputer based systems continues to accelerate.

- The low cost of microprocessors is stimulating the development and marketing of off-line circulation systems for small libraries.

- Flexible system design, maximizing the library's options, is emphasized in the newer systems.

- While many libraries employ several automated systems autonomously, several are making circulation the hub of automated processes, using circulation terminals to interact with other data bases.

---

[2] "The Age of Miracle Chips," *Time,* 111:44 (February 20, 1978).

[3] Markuson, "Granting Amnesty," p. 207.

● Most users have not had sufficient time to exploit all the potential of their circulation systems.

● The emphasis on networking will continue to stimulate interest in automated library circulation control systems.

● While home-grown systems continue to be developed and to influence the market, a number of libraries initially using them have switched to packaged systems.

● The main impetus for automation of circulation remains the desire to provide better service and maintain better control over the collection.

* * * * * * * * * * * * * * * * *

In 1977 Dranov provided an excellent survey of the automated circulation control system's development. She traced its origin from the in-house developed, off-line system (one designed to capture, store and later print out data about materials out of the library in circulation) developed by universities and municipal data processing departments in the early 1960s to the on-line, minicomputer-based inventory control systems. These were made possible in the 1970s by the simultaneous development of both minicomputers and light pens able to read and transmit data from bar-coded labels to a minicomputer.[4] Documenting transitions, Dranov indicated that the University of South Carolina's McKissick Library was the first to use light pens for circulation and that the first packaged, commercially available system was (and still is) offered by C L Systems, Inc. (CLSI) in Newtonville, Mass.

Building on that history, this chapter will clarify the terminology and the issues involved in the automation of circulation: terms like home-grown, packaged, absence, inventory, off-line, on-line and issues like call number vs. access number, OCR labels vs. bar-coded labels, conversion, electronic security system interface and cost. Preceding that, however, is a synopsis of why libraries have and have not automated.

In 1975 Butler estimated that 800 libraries were involved in some automated procedures.[5] Small as that figure is and despite some libraries' increasing transaction figures,

---

[4] Paula Dranov, *Automated Library Circulation Systems, 1977-1978* (White Plains, NY: Knowledge Industry Publications, Inc., 1977), pp. 13-15.

[5] "Butler Says 800 Libraries Involved in Automation," *Advanced Technology/Libraries* (October 1975), p. 10.

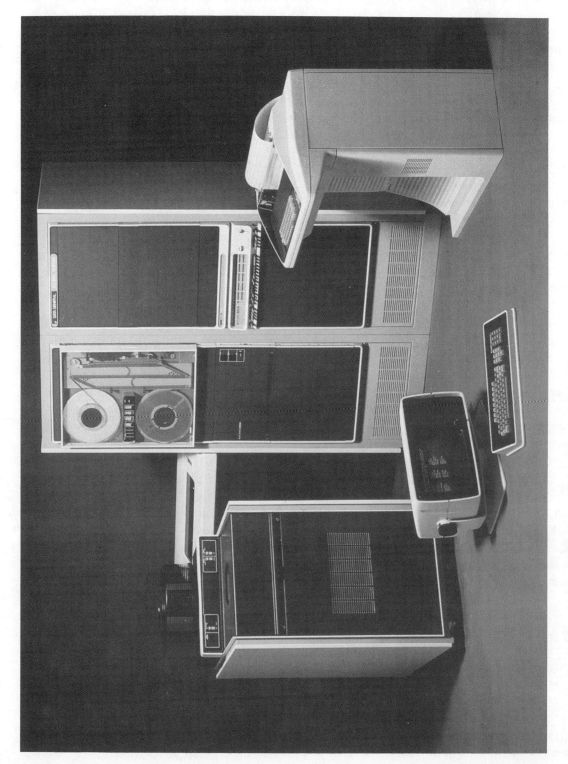

ECLIPSE S/100 hardware supplied by Data General for DataPhase Systems, Inc. (Courtesy Data General.)

less than half that number now have automated circulation processes. Why? The slow response is a matter of cost, expertise and size. Unless the library is joining a circulation network, average costs for an on-line system are about $100,000. Few libraries can afford that outlay unless they can demonstrate the system's cost effectiveness, are awarded a grant or special funding or are faced with major equipment replacement. Even those with funds often prefer to live with the system they know rather than combat the less known exigencies of the computer. Lastly, one rule of thumb is that transactions under 200,000 a year may be handled manually without great difficulty. For some, the manual and photographic systems perform well enough and at a reasonable cost.

For libraries with annual transactions exceeding 200,000, the limitations of the typical manual or semi-automatic systems become increasingly evident. Except for batch processing systems, preparation of overdue notices is a time-consuming and troublesome task. In manual and photographic systems, files must be searched manually and notices either typed or written out. One reason the University of Pennsylvania's Van Pelt Library switched from an IBM System 7 to CLSI was that the off-line batch-processing system afforded no control over fines after first notices were generated.

Another time-consuming manual task is filing. In 1977 the Commack (N.Y.) Public Library circulated 267,640 items. On a particularly busy day when 1200 items circulated, the staff knew that half of the next day would be devoted to filing. Usually four people were needed to file the previous day's book cards, which were separated into a number of categories. For example, children's fiction was separated from children's nonfiction. Now, using Gaylord's Automated Library Circulation Control System, the library's filing is eliminated and overdue notices are mailed within 10 days rather than after two or three months.

Photographic systems eliminate the necessity of filing, but like the manual systems they pose serious collection control problems. Until book cards are sorted and filed and microfilm records of transactions are developed, the staff cannot determine whether a book is out. The process is even more difficult with microfilmed transactions since they are recorded as they occur, not in call number order. Off-line systems, like manual card file systems, involve a time lag between checkouts and available library records. Moreover, placing a reserve on an item in any of those systems is a difficult, unwieldy task.

In addition, there are a number of tasks that manual and semi-automatic systems do not perform. None calculates fines automatically, records borrower statistics, places reserves automatically, catches delinquent borrowers or handles inquiries about the status of a particular item.

Traditionally, then, libraries turn to automation to reduce time-consuming clerical routines, to provide better service, new services and greater control over the collection. A few can justify automation on a cost-containment basis alone. For example, the Greensboro (N.C.) Public Library determined that an automated circulation system would reduce staff by three or four full-time persons, an annual saving of between $40,000 and $45,000. When the Tucson (Ariz.) Public Library's 15-year-old, outdated Regiscope equipment deteriorated, the library discovered that an automated circulation package was not much more costly than comparable equipment replacement. Similarly, when the Dallas (Texas) Community College District decided to open three new campuses, it faced the option of purchasing expensive semi-automatic equipment, Standard Register equipment to take IBM punched cards, or an on-line package; again, the cost differential among them was insignificant.

New buildings open up new possibilities. Just as the Dallas Community College District switched to DataPhase when opening its new campuses, the Northland Public Library (Pittsburgh, Pa.) commemorated its 10th anniversary with a new building and a ULISYS automated circulation control system. Purchased to offset a growing circulation rate in a new building with multiple exits, ULISYS has become the lever for automating other functions in the library. Laura Shelley, library director, now plans to contact BALLOTS for cataloging, and Baker & Taylor and Brodart for acquisitions. Moreover, she hopes to convince local school libraries to purchase terminals to make inquiries of the public library's data base, thereby facilitating interlibrary loan requests. A final reason for automating circulation, then, is to provide a hub or nucleus for further automation and to tie together community resources.

IN-HOUSE DEVELOPED SYSTEMS

In-house or home-grown systems, those designed by libraries around commercially available equipment, were the first automated circulation systems. Usually they relied on punched book cards being read at circulation terminals which stored patron ID, book ID and due date for transferral to a host main computer. Whether at a university, municipal or commercial data processing center, host facilities use the collected information to produce printouts of checked out materials, usually arranged by call number. Frequency of printouts is determined by the library and sometimes by the center's own workloads and priorities. Typically, printouts are issued daily, semi-weekly or weekly.

The capabilities of such systems vary, and the early systems became prototypes for later ones. For instance, a few early systems had some on-line capabilities. Today Checkpoint/Plessey offers an off-line system with optional on-line book status. In other words, printouts continue to be generated on a predetermined basis; however, should the library need to know the status of a book immediately, it may do so. Similarly, host facilities of many early systems prepared overdue notices at specified intervals. This is the distributed processing concept behind Gaylord Bros.' current automated library circulation control system. While all borrower and staff transactions are recorded immediately, they are transferred nightly to the host computer, which prepares all notices.

The impetus for a library to design its own system seems to be fourfold:

- No other acceptable systems are available.
- Knowledgeable data processing staff are available.
- There is a need for greater flexibility than available systems offer.
- Self-design appears to be less expensive.

In the late 1960s the University of Pittsburgh designed an off-line, batch-processing system relying on an IBM 11/30. Transactions were processed every three or four days. Pittsburgh had little other choice: No commercial, packaged systems were then available. In the early 1970s both Bucknell University and Syracuse University developed their own off-line systems for the same reason. With time, all have made major modifications in hardware and software, some quite costly. At present, all are planning some future on-line capabilities.

Another reason universities design their own systems is that most have computer equipment and staff already available to them. For example, the library circulation system developed in the late 1960s at Ohio State University by library and IBM staff ran on the university's IBM 360/50 computer system. Now called the Library Control System, LCS has been transplanted to the State University of New York (SUNY) at Albany and the University of Illinois.

However, even though a plethora of commercial systems are currently available, home-grown systems continue to be developed, whether for independence or because they are cost effective. For some it is both. The East Brunswick (N.J.) Public Library was fortunate in two respects. First, the township's data processing center is next door, providing unusually convenient expertise and service. Second, the township did not bill the library for its programming time, which was the equivalent of one man-year. As a consequence, the library's on-line inventory system, which includes three IBM 3277 CRTs and two Recognition Products, Inc. Model P130 OCR wands tied to an IBM 3/15 at the data processing center, cost only $28,000 to develop. The least expensive, comparable packaged system was approximately $100,000. Therefore, even if programming time were assessed at $40,000, the library saved money.

The same was true for the Macon/Bibb County (Ga.) Public Library. Modeled after a system developed for the Oklahoma City Library, the Macon/Bibb County Public Library's automated light pen system, comprised of IBM and NCR hardware and Monarch bar-coded labels and wands, cost only $18,000 to install in the main library and in four branches. [6]

In addition to potential cost effectiveness, however, there are still other reasons for designing a system in-house. As East Brunswick library director Edward Whittaker explains, "The system devised for the East Brunswick Public Library gives us greater flexibility and allows us to cull from the system exactly what we want." As an example, the library is currently pulling out all circulation statistics for the past two years by location code (adult, etc.) and by Dewey classification number. This information, providing a profile of patron reading habits, is an effective tool for collection and special program development.

The impact of custom in-house systems on automated library circulation can be phenomenal. For example, the University of Chicago Library-designed terminal, the

---

[6] " 'Home Brew' Saves Money in Georgia," *Library Journal* (March 15, 1977), p. 673.

JRL-1000, was the beginning of Cincinnati Electronics' on-line circulation system, CLASSIC.

Although sometimes cost-effective and usually more flexible, custom systems have not always proven more desirable than the commercial packaged systems. At least one large university currently using an off-line system it developed would eagerly purchase a packaged system if funds were available. This would give the library greater control over its operations. Independent of the university's computer center, the library could set its own priorities instead of having them established by the university. American University (Washington, D.C.) and the University of Pennsylvania switched from their own systems to CLSI. The ultimate value of self-design is determined largely by environment. If hardware and programming expertise are available, relatively inexpensive and capable of meeting library specifications, the home-grown system is a viable alternative to the packaged system.

PACKAGED SYSTEMS

Packaged systems, those designed by commercial vendors who offer hardware, software and often maintenance in one total systems package, free the library both from choosing hardware and from programming, which is often more expensive than equipment outlay. These systems are referred to as turnkey systems; presumably the librarian merely turns a key to activate the entire system. While that is a simplification, the packaged system's drawing card is that the vendor, not the library, is responsible for system development and maintenance. Ironically, as time goes on, libraries are becoming increasingly interested in controlling the computers that control their operations; hence, a number of vendors now allow libraries to maintain their own software and thereby to modify and enhance programs.

Vendors

The first available packaged system was introduced by C L Systems, Inc. (then called Computer Library Services) in 1973. Since then 12 other vendors have entered the market. Many more are planning to join them, but there has also been an exodus of some who have not met with the success they had sought.

One of the 12, Check-a-Book, sold its on-line minicomputer-based system to 3M Co. in 1975. In February 1978 3M Co. announced that its Inventory Control System (ICS), already installed at the Arlington County (Va.) Public Libraries and at Princeton University, would be withdrawn. A second vendor, IBM, withdrew software support for its System/7 computer after assisting in development at the University of Pennsylvania. Although several libraries continue to use IBM hardware for custom designed systems, the University of Pennsylvania eventually adopted CLSI. A third vendor, Mohawk Data recently announced that it was not accepting new customers for its 4400 system, a batch-processing system relying on punched cards. A fourth company multiplied rather than reduced the number of vendors on the market. Plessey Telecommunications, an English concern, markets its three off-line and partially on-line systems through Checkpoint Systems, Inc. and its fourth, totally on-line system, through International Computing.

At present, then, eight vendors are marketing four different types of automated circulation control systems:

1)   Off-line batch processing systems relying on host computers to generate circulation printouts (Checkpoint/Plessey).

2)   Off-line batch processing systems with optional on-line book status inquiry (Checkpoint/Plessey).

3)   Distributed processing systems in which all local functions are on-line, but certain tasks like issue of overdue notices are handled by a host computer (Gaylord).

4)   Stand-alone, on-line systems (C L Systems, Cincinnati Electronics, DataPhase, ICC/Plessey, Systems Control and Universal Library Systems).

ABSENCE SYSTEMS

Most libraries with a manual book card or photographic charging system already have an absence circulation system, one which records only those items checked out of the library. Absence literally means absent from the library. With such systems, full bibliographic records of checked-out items need not be kept. Enough information must be recorded to permit access to the library's full bibliographic record of its holdings, the shelflist. Usually that means call number. However, author and brief title provide a double check on records' accuracy and permit staff and patron alike another access route to the shelflist (i.e., in the case of lost but not overdue books when the patron does not know the call numbers). Because a great amount of data need not be stored, automated circulation systems which work around the absence design require less storage space and are consequently less expensive than those working around the inventory design.

Librarians seem to want more and be willing to pay for more today. None of the systems described in this report are absence systems, which effectively constitute the first step in automated circulation control. What absence systems eliminate is the manual drudgery of filing and preparing overdues. For some, that is all that automation is required to do and a number of in-house systems continue to operate in the absence mode.

Such systems speed up traditional circulation routines, but hardly redefine the department's role. Instead of patrons having to wait while a librarian culls endless card files to locate a book, an irrevocable black and white printout has an immediate and definite result. Inventory systems, on the other hand, can alter the nature and function of the circulation department, making it the hub of most library activities.

INVENTORY SYSTEMS

Like absence systems, inventory systems require that at least the library's circulating materials be identified in machine-readable form. While some rely on punched cards, as do most absence systems, the majority rely on bar-coded labels — unique machine-readable

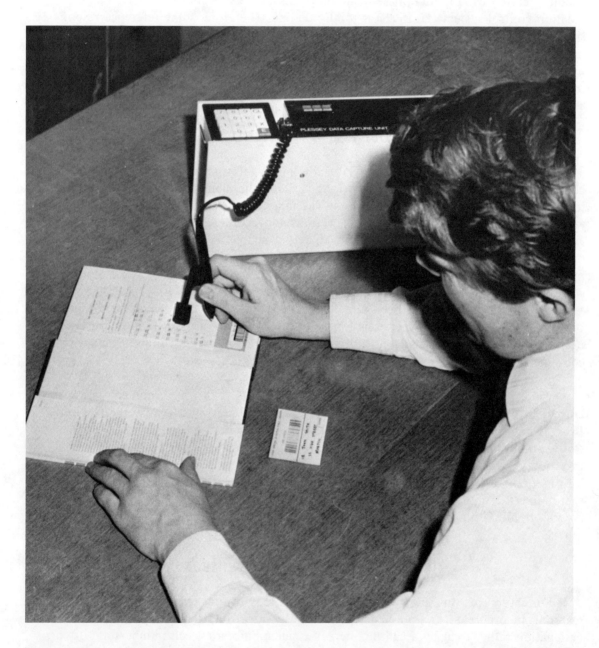

USING THE CHECKPOINT/PLESSEY portable terminal to record a checkout. (Courtesy Checkpoint/ Plessey.)

numeric identifiers providing access to more complete bibliographic files stored in the computer's data base of holdings. The main distinction between an absence system and an inventory system is that an inventory system maintains a permanent file of all holdings converted to machine-readable form.

What that means to the library depends on how complete holding files are, what kind of access is provided to them and how the library plans to employ such information. For instance, the Northland Public Library near Pittsburgh decided to include subject heading references in its data base of holdings. Its Universal Library System, Inc. circulation control system (ULISYS) is totally on-line. Therefore, some reference responsibilities may be partially assumed by circulation attendants. The degree to which automation affects the library's organizational structure is determined by the library. What inventory systems mean technically is that a larger computer is needed; what they mean managerially is that a greater variety of statistical and managerial reports are available.

OFF-LINE VS. ON-LINE

While absence and inventory refer to how much information about the library's collection should be recorded and how long it should be maintained, on-line and off-line refer to how that information is accessed. The majority of currently available systems are on-line and real time; that is, as transactions are recorded, files are instantly updated and the most current information is immediately available to library staff. In off-line or batch-processing systems, information is stored or captured at terminals and processed by a central computer at a later time. It cannot be directly accessed by staff. Simply stated, the off-line system records data, but does not interact with it. The on-line system, which, for example, has been directed to trap delinquent borrowers and catch overdue books that are on reserve, is forced to interact with all new data. Because it is asked to do more, it demands more from the library: a larger computer and more equipment, such as video display terminals and random access storage.

While most systems are advertised as totally on-line, that is a misnomer. It is more correct to think of functions rather than systems as on-line. For instance, the Gaylord Bros. system places files of delinquent borrowers, certain statistical reports and item status on-line. Library staff can identify all delinquent borrowers listed in the file and may query the data base for an item's status at any time and receive the most current information. However, a patron who becomes delinquent on a particular day is not in the on-line file until the following day when the host computer updates the delinquent borrowers' file. In most other systems, some functions are off-line, usually detailed reports.

ACCESS NUMBER VS. CALL NUMBER

For several reasons, most automated systems require that circulating materials or materials incorporated in a permanent data base be identified by a unique numeric designation rather than by a call number. In academic libraries, call numbers are often complex or too long to fit the allowed character space and too prone to error when keyed in manually. In public libraries, call numbers often do not uniquely identify an item. To assure that every item may be identified uniquely, each is assigned an access number.

There are several advantages to unique numeric designators. Since only numbers need be entered, additional keyboarding is unnecessary. A simple number keyboard, less expensive than a full keyboard unit, can handle transactions. Moreover, such access numbers allow the library to circulate materials prior to cataloging, especially when pre-punched cards and sequential machine-readable labels are available from vendors. Preparing either in-house would be costly.

For those libraries that still find call number access useful, some vendors do make such systems available: CLSI, Cincinnati Electronics, ICC/Plessey, Systems Control and Universal Library Systems.

OCR LABELS VS. BAR-CODED LABELS

Most automated systems use bar-coded labels to identify both patrons and items. In several systems, however, OCR (optical character recognition) labels are an option: CLSI, DataPhase, Systems Control and Universal Library Systems. Both are in common use today. Bar codes are found on most food products and magazines today, while OCR numbers are on the bottom of bank checks. Both serve the same purpose: They uniquely identify an item or person in a form that the computer can translate into its own language.

While some vendors (who have incorporated bar codes) are not sure that OCR technology has proven itself, libraries choosing such labels accrue certain benefits. For one, they are cheaper than bar codes, whose production must conform to more rigid technical requirements. Second, unlike bar-coded labels, they may be produced in-house using a typewriter (such as an IBM Selectric) with an OCR font. On the negative side, OCR labels smudge more easily than bar-coded labels, which are produced by a photographic process. In some instances, the OCR wand requires a steadier hand than does the bar code reading light pen to get a successful read.

CONVERTING TO AUTOMATION

Those who have undergone the traumas of bringing an automated system into operation would likely agree with one library director: "Conversion does not go as smoothly as any vendor tells you it will." It would be surprising to hear the contrary, since years of effort go into the construction of a library's bibliographic records. Converting even a shortened version of those to machine-readable form is a monumental undertaking requiring great forethought. Even with 25 employees paid under the Comprehensive Employment and Training Act (CETA) and working 13 hours a week, six hours a day on 20 terminals, the Tacoma Public Library anticipates that it will take a full year to convert its 500,000 volumes.

Like automation itself, conversion techniques have evolved. Initially, conversion meant keypunching cards based on shelflist information and then transferring the data to tape. The amount of information recorded depended on available field space and on the uses to which the data base would be put. Costs were estimated to be $1.50 or $1.60 per title.[7] Prior to going on-line in September 1977, the Manhattan (Kan.) Public Library, which uses the Gaylord System, converted its 100,000 titles in this manner.

Today, more common than the error-prone keypunching approach is the matching of library holdings against another library's holdings which are already in machine-readable form. And sometimes, data bases are supplied by vendors. For example, Systems Control, Inc. provides a data base of 300,000 titles as part of its circulation control system package. C L Systems will assist the library to develop a holdings profile and then search for a compatible data base. Oftentimes, however, that is the library's responsibility. When the Tacoma Public Library went on-line in April 1978 with DataPhase System, it purchased Blackwell North America, Inc.'s tape data base of 1.9 million titles. Tacoma estimates that 80% of its titles could be matched to the Blackwell base, which has been stripped to an abbreviated record so that it could be entered into Tacoma's minicomputer.[8]

For titles not matching entries in another library's data base, the usual approach is to key data in manually via circulation terminals; only Checkpoint/Plessey I does not permit the data base to be built this way. Some libraries select manual keying as the sole conversion technique. When the Phoenix Public Library purchased a Universal Library Systems, Inc. on-line circulation control system, it keyed in its 1 million volumes. The task was somewhat easier for the Northland Public Library. Installing its ULISYS system in October 1978 entailed keying in only 70,000 titles. Of course, few libraries keying data in manually have a complete data base before going on-line. Typically, a number of books will be converted while in circulation: bar-coded labels are affixed when an item circulates; when it is returned, it is flagged by the terminal for full data entry. Tacoma's director, Kevin Hagerty, estimates that manual keying takes "10 times as long" as matching titles.[9] Regardless of how the title base is constructed, however, some manual keying is inevitable when data specific to the library is entered.

For libraries with data already in machine-readable form, there are three options. Keypunched cards can be transferred to tape by the vendor or a service bureau. Keypunched cards may also be used to transfer data directly to the library's disk storage file during checkout with the help of a special terminal manufactured by Epic Data and distributed by CL Systems. Called a Circulation/Conversion Station, it is used by both the University of Pennsylvania and American University. Finally, if the library's data base is already on tape, a number of vendors will reformat data to make it compatible with their systems.

Thanks to an innovative San Jose Public Library employee, OCLC members may now simultaneously enter circulation code numbers while cataloging new acquisitions.

---

[7] "Library Saves $370,000 on System Conversion," *Computerworld* (May 1, 1978), p. 19.

[8] Ibid.

[9] Ibid.

The unit which makes that possible reads both OCR and bar-coded labels and is currently available from TPS Electronics. DataPhase also has an OCLC interface under development that would allow information on OCLC screens to be transferred to circulation terminals and entered in the circulation system data base.

While the future is bound to afford even more innovation and greater expertise in developing and refining conversion techniques, librarians should keep two things in mind. First, while vendors assume varying degrees of responsibility for conversion, the ultimate burden falls to the library. Automated circulation is still too new for many vendors to have had complete experience with all conversion techniques in a variety of different environments. A few libraries which converted early and allowed vendors to convert their shelflists for them were not totally satisfied with the end result. Consequently, many libraries' specifications detail the conversion technique they wish to use.

Second, one reason for dissatisfaction with vendor-controlled shelflist keypunching was inadequate shelflist preparation. If the shelflist has been variously marked and coded over the years, detailed explanations regarding what is to be entered must be compiled. If only brief data will be recorded, the library must realize that such an abbreviated data base would not be serviceable for any future on-line cataloging plans. Automating circulation provides a good excuse for taking inventory. A few smaller libraries now regret not having taken inventory prior to converting; larger institutions appear more willing to live with a few errors.

ELECTRONIC SECURITY SYSTEM CONNECTIONS

There is little, if any, difficulty in having electronic security systems located close to automated library circulation control systems. The Commack (N.Y.) Public Library has Gaylord Book Theft Detection System screens three feet from its Gaylord Circulation Control System terminals and has experienced no difficulties with interference. The San Jose Public Library employs the 3M Tattle-Tape Detection System in conjunction with a Systems Control, Inc. circulation system (SCICON) and reports no problems.

However, a few libraries did have problems with their electronic security systems when their circulation systems were first installed. For instance, the Dallas Community College District reported an initial problem with Tattle-Tape screens and DataPhase CRTs. The Biomedical Library at UCLA had similar difficulties with Tattle-Tape screens and CLSI CRTs. In no case was the problem prolonged, nor was data recorded via circulation terminals hampered.[10] Radiation emitted from CRTs (placed too close to detection equip-

---

[10] A number of automated circulation systems have been integrated with electronic security systems. For example, the Innovated Systems circulation system at the University of Texas at Dallas is combined with the 3M Tattle-Tape Book Theft Detection System. Cincinnati Electronics' circulation system (CLASSIC) provides a connection with the Checkpoint/Mark II Book Theft Detection System, and other system combinations are being developed. Finally, the Knogo/ALS circulation system will be compatible with the Knogo Book Theft Detection System.

ment) interfered with detection equipment operation; in some cases, sensitized materials failed to signal alarms. The solution was a simple one: moving detection screens farther away from CRTs.

COST

Cost effectiveness of automated circulation systems is only one reason for their attractiveness. Some libraries, however, do report impressive savings. For example, the San Jose Public Library anticipates paying for its $465,600 Systems Control system within three years, based on the 17 employees it expects to eliminate through attrition. The Dallas Community College District and the Northland Public Library estimate that their systems will pay for themselves in about five years. According to Markuson, these payback results are about the best that can be hoped for. "If a system is at the *current* state of the art, is readily expandable in terms of added storage and terminals, and is cost-effective over a five to seven year period, that is about all the certainty one can expect in this uncertain world."[11]

For the most part, however, libraries are at least as interested in improving services as in realizing savings. In the early 1970s when IBM helped develop the Library Circulation System at Ohio State University, A. Robert Thorson, head of OSU's circulation department, defended development and maintenance costs of the home-grown system primarily on the basis of improved services. Although development and maintenance were each in the neighborhood of $400,000 (the latter continuing on an annual basis), Thorson acknowledged: "It was known that costs would exceed those incurred under a manual system but given the climate prevalent in the late 1960s, the automation of circulation functions appeared to be inevitable.[12]

With so little emphasis on cost, it's not surprising that so few cost benefit analyses have been done. Only one recent study has pinpointed costs for a particular type of system: shared time. At the Suburban Library System in Burr Ridge, Ill., 13 member libraries are linked together in a network by four C L Systems LIBS 100 systems. Members pay $750 a month for the first five years and $280 a month thereafter.[13] Rates are based on each library having one light pen terminal and one CRT terminal.

It is difficult to determine what, if any, dollar savings are realized by a library's use of an automated circulation system. A year ago, member libraries using manual systems discovered that the cost of circulating an individual item was between $.23 and

---

[11] Barbara Evans Markuson, "Granting Amnesty and Other Aspects of Automated Circulation," *American Libraries* (April 1978), p. 207.

[12] A. Robert Thorson, "The Economics of Automated Circulation," in *The Economics of Library Automation,* ed. J.L. Divilbiss (Clinic on Library Applications of Data Processing, 13th, University of Illinois, 1976), p. 40.

[13] "Online Circulation: Costs Pegged," *Library Journal* (April 15, 1977), p. 867.

$.35. Cost variation was partly due to who manned the circulation desk; in small libraries, in which professional librarians staffed the desk, costs accelerated. While the study was not conducted uniformly, each library measured different items to arrive at its calculation. The agreed-upon average cost to circulate one item was $.26.

One not-yet automated library in the system, the Blue Island Public Library, circulated 118,392 items in fiscal year 1978. At $.26 an item, total circulation costs for that year were $30,781.92. A comparable system library, the Harvey Public Library, circulated 105,892 items in the same fiscal year. At $750 a month, the cost of their automated circulation system, annual circulation costs were $9,000. That figure, however, is exclusive of staff salaries. At Harvey, that includes two full-time clerks, two part-time clerks and a head of circulation. Although it is unlikely that those salaries total less than $21,000, Donna Sundstrom, head librarian at Harvey, says, "I'd never go back to stamping, regardless of price."

Most libraries are content to gauge savings roughly. For example, one CLSI user, the Lewis and Clark Library (Helena, Mont.), increased circulation 80% with no additional staff. A second CLSI user, New York University, handled a 243% circulation increase one year after the system was operational.

Moreover, estimates often overlook a number of expenses not included in either purchase or service costs. Accordingly, potential purchasers should keep an eye on:

- Telecommunications costs: the continual telephone line changes to the distant network computer or among library branches or from mini to main computer.

- Conversion costs: the one-time expense of getting on the system.

- Supply costs (labels): small but ongoing.

- Site preparation costs: one time, but may be substantial for some facilities.

- Upgrading costs: adding capacity to meet new demands of growth in branches or transactions.

- Additional programming costs: to add features not included by the vendor.

SUMMARY

Both the market and technology for automated circulation control systems play integral roles in the on-going change characterizing the field. The first systems, mostly off-line absence systems, were developed in the early 1960s. In-house developed systems (ones designed by libraries around commercially available equipment) were usually designed by large universities or by municipal data processing staff which had technical expertise readily available. They were responding to manual systems which became increasingly cumbersome and costly to operate when transactions reached 200,000 annually. The early systems eliminated the time-consuming chores of filing cards and preparing overdue notices.

In the mid 1960s the minicomputer arrived, but only in the 1970s were packaged systems (ones developed commercially offering hardware, software and maintenance from one vendor) made available. Such on-line inventory systems, permitting direct access to a data base of the library's total holdings, did more than eliminate clerical routines: They provided greater collection control and new services. Patron receipts, bibliographies, and other notices could be printed, as could a greater variety of statistical and managerial reports. Delinquent borrowers could be trapped and the fines they incurred could be computed automatically. Data base inquiries to determine book and patron status could be made, and messages could be sent from one library to another via the systems' visual display units. While minimum costs for such systems are approximately $100,000, many librarians feel the qualitative service they make possible offsets both their initial outlay and on-going operating costs.

In the future, microcomputers will make available even more less costly alternatives. The present eight vendors offer everything from off-line inventory systems, some with certain on-line capabilities, to stand-alone systems. In the developmental stage, however, are on-line microprocessor-based absence systems for $10,000 or less. Eventually, the microprocessor-based systems will rival the capacity of present minicomputers. Simultaneously with these developments is the ever-present influence of in-house systems. Newer, on-line ones, like that devised by municipal data processing staff for the East Brunswick Public Library at a cost of $28,000, probably will be entering the marketplace in the near future. In addition to cost savings, such systems allow the library to tailor design a system for its unique needs. To rival those capabilities, commercial vendors are making software design less proprietary, and a number of vendors now sell software separately.

X

Criteria for Circulation System Acquisition

by Alice Harrison Bahr

Serious attention to automating circulation accelerated in the early 1970s with the advent of the first packaged systems. While few libraries purchased systems in those early years, several formed committees to monitor developments in the field. For example, in this period the city manager of Greensboro, N.C., formed a group to investigate automation. Almost six years later the Greensboro Public Library decided to automate.

In some cases the wait was for economic reasons. Only special grants or Library Services Construction Act (LSCA) funding made implementation of plans possible. As Richard DeGennaro points out, "In the end the purchase and implementation of such a system may be the single most expensive purchase a library will make."[1] Technological advances, spurring the growth both of internally developed and packaged systems, coupled with decreasing costs, however, have renewed interest in acquisition of such systems. While new products and new vendors with untested product performance pose difficulties, sufficient experience exists to offer at least broad outlines of how librarians arrive at acquisitions decisions.

THE DECISION PROCESS

Surveying the Literature

The first step is to gauge the state of the art by reading the available literature. Such was the drive behind the early automation committees. At present, there are a number of available reports. For example, the American Library Association's *Library Technology Reports* for May 1975, September 1975 and May 1977 cover the then available systems. There is Knowledge Industry Publications' *Advanced Technology/Libraries* newsletter and the Professional Librarian series of monographs.

---

[1] *American Libraries*, April 1978, p. 212.

Reprinted from *Automated Library Circulation Systems, 1979-80* (White Plains, NY: Knowledge Industry Publications, Inc., 1979).

A report on the experiences of 38 of the 50 public libraries using turnkey, automated circulation systems contracted by the Fairfax County, Va., Public Library and published in June 1978 by the Mitre Corp., found that 47% reported significant operational Problems, but 70% could still say that their system provided the expected benefits. Over three quarters also said they would purchase the same system again.[2]

The Tacoma Public Library has made available the report done for the library in 1977 by Blackwell North America. That report, which sparked some controversy, is a detailed analysis of proposals of the four vendors most responsive to Tacoma's proposal. On the basis of hardware configuration, terminal cost, upgrade implications, central processors, supplies and functional specifications, the consultants decided that while Systems Control offered the most technically sophisticated system, DataPhase was as sophisticated as was 3M's, but at significantly lower cost. At that time, CLSI's programming language was proprietary, and it could not be upgraded to accommodate more than 15 terminals economically. Systems Control was too expensive. DataPhase had two benefits: it was the low bid, and the availability of OCR promised cost savings for supplies, at least $250 a year for 25,000 labels.

In addition, there are several recent journal articles, particularly in *American Libraries*, April 1978. A literature survey does not afford an adequate basis for acquisition in itself, however, for all printed sources are somewhat out of date. What the survey will do is alert potential customers to the general capabilities of systems and the experiences of users.

Requests for Proposals

After obtaining a general notion of what systems can and cannot do, the library staff must analyze its own needs and determine what particular requests it would make of an automated system. Such discussions and planning are part of preparation for writing specifications for bid. The Tacoma Public Library, working in conjunction with the Washington Library Network, developed a list of general specifications. Then the public library differentiated its needs from the network's. The result was a preliminary specification. In other words, Tacoma specified what it wanted, but was open to alternative vendor suggestions. Those tentative specifications afford a good outline of what should be included.

For example, included in the Tacoma *Request for Proposals for a Computerized Library Circulation Control System* are the following sections:

> 1. Acceptable procedures for bids: how forms are to be filled out; to whom questions should be addressed and what factors will determine bid award; a list of vendor's founders, names of company officers; number and type of professional employees; vendor's organization; bank references; annual report; name of investment banker; balance sheets

---

[2] *Automated Circulation Systems in Public Libraries* (McLean, Va.: Mitre Corp., June 1978). Expanded December 1978.

for last two years; Dun & Bradstreet report; opinions concerning last two years' financial statements from a CPA.

2. The library system's operations and history: size; circulation statistics; interlibrary loan relationships.

3. General instructions to bidders: vendors may bid on software only; price is not the sole criterion; a list of users should be supplied, including the quantity of disk storage each requires in relationship to size of collection; vendors should supply a list of supplies needed, including recommended stock level; vendors should detail any site preparations on system standards (turnkey);

4. Functions required — system should: permit charging on initial patron visit; accept varying loan periods; signal when bar codes have not been read; provide a borrower list at certain intervals; have a claims return key; permit circulation of uncataloged materials; interface with WLN data base with full MARC II content.

5. Technical requirements: storage capacity; number of terminals.

6. System configuration: where hardware should be housed, etc.

The Tacoma request also included a notarized non-collusion affidavit, a performance bond and an acceptance test. The latter specified that after the system became operational, it must run for 60 days with less than 2% downtime. The Tacoma proposal also defined the date by which the equipment was to be operational.

Library staff may write the functional specifications, detailing what jobs the system should do and the preferred way of doing them, but some technical assistance is usually required to write the technical specifications. The San Jose Public Library had the help of a city technical agent; the Tacoma Public Library had the assistance of two consultants; the Northland Public Library hired a consultant. At least half of the 20 librarians interviewed for *Automated Library Circulation Systems* employed consultants during some part of the acquisitions procedure. Some libraries are fortunate enough to have municipal data processing personnel or highly qualified technical services personnel already available to them. Others must look outside. The cost is well worth it, for as DeGennaro advises, it is essential to obtain "the advice of experienced consultants the way businesses and governments do when they are faced with similar complex technical, financial, and managerial decisions."[3]

In addition to offering suggestions for technical specifications, consultants play another large role. For instance, the Tacoma Public Library employed a consultant from Blackwell North America, a library wholesaler and cataloging service, to assess bids in

---

[3] *American Libraries,* p. 221.

light of the library's specifications. It was probably because of outside assistance that Tacoma was able to make its purchase decision one month after bid opening. The North-land Public Library hired a consultant for other reasons. While the consultant reviewed vendors' software plans for the library, he also offered both maintenance and, if necessary, ongoing program development and support. In short, good consultants become the library's safeguards, redressing the present disadvantage of librarians in the technical marketplace. Otherwise, DeGennaro characterizes the transaction as "an uneven contest between hard-selling vendors and naive, inexperienced librarian-customers. Not surprisingly, the vendors are ahead."

While specifications are being written, the library should give consideration to the conversion process. If specific vendor assistance is required, that should be included in the specifications. If conversion is going to be handled by a service bureau, bids should be received before or simultaneously with vendors' bids so that a full financial analysis of costs may be tabulated. Writing specifications usually takes about three to four months; the actual decision process varies from one month to two years, with most decisions taking place in about six months.[4]

On-site Visits

After bids are received, the library might choose to make site visits, investigating systems in which they are most interested. Most librarians who have already purchased automated circulation systems highly recommend on-site visits. Important and valuable as they are, however, some caution should be exercised. First, as DeGennaro suggests, "It is particularly dangerous to blindly copy the decision of another library by reasoning that if a particular system was good enough for Library X, then it should be good enough for your library."[5]

Second, the drawbacks itemized by a user may or may not be accurate for any number of reasons. At times, staff misunderstand the nature of certain problems and options available to them. Therefore, the complaints of any user must be taken back to the vendor before an accurate assessment of a system's weaknesses can be made. Third, it should be remembered that libraries that purchased their system several years ago made their decision based on the technology present then; often that technology has changed. For example, when the Dallas Community College District was investigating automated systems, it eliminated C L Systems because at that time it did not offer OCR labels; today C L Systems makes these available.

The site visit may also be used prior to writing specifications. When used in preliminary fashion, it supplements and sometimes updates printed reports relied on for background information.

---

[4]   For more on designing requests for proposals, see Audrey Grosch, *Minicomputer in Libraries, 1979-1980* (White Plains, NY: Knowledge Industry Publications, Inc., 1978). Chapter V.

[5]   *American Libraries*, p. 221.

ORGANIZATIONAL FACTORS

Furthermore, certain questions such as organizational constraints are rarely addressed. Frequently, automation affects the library's organizational structure. In one large university library, automation meant upgrading the positions of desk attendants operating terminals. Sixty percent of the 38 libraries answering Fairfax County Public Library's questionnaire indicated a reduction in circulation personnel after automation.[6] However, such reductions are but part of the total picture. While one of those libraries reduced a circulation position, it added one in cataloging; another found it necessary to create a totally new position, that of Computer Console Operator.[7] Other libraries, those whose circulation staffs rose after automation, have found it necessary to create new positions. For example, when the Harvey (Ill.) Public Library added book ordering to its CLSI system, two additional part-time clerks were hired. Staff increases are likely when the circulation system is used for more than the traditional circulation functions, which is often the case when such systems permit the library to offer new services. Because the circulation functions have become increasingly complex at Harvey, some consideration is being given to the creation of a new position: Assistant Head of Circulation. Organizational changes depend upon how tasks were performed previously, so the changes effected by automation will vary from library to library. However, they should play as large a role as system capability in the library's decision process.

The decision process itself involves a series of dialogues, beginning with staff from all library departments. Sometimes special on-going review committees to investigate automation developments are formed prior to actual automation. The city manager of Greensboro formed such a committee six years prior to the library's automation of circulation procedures. At other times committees are formed solely to select an automated system and are disbanded after a purchase is made. Whether or not committees are actually formed, extensive staff discussion is essential to assess current systems' capabilities, and more importantly, to clarify what the library wants its system to do. For example, if the data base constructed for the automated circulation system is to be used to prepare bibliographies for patrons, then a system permitting subject access or call number access is desirable. If on-line cataloging is a future possibility, a system with full title file capability is essential. A review of the current literature will define systems' capability broadly; vendors' literature will supply more specific information.

THE FINAL DECISION

The final decision rarely depends on price alone. Important as cost is, system capability and options for future enhancements are vital considerations. Most often, then, costs are adjusted by purchasers to reflect what the system offers. For example,

---

[6] *Automated Library Circulation Systems in Public Libraries*, p. 6.

[7] Ibid, p. 13.

when comparing the various terminals proposed by bidders, the Tacoma consultant also weighed the strengths and weaknesses of each. Likewise, the storage capability of the central processors was compared before prices. Only then do prices become meaningful.

Generally, the current market offers different options with each system. For instance, Systems Control, Inc. (SCICON) and ICC/Plessey are not generally considered cost effective for small libraries requiring few terminals. Gaylord, CL Systems, Data-Phase and ICC/Plessey offer the most packaged systems of hardware and software, but despite certain options, their flexibility is still determined largely by the predetermined parameters set by the vendors. Decicom and Plessey allow a library to begin with an off-line system and gradually convert to an on-line system. Only C L Systems, DataPhase and Universal Library Systems (ULISYS) permit subject access to the data base. Only Gaylord has a true lease option, while other vendors offer a lease/purchase plan. Whether these or other options are advantages or disadvantages depends on the buyer's needs.

SUMMARY

A review of currently available systems often entails dialogue with consultants. Usually data processing personnel will assist in the writing of technical proposals as well as in the analysis of vendors' bids. Blackwell North America, consultants for the Tacoma Public Library, asked vendors to specify whether hardware could be bought directly from the manufacturer by the library, thereby saving the library any middleman costs. Blackwell also analyzed the vendors' bids. Included in any proposals should be some consideration for conversion. Some vendors have not always supplied the best counsel for conversion procedures. Hence, the library must decide what role the vendor should play in conversion. Furthermore, if the data base may be used for future on-line cataloging, some shelflist preparation may be necessary.

After the decision is narrowed to a few vendors, a site visit is helpful. Discussions with other librarians actually using a system prepares the staff to conduct more meaningful vendor interviews. Some caution must be exercised, however, since technology often eclipses problems encountered by early system users. When the search is earnest, the decision process takes anywhere from one month to two years, usually closer to six months. Ordinarily, specifications or proposals for bid take between three and four months.

XI
Microforms: Traditional Uses

by Alice Harrison Bahr

THE USER

Microforms are not quite what some in the industry claim — "*the key* to fulfilling, today and in the future, the need for storage and retrieval of vast amounts of original information."[1] Based on a library's particular needs and goals, however, microforms can be *one* of the keys. Whether they are or not depends in large measure upon the library's users. Therefore, a user and use study should be a part of every microform acquisitions program.

One of the most intelligent, if not the fairest, user surveys was conducted by the New York Public Library between July 1971 and March 1972. After interviewing patrons who used a small portion of the card catalog on microfilm, the library determined that such a catalog would provide insurmountable problems for its patrons, "who do 'serious browsing' through the catalog."[2]

Although a microfilmed catalog is not a traditional use of microforms in libraries, the New York study highlights the fact that what one set of users will accept on microfilm will not necessarily be accepted by another group of users. Hence, even traditional uses of microforms must be selective. One library's experience is not necessarily a guide to another's. For instance, it is standard practice to provide access only to microfilmed copies of theses and dissertations in many libraries. Yet, such a procedure is justified only if those materials are skimmed, rather than studied in great detail. It is the way information is used that makes it a candidate for microform storage and retrieval. If dissertations and theses, like the New York Public Library's card catalog, must be perused for long periods of time, annotated and studied in leisurely fashion, then they should be made available in hard copy, and the microfilm copies should be held in that office responsible for record integrity.

Since most microforms are used in the library, the second part of a successful user-oriented microform program entails creating a pleasant, comfortable, properly lighted environment, maintaining equipment, and enthusiastically promoting the

Reprinted from *Microforms: The Librarians' View, 1978-79* (White Plains, NY: Knowledge Industry Publications, Inc., 1978).

collection. Failure to provide such an environment was one of the weaknesses found by the New York study. Studies in 1969 and in 1970 found that hard copy was universally preferred over microform because of browsing difficulties, damaged microforms, misfiled microforms, equipment failure, number of readers available and eye strain.[3] Most of those problems are failures in microform management.

In 1964, when Cathryn C. Lyon investigated those National Aeronautics & Space Administration (NASA), Atomic Energy Commission (AEC), and Defense Documentation Center (DDC) libraries in the Washington area then using microfiche, she discovered that "none of these agencies were equipped with enough readers to make the use of microfiche convenient."[4] That is a typical situation. One small Southern junior college visited by the author has ordered backfiles of *The New York Times* to enhance its research facilities. An old microfilm reader, without a dust cover, was situated next to the film; both were in a dark corner of the library, under a stair-well. No copying facilities were available and the reader was on a four-and-a-half foot high table, so that a patron would have had to stand to read any microforms.

Although user response to microforms has often been unfavorable because the wrong materials have been recorded on the medium and then housed in unpleasant surroundings and neglected, a 1973 Xerox University Microfilms' questionnaire sent to 15,000 secondary schools nationwide found that 42% of the 2500 schools responding had active microform collections, although this represented only 6% of the schools surveyed.[5] Some have advocated using microfilm in elementary and secondary classrooms, where its larger-than-print page size and the medium's appeal to students turned off by conventional print materials could be assets.

However, only one study of microform's impact on elementary students found it to be unquestionably successful. Not surprisingly, the study involved supplemental materials on microforms, not microform replacements for hard copy texts. In other words, some care was exercised to match the information's use to the storage medium. What Michael Ahern discovered was that rural sixth graders retained more information about a career information presentation when they read it on microform than when they read it in hard copy.[6] Since that investigation, comparable career information programs on microform have been developed in Georgia for high school students.

The favorable attitude of children toward microforms is consistent with findings that in general, younger people, when properly introduced to the medium, enjoy working with it. A survey of microform users at the Pennsylvania State Library revealed that while 15 to 25 year olds were in favor of the medium, 25 to 35 year olds preferred hard copy.[7] Similar results were reported by the Georgia Tech Library survey of its microfiche card catalog users. Faculty members under 30 years old had more positive attitudes than did those 30 years old.[8] Those various reports confirm Harold Wooster's surmise in his 1969 user survey: "we may . . . have to wait for a generation to grow up that by habit is used to spending much of their time looking at images on a glass screen — that has no capital investment in the totality of physical and mental skills that go with reading old fashioned linear prose in black ink on good white paper."

Factors other than age also play a role in a reader's acceptance of the medium. Discussing the questionnaires Xerox sent to the nation's secondary schools in its 1973 survey referred to earlier, Richard Whalen says, "There is mounting evidence that the usage level may be a function of how the medium is introduced to the student." The two largest user problems Pennsylvania State Library microform patrons pointed out were environment and microform handling. The latter is closely related to how the medium was introduced.

TRADITIONAL USES

There are certain traditional uses to which microforms have been put in libraries, but as the preceding brief review of reader response indicates, tradition alone should not determine a library's practices, especially since microforms are a special medium, requiring special care and promotion. The following sections describe some principal uses.

Newspapers

The best way to test the efficacy of storing information on microform is to ask what particular user need is being met. In the case of newspapers, users want to consult back issues that are readable and manageable. Almost all libraries have found film preferable to the original for the following reasons:

- the size of originals makes handling difficult;
- the bulk of originals makes shelving difficult;
- binding is costly and replacement issues difficult to obtain;
- since the late 19th century, newspapers have been printed on friable paper, and
- microforms preserve file integrity, maintaining proper sequence of data and discouraging theft.

Clearly, newspapers on microform offer more advantages than disadvantages to the user and to the library. They make available information which the library otherwise might not have the space to house, and even if space were available, originals would be cumbersome to handle and subject to theft and deterioration. It is not surprising, then, that the Library of Congress publication *Newspapers in Microform*, which covers information received through 1972, lists 34,289 papers available in microform. Meanwhile, the British Library has announced a plan to place its more than 500,000 volumes of newspapers on microform.

The one major user drawback in newspaper research is indexing. For that reason, most libraries prefer to keep on file only those papers for which printed indexes are available, namely *The New York Times, The London Times, The Wall Street Journal, The Christian Science Monitor, The Washington Post, The Los Angeles Times, The New Orleans Times-Picayune* and *The Chicago Tribune* (the latter four are indexed in a combined index). Since indexing is needed whether or not a paper is in microform, the requirement of an index is no impediment in itself to acquiring papers on microform.

Journals

The second traditional role microfilm has played in library collections is in replacing or backing up journal collections. The advantages and disadvantages are less clear-cut in this area of microform collection and more dependent upon the individual library. For example, if more journals, supplying real information needs, can be bought on microform than would be otherwise possible to collect because of space savings or because present collections have no room to expand, then microforms are making available added information. Other cases in which advantages outweigh disadvantages include:

- if theft and mutilation are overwhelming problems;

- if microforms are bought in sufficient quantity to offset equipment outlay;

- if articles in the periodicals are short and a copier is available, microforms offer optimal service; if the periodicals are scholarly and articles run from 20 to 30 pages in length, then microfilm is more advantageously used as a back-up system.

Research Materials/Preservation

In the broadest sense, journals and newspapers are research materials; however, most are far less specialized than are Xerox's microfilmed dissertations, the million reports from the National Technical Information Service (NTIS) and the Educational Resources Information Center (ERIC) educational reports. Although the impetus behind large research sets on microform is the same as that behind newspapers on microform — preservation — both have made vast amounts of hitherto uncirculated information available.

Micro-republishing, publishing microform copy from existing printed publications, has been in progress since the early 1930s and is largely responsible for the availability on microform of titles listed in bibliographies like A.W. Pollard's and G.W. Redgrave's *A Short-Title Catalogue of Books Printed in England, Scotland and Ireland and of English Books Printed Abroad, 1475-1640* and Charles Evans's *Early American Imprints*. This is one aspect of publishing that continues to grow. In March 1978, for instance, Readex Microprint announced forthcoming publication of a new microprint series, *Lenin to Khrushchev*, a collection of books, pamphlets and brochures relating to the development of the Soviet Union from 1917 to 1956.

More recently, there has been a trend to collate, index and issue original papers in microform only. This is micropublishing, publishing materials for the first time in microform. A notable example is the collected papers of America's first architect, Benjamin Henry Latrobe. While previous historical manuscripts had been issued on microfilm, the Maryland Historical Society chose to issue the Latrobe papers on microfiche. Both micropublishing and micro-republishing have enriched the resources of research libraries.

In the past few years, increasing attention has been given to the preservation of all library materials, regardless of their age. A study undertaken for the Council on Library Resources during 1957-58 indicated "that most library books printed in the first half of the twentieth century will be in an unusable condition in the next century."[9] Similar studies showed that of a sample of books printed in the United States during a 40-year period, 1900-1939, 40% were found to be so weak that given only moderate use they would be unusable by the general reader within another 20 years, and another 50% would be too weak for general use within 45 years.

What is the role of microforms in the current preservation dilemma? It varies from institution to institution; either original documents are discarded after copies have been filmed or filmed copies are used to preserve originals. For instance, a 1963 law permits the British Museum to destroy materials published after 1850 following microfilming, and the Library of Congress destroys original copies of newspapers after filming. However, the Royal Library in the Hague, Netherlands, uses hard copy newspapers for day-to-day work and keeps microforms for preservation purposes only.

Smaller libraries facing preservation problems have recourse to cooperative microform efforts. The Center for Research Libraries, for example, not only stores and provides access to lesser used materials for member libraries, but in many cases makes microfilm masters of materials on deposit. In 1971, the Northwest Association of Private Colleges and Universities initiated its own Microforms Center. Begun to alleviate acute space problems of member libraries and to fill serial collection gaps, it also fills preservation needs by collecting complete runs of some serials already held by libraries, which are in deteriorating condition.

Finally, microfilm plays a vital role in the preservation and security of archival materials. The National Archives would have lost valuable letters from the U.S. Attorney General's files in 1962 had not a Stanford University professor microfilmed the bulk of the folder a short time before their disappearance. Today, many archives systematically store valuable items in vaults and make microform duplicates available for use.[10] Often, library ownership of manuscripts is difficult to prove; some manuscripts would be defaced if marked. In that instance, microfilming serves as a mark of identity, necessary if libraries wish to prosecute thieves. Based on a letter received by the Dominion Archivist of Canada from a researcher who admitted that she decided not to steal a manuscript embarrassing to her family because it had been microfilmed, Philip Mason suggests in the previously cited article that microfilming archival material also "discourages the purging of embarrassing information from the record."

College Catalogs/Technical Reports/
Government Publications/Telephone Books

Information of current interest only is increasingly being offered in microform to library users. The benefits are not just space savings but tremendous savings in staff time, too often wasted by ordering, maintaining files, shelving, searching and reordering catalog and directory-type information that is quickly out of date. Depending on use patterns, the improved control over such collections that microforms make possible is a strong argument for their purchase.

In 1973 Dataflow Systems offered approximately 500 college catalogs on microfilm; the *College Suggestor*, part of the package, provided data on over 200 schools and cross referenced to the microfilm set. One year later, the National Microfilm Library made almost 2000 college catalogs with two- to three-month revisions available on microfiche for $400. Today the set sells for approximately $600.

Although many large reference libraries have telephone directories microfilmed for historical and reference purposes, a commercial set, *Phonefiche*, became available in 1977. Produced by Bell & Howell Micro Photo and representing 360 directories from the associated companies of the Bell System, several different purchase plans are available. For instance, either a basic collection of the 10 largest metropolitan areas or 25 of the largest cities is available. All in all, there are five purchase plans, and in each, costs for small cities are $2.00; for medium-sized cities, $5.00; for the largest cities, $25.00. The total collection comprises 3200 fiche at a cost of $639.

Technical reports which are costly and often difficult to catalog and which are quickly out of date represent another kind of information which is more efficiently handled on microfiche, especially when the library makes portable readers available. Photo-reduction of those materials is common in industry, government and micropublishing in professional areas.

Photographic Charging

Photographic charging, the process by which a borrower's identification and information about a borrowed book is filmed, is a cost-saving circulation procedure used by many public libraries. After a certain number of transactions are photographed, the film is processed and used to determine which books are overdue. Since each transaction is numbered, overdue slips include that number to facilitate proof to the library patron that a particular book was discharged to him or her.

While cost savings are realized because manual card files are eliminated, such a system is not workable in either school or academic libraries which need to know which borrower has which book and when the book is due back. Photographic charging systems can answer neither question.

Cataloging

For years, microform versions of basic cataloging tools like the *National Union Catalog* and the *Library of Congress Catalogs* have existed. Their market, for the most part, has been the small library which has neither money nor space for the full-sized editions. More recently, however, several companies have offered microform catalog data retrieval systems, either fiche or film, with indexes.

The primary market for these sets are libraries that:

- want access to information on MARC tapes, but that do not have computers;

- do not want to maintain files of Library of Congress (LC) depository sets or proofsheets;

- facilitate search procedures by having indexes available to LC cataloging information;

- want to reproduce catalog cards quickly.

At present, three companies are offering microform catalog data to libraries that wish to speed up cataloging processes but not to automate. They are Information Design, Inc.'s Cardset (Menlo Park, CA); Marc Applied Research Company's Marcfiche (Washington, DC) and 3M Library Services' MCRS (previously offered by Information Dynamics).

The systems have been reviewed several times, in *Library Technology Reports* (LTR), May 1975, and one year later, as well. Marcfiche was also reviewed in the October 1976 issue of *Microform Review*. While the systems vary in price, coverage of cataloging data and microformat, all can be used for quick access to cataloging information and for actual card reproduction, although LTR indicated quality is not always satisfactory.

Larger libraries, those internally producing more than 500,000 cards annually, have relied on a combination of micrographic and electrostatic techniques to reproduce cards. Basically, LC cards or proofslips are photo-reduced, duplicated on an electrostatic copying machine, cut, and drilled. In the user survey at the New York Public Library referred to earlier, offset printing from photo-reduction is recommended for libraries adding 15,000 or more titles a year.

SUMMARY

Traditionally, then, microforms have been used

- to reduce circulation costs in some libraries;
- to eliminate files for current materials too costly to maintain or to catalog fully, like college catalogs, telephone directories and technical reports;
- to reduce theft and mutilation;
- to secure file integrity;
- to create necessary shelving space;
- to make cataloging speedier, in the absence of computers;
- to enhance a collection's research capabilities;
- to preserve older materials in danger of deterioration, like newspapers and manuscripts.

FOOTNOTES

1. Stephen R. Salmon, "User Resistance to Microforms in the Research Library," *Microform Review* 3:194 (July 1974).

2. "The Use of Microfilm in Relation to the Retrospective and Prospective Catalogs of the Research Libraries of the New York Public Library," in *Microforms and Library Catalogs,* A.J. Diaz, ed. (Westport, CT: Microform Review, 1977), p. 9.

3. Frederick C. Lynden, "Replacement of Hard Copy by Microforms," *Microform Review* 4:19 (January 1974).

4. Harold Wooster, *Microfiche 1969 – A User Study* (Springfield, VA: Clearinghouse for Federal Scientific and Technical Information, AFOSR-69-1847 TF, 1969), p. 25.

5. Richard Whalen, "Microfilm in the Secondary School? Definitely!" *The Journal of Micrographics* 8:153 (January 1975).

6. Dr. Michael J. Ahern III, "A Comparative Study of Microform and Hardcopy as Methods of Presenting Career Information Materials," *The Journal of Micrographics* 9:184 (March 1976).

7. Mary Jane Edwards, "Microforms: A View from the State Library of Pennsylvania," *The Journal of Micrographics* 8:247 (May 1975).

8. Robert J. Greene, "Microform Attitude and Frequency of Microform Use," *The Journal of Micrographics* 8:133 (January 1975).

9. G. Williams, "The Preservation of Deteriorating Books," *Library Journal* 91: Pt. 1 (January 1966).

10. Philip P. Mason, "Archival Security: New Solutions to an Old Problem," *The American Archivist* 38:484 (October 1975).

XII

Microforms: Innovative Uses
by Alice Harrison Bahr

Nearly every small public or school library has a microform reading machine for newspaper and magazine back files. Yet, standard as *The New York Times* on roll film and the ERIC reports on fiche have become, microforms are becoming more important to the library's educational role, the format of its collection and the management of collections and collection records.

EDUCATION

Reserve Readings

One basic problem faced by school libraries on all levels is the inability to supply required texts in sufficient quantity. That dilemma gave rise to the reserve reading system, a system devised to benefit users, but one which is almost always fraught with difficulties, especially for commuting and working students. Attempting to make materials more available, two schools which experimented with microfiche came to similar conclusions: prolonged use of microfiche results in eye strain, but that is worth the convenience of having materials when they are needed.

Because varying enrollments in the University of South Africa's correspondence schools made ordering sufficient texts for up to 30,000 students difficult, and because mailing texts was time consuming and costly, the library (after securing copyright permission) made required materials available on microfiche. The more than 300 students participating in the experiment were automatically provided with fiche readers after registration. Results indicated that only 14.5% of the students did not readily accept microfiche.[1]

Although the program was successful, three problems have kept it from becoming standard university policy. For one, not all publishers will give copyright permission. Second, readers are too expensive for either the university or the students to purchase on a broad scale. Last, some students find the medium unacceptable. Although

Reprinted from *Microforms: The Librarians' View, 1978-79* (White Plains, NY: Knowledge Industry Publications, Inc., 1978).

using microfiche only when hard copy is not available would not be cost effective, substituting microforms on a broad scale can lower the high cost of educational materials.

The Department of Librarianship at San Jose State University (CA) conducted a similar, but less complete, study. Reserve readings for one basic library science survey course were microfilmed and the results were surprising: "Convenience of the microreadings was rated better than the print reference system by two-thirds of the test class."[2]

Replacing Slides

In medical education, Dr. Chandler Smith championed the instructional use of color microfiche on the grounds that expensive illustrated reference works would be easier to use if reproduced on fiche, and that color microfiche images are much less expensive than color slides — only 5% the cost .

Color microfiche, infrequently used before 1972, are now a part of medical education at the University of Texas Medical School in San Antonio, the University of Missouri, New York University, the Medical College of Georgia at Augusta, the Ohio State College of Medicine, Ohio State University, the Veterinary Medical Library at Washington State University and the Yale Medical School. As of 1975, they were in use for a basic accounting course at the University of Wisconsin. Students there actually reported less difficulty with microfiche equipment than with warped slide mounts, jammed slides and burned-out bulbs.[3]

Conversion from the slide to the microfiche format is a relatively simple and already well-documented process. Guidelines appeared in the November 1974 issue of *The Journal of Micrographics*; guidelines for in-house production were published in the January 1975 issue of *Consumer and Library Microforms.* At present, the Eastman Kodak Laboratories at Rochester charge $1.50 an image, and copies range from $1.50 (for one to 74 copies) to $.66 (for more than 1700 copies). For conversion and duplication, the minimum charge is $75.00 .

The volume of duplicate copies required determines whether microfiche will lead to savings. If one copy of each slide is required, the cost will be between $.30 and $.60 per image, or an average of $44.10 for each 98 slides. Converting those slides to color microfiche and making one copy would cost $147 for the master, plus $1.50 for each copy. If four copies of each image are required, however, slide copies would cost $176.40, whereas microfiche would cost $153. Thereafter, each copy made of the microfiche would represent a saving of $42.60.

Using color microfiche is a simple matter. Color microfiche can be viewed on most black and white microfiche readers, provided that they do not have tinted screens, and that they use the appropriate reduction ratio.

Microforms' educational applications expand with advances and refinements in hardware and software. For instance, experiments are in progress with microfiche projectors that are linked to automatic, synchronized sound as well as to computer-assisted instruction terminals. Becoming an integral part of audio-visual curricula, microforms are destined to play an increasing role in library and media center collections.

LIBRARY COLLECTIONS

It is not just audio-visual services and collections that microforms are affecting; they are changing the character of traditional library collections, services and operations as well. In the early 1970s, for example, Butler suggested that computer-output-microfiche (COM) would be the ideal way to update reference texts. Since libraries pay more than $500 million a year for texts that are six to nine months out of date before they are printed, not only would microfiche make data more current, but it would also eliminate the time-consuming project of filing looseleaf updates and reduce cost-consuming computer searches.[4]

Although no reference books are currently updated in that manner, microfiche is invading the reference collection in other ways. As of January 1978, Whitaker's is making *British Books in Print* available on COM. While the fiche is more expensive than the hard copy, it is always up to date; every subscriber receives a new set of fiche each month.

Commentators have wondered why R.R. Bowker Co. has not followed Whitaker's lead. Actually, both *Books in Print (BIP)* and *Forthcoming Books (FB)* were generated on microfiche during 1974 and 1975 on a test basis. Lehman College of the City University of New York tested their efficiency in acquisitions searching. Results were surprising: without altering normal procedure, that is, the randomized title search, "microfiche proved to be more efficient than hard copy."[5] Searchers' comments were equally interesting. While prolonged use of microform usually results in complaints of eye strain, Lehman Library searchers reported less eyestrain with fiche than with hard copy, due, perhaps, to the capability of microfiche images to be enlarged to any desired size.

Lehman Library staff made some excellent suggestions. Since one-sixth of all titles searched in *BIP* must subsequently be searched for in *FB*, the staff suggested that the two titles be merged. The forthcoming titles could be tagged to differentiate them from titles already in print. A merged, continuously updated *BIP* and *FB* would contribute significantly toward improving both library ordering processes and references services. After conducting tests, Bowker did a survey of stores and libraries to determine their interest in receiving *BIP* and *FB* on fiche, updated every two months, at an annual cost of $300. Most respondents were interested in fiche only if it would be cheaper than the current price of $151.50 for six volumes. Since publishing costs could not be reduced (preparation time, not production cost was the primary factor) and since fiche may be duplicated easily, Bowker is assessing Whitaker's results carefully before determining future micropublishing plans.

Standard indexes are also appearing in microformats. For example, in 1974 the nonprofit National Information Center for Educational Media (NICEM) began to micro-publish its annotated indexes to non-book media. That year more than 5000 schools, libraries and individuals were subscribers to some of NICEM's 17 catalogs, and shortly after the venture began, more than 10% of those subscribers ordered fiche only, bypassing the hard copy edition. Space was one consideration — 15,000 pages were reduced to 150 film cards — but cost was another: microfiche sold for 20% to 30% less.[6]

In April 1978 an index never available in hard copy was published in 16mm micro-film. *Magazine Index* is a computer-generated index to 400 popular magazines, including those covered in *Reader's Guide to Periodical Literature*, and is totally cumulated each month. In a short time the microform publication attracted a large number of subscribers. Customers receive 12 monthly issues, use of the ROM viewer (a 16mm open-reel, motorized reader available from Information Design) and four looseleaf product lists from Information Access Corporation (Los Altos, CA) for $1480 a year. Product lists expedite searching, thus minimize long waits to get access to the *Index*. The lists include information on products of current, univer-sal interest like particular car models. Because information is current and only one file ever needs to be searched, *Magazine Index* is an innovative application of COM technology to library reference collections, one that can improve the quality of reference services.

COLLECTION MANAGEMENT

Because they are overwhelmed by the impossibility of maintaining paper files, banks, courts, map depositories, patent offices, newspapers and hospitals have turned to alternate modes of storing and retrieving information. Many of their experiments with data processing and manual and automated microform storage and retrieval systems are relevant to libraries.

For example, if medical records librarianship follows the lead of St. Luke's Hospital Medical Center in Phoenix, AZ, paper records will be maintained for only one year after a patient has received treatment, and all inactive files will be photo-reduced on 3x5 inch or 4x6 inch microfiche jackets.[7] If a patient is readmitted, the fiche is duplicated and routed via pneumatic tube or dispatch to the appropriate nursing unit. St. Luke's estimates that microform storage reduced storage space needs by 98%.

Likewise, libraries with large collections of engineering drawings and maps, space-consuming, oversize materials, will be replacing long drawers full of crumbling papers with aperture cards, i.e., tab punch cards with 35mm film inserts. Indexing this microform is an easy process, since aperture cards can be keypunched with all required retrieval information. Most often it is done at the same time that materials are photo-reduced. For example, when the Pittsburgh Map Repository photographs a map, it assigns a document number to it. That document number appears after the state, county and the name of the mine in a computerized index. Cards are filed by that number which appears in the upper left-hand corner.[8]

Various experiments have been tried with newspaper clippings as well. Instead of devoting thousands of square feet to morgue file storage, some news libraries rely on CRT terminals, but others have turned to easily updated microfiche and computers and some rely on microforms stored within terminals. In the last system, fiche are not handled manually and can never be misfiled.

Changes in information storage and retrieval have the greatest impact on large libraries, yet even the smallest of libraries, the personal library, will eventually feel the impact. To get an idea of the capability of modern micrographics systems, the National Micrographics Association Resource Report Number 10, *Automated Micrographic Retrieval Systems,* should be consulted. More than 40 systems are described: type of microform handled, capacity, access time, coding and indexing, search mode, output, specifications and special features.

The marriage of computers and microforms for information display has long intrigued information users, and developments are coming at a rapid rate. For instance, Eastman Kodak announced in August 1978 the introduction of an "intelligent" terminal that combines microfilm storage with computer logic. The terminal, the Kodak IMT-100 (reader only) and IMT-150 (reader/printer), can be used for automatic retrieval either on-line to a computer or alone. More than 10,000 8½ x 11 inch images are stored in a microfilm magazine measuring 4 x 4 x 1 inch. An operator can enter the addresses for a series of documents in the keyboard and the terminal will automatically search and display the images in order.

COMPUTER-OUTPUT-MICROFILM (COM)

Computer-output-microfilm continues to be the fastest growing segment of the micrographics industry. International Data Corporation reports that in 1974 16% of all computer output was in microform, but predicted that by 1979 it will grow to account for 24%.[9] The reasons behind the increase are numerous. First, paper costs have risen far more dramatically than have film costs. Second, the maintenance of film is often less complex. Third, COM has a greater character repertoire than do conventional hard copy line printers, which often have upper case only. Fourth, in some cases, COM means faster access to information at lower cost.

Given COM's advantages over video display terminals and hard copy computer output, what has it been used for to date and what library applications exist for its use? According to a 1974 industry survey, financial reports comprise 50% of COM use.[10] Another 18% was devoted to reproducing printed material, including in-house catalogs. Both figures suggest that COM is most useful when multiple copies of large computer files must be disseminated. Diaz' study cited earlier notes several specific cases:

• Illinois realized a cost saving of 50% when it transformed a 17-volume set of automobile registrations to 100 microfiche. In addition, many companies have saved money and time by mailing microform service catalogs instead of paper updates. The most prevalent library application is card catalog distribution.

• An early study of microform and card catalogs, done by the Hughes Aircraft Company in 1963, compared costs for three alternative catalogs over a 10-year period. It figured a traditional card catalog would cost $48,000; a book catalog, $30,000; and a microform catalog, $22,000. In 1978, a library with 250,000 titles, adding 20,000 annually, could buy 100 readers and still save $24,000 after three years if it produced 100 COM catalogs monthly, rather than 100 copies of a computer-generated book catalog.

• The first large-scale use of COM catalogs in libraries was in 1966 at the Lockheed Missiles and Space Company's Technical Information Center. Since then, several consortia and large academic and public library systems have turned to microform and COM catalogs with less cost and more timeliness than paper output provides.

• As early as 1964 the New Jersey State Library microfilmed its card catalog. Shortly thereafter, the Illinois State Library put its holdings onto 30 sets of 64 16mm cartridges at a cost of $633.03 a set. Libraries receiving sets purchased a reader/printer (usable with other 16mm cartridge library collections) and a cartridge carousel to display the collection.

No computer was utilized in those early conversions; even so, many benefits were realized: interlibrary loan work time was reduced and the system libraries had greater cataloging data available. Today, both libraries continue to produce microform card catalogs which indicates that they have proven satisfactory over a long time span. While the Illinois library maintains a traditional card catalog and generates microform duplicates for system libraries, the New Jersey State Library is presently preparing its first COM catalog, having joined OCLC in June 1977.

Again, without computer assistance, the Ramapo Catskill Library System in New York produced a subject catalog of 60,000 entries on microfiche in 1970. The fiche were distributed free of charge to all of the 45 member libraries.[11]

As more library functions are automated, computer-output-microfilm catalogs have outpaced manually photo-reduced catalogs. For instance, one major university, Tulane University (New Orleans), produced a short-title catalog of 80% of its holdings as an offshoot of its automated circulation system. The duplication was to facilitate research at many points within the library; copies were made available at two locations distant from the card catalog.[12]

Georgia Tech expanded the usefulness of multiple access to the card catalog by combining telephone request and delivery service with 35 sets of COM microfiche placed at different locations on campus. (The basic catalog was filmed; however, supplements are COM produced.) Georgia Tech, recognizing the potentially dynamic quality of the medium, uses it as part of a total service system.

In 1973, one year after the inauguration of Georgia Tech's **Lends** program, the Louisiana Library Association produced a COM (microfiche) union catalog of more than 1 million volumes held in 21 libraries.[13] A few years later, the Los Angeles County Public Library, one of the first libraries with a machine-readable bibliographic data base, converted to a COM catalog, purchasing 500 readers for its 94 branches.[14] By 1987, the University of California at Berkeley will change to online cataloging; nevertheless, included in future plans is the annual, concurrent production of a microfiche catalog for a backup. Similarly, on-line cataloging at the Rochester Institute of Technology (NY) also includes production of a microform catalog.

Rochester and Berkeley practice demonstrates that even if on-line cataloging is the way of the future, it will not displace the value and function of microform catalogs. In addition to providing a backup, they remain the most economical mode of distribution, especially for preparation of bibliographies, selective dissemination of information services, and home use of catalog holdings.

With the advent of the Anglo-American Cataloging Rules (AACR) and the Library of Congress's adoption of them and subsequent closing of its card catalog planned for 1981, microform catalogs become an attractive alternative to large libraries that want to close their own catalogs. And the successful practice of those already using microform catalogs should provide an additional boost. For instance, public acceptance of microform catalogs in British libraries was said to be exceptionally good, while acceptance at the University of Toronto was tremendously popular.[15] Fifty-nine percent of the users of the previously discussed Georgia Tech Lends program had above average attitudes toward the catalog. Only one test-pilot study of microform catalog implementation concluded that such catalogs would not adequately meet users' needs. Last, while some surveyed users of the University of Texas at Dallas Library's microform catalog expressed concern over equipment failure, library staff concluded that purchase of low-maintenance machinery could correct that problem.

The success of these large scale investments is the result of careful planning — a deliberate implementation of microform systems that aid, rather than impede, library operations and services. Part of that careful planning includes a staff willing to experiment to provide better and more library services, a staff enthusiastic about the role microforms play in those services. Without that, no project can succeed. Studies show that users provided with more and better services rarely find machines unmanageable.

At present, the following American libraries are among those producing COM catalogs:[16]

Black Gold Library System (CA)
*Boeing Company
*Council of Research and Academic Libraries (South Texas Area Consortium)
Cumberland County Public Library (Fayetteville, NC)
Enoch Pratt Free Library (Baltimore, MD)
El Centro College (Dallas, TX)
*Georgia Institute of Technology
Hawaii State Library
Huntington Beach Public Library (CA)
Learning Resources Center (University of Texas of the Permian Basin/Odessa, TX)
Library Services Division (Boys Town Center for the Study of Youth Development/
   Boys Town, NE)
Lockheed Missiles and Space Company (Technical Information Center)
Raisin Valley Library (MI)
Salt Lake County Library System (UT)
State Library of Kansas (Topeka)
*Temple University Libraries (periodical holdings)
*West Virginia Library Commission (Charleston, WV)
Yale University

* fiche catalogs

COM Additional Library Services

Finally, COM has been used frequently for other than card catalog production or reproduction. In addition to COM-produced tools like the *Library of Congress Subject Headings in Microform* and the *Register of Additional Locations*, Connis O. Brown, Jr., head of the Local Records Branch of the Virginia State Library's Archives Division, envisions COM as a major tool for the modern state government archivist. Brown argues that too often paper records are destroyed under the assumption that the record copy exists on tape; however, since reusable magnetic tapes are recycled as quickly as possible, valuable information is being lost that COM could retain.[17]

UPDATABLE MICROFICHE

One of the most interesting technical developments in micrographics in the past decade has been the introduction of updatable film. The leading company supplying such film at present is: Dick/Scott (Holyoke, MA), a joint venture of Scott Graphics and the A.B. Dick Company. The Scott system, including a special camera processor, uses a transparent electro-photography process to add new images onto an already exposed master microfiche, from which new distribution copies can then be made. The U.S. Army was an early customer for the system, which it used for personnel records. Although no library applications have been reported to date, Dick/Scott announced in 1977 that a Boston newspaper had purchased the system in order to update its morgue (clipping) files.[18] This application suggests some possible publishing uses of updatable microfiche, whereby new information could be adding to existing masters without the need to completely re-film all the previous pages.

SUMMARY

Use of microforms in education, e.g. for reserve readings in the library, and to replace card catalogs, are among the more innovative uses of the medium today. Color microfiche offers dramatic savings for certain limited publishing applications. Updatable microfiche and computer-controlled microfilm retrieval systems, although not directly used by libraries yet, are examples of micrographics technologies that promise to extend the uses of microforms in publishing and information retrieval in the years to come.

Whatever the applications of microforms, however, libraries using them must carefully analyze costs, prepare for their proper handling and make a series of decisions about acquiring and maintaining the required equipment.

FOOTNOTES

1. John Willemse, "Microfiche as a Means of Providing Students with Literature," *Microform Review* 3:28 (January 1974).

2. Martha West and Brett Butler, "Microreadings: Easing Obstacles to Library Distribution of Information," *The Journal of Micrographics* 8:20 (September 1974).

3. Philip J. Schwartz, "Use of Color Microfiche as a Replacement for Slides in a University Elementary Accounting Course," *The Journal of Micrographics* 11:219 (January/February 1978).

4. Brett Butler, "Updating the Reference Book Through Microform Supplements," *Microform Review* 3:30 (January 1974).

5. Harold B. Schleifer and Peggy A. Adams, *"Books in Print* on Microfiche; A Pilot Test," *Microform Review* 5:13 (January 1976).

6. Dr. M. Thomas Risner, "Micropublishing Helps Increase Availability of Non-Book Media References," *The Journal of Micrographics* 9:32 (September 1975).

7. Harold J. Franceschi, "On-Line Microfilm System for Medical Records," *The Journal of Micrographics* 11:16 (September 1977).

8. Curtis Edgerton, "The Mine Map Repository — A Service of Mine Map Data," *The Journal of Micrographics* 8:239 (May 1975).

9. Joan Ross, "The Great Output Race: COM Joins the Winners' Circle," *The Journal of Micrographics* 10:11 (September 1976).

10. *Industry Survey: Computer Output Microfilm* (Silver Spring, MD: National Microfilm Association), 1974.

11.   Katherine Gaines, "Undertaking a Subject Catalog in Microfiche," *Library Resources and Technical Services* 15:297 (Summer 1971).

12.   Robert J. Greene, "Microfilm Catalogs and the *Lends* Microfiche Catalog," *Microform Review* 4:32 (January 1974).

13.   Diaz, p.147.

14.   "L.A. County PL Establishes a Series of Firsts," *Advanced Technology/ Libraries* 6:2 (September 1977).

15.   "Closing the Card Catalog," *Advanced Technology/Libraries* 6:5 (November 1977).

16.   For expanded treatment of this topic, see S. Michael Malinconico and Paul J. Fasana, *The Future of the Catalog: The Library's Choices* (White Plains, NY: Knowledge Industry Publications, Inc., 1979).

17.   Connis O. Brown, Jr., "Computer Output Microfilm and the State Archivist: Opportunity and Responsibility," *The Journal of Micrographics* 9:39 (September 1975).

18.   "A.B. Dick/Scott Outfits Newspaper Morgue with Updatable Microfiche," *Advanced Technology/Libraries* 6:7 (July 1977).

XIII

Book Theft and Library Security Systems
by Alice H. Bahr

INTRODUCTION: THE UBIQUITOUS THIEF

Book theft is on the increase and its cost is formidable. A 1969 survey at Carnegie Mellon University Library indicated that of 5000 monographs, 10.2% had been lost. Estimating replacement cost at $15 a book, that library lost $7500 in materials in one year.[1] A few years prior to the Carnegie Mellon study the Suffolk County Senior High School Libraries discovered that 22.7% of newly acquired books had been stolen.[2]

A 1973 inventory at the C.W. Post Center Library of Long Island University revealed a loss factor of 10%.[3] In 1977 newspapers reported that a middle-aged man's abandoned apartment in New York City contained 7000 books stolen from East Coast libraries. The books covered a multitude of subjects, from birth control to Cicero. Two years earlier another New York apartment housing 15,000 books valued at $125,000 had been discovered.[4]

The preceding examples suggest that for individual institutions, loss rates of between 2% and 10% are not uncommon. While the cost to any one library is high enough, the loss on a national scale becomes impressive.

In the United States, where the nation's libraries contain an estimated 1.5 billion volumes, a loss of even 1% annually amounts to some 15 million books. Again, using an average cost of $15 to replace a missing book, the total annual replacement cost would be $225 million. This is more than 10% of what libraries spend annually. The 15 million volumes are almost 16% of the 95 million volumes added annually by the nation's libraries.[5]

And many of the items stolen from libraries are worth far more than $15. Rare books

Reprinted from *Book Theft and Library Security Systems, 1978-79* (White Plains, NY: Knowledge Industry Publications, Inc., 1978).

and manuscripts present an especially inviting target. Well-known book theft scholar Lawrence S. Thompson notes the increasing activity of professional thieves which has made "the record of major thefts in the last 15 years . . . little short of appalling." Current reports back him up.

On July 16, 1971, the FBI recovered the first volume of the elephant folio edition of Audubon's *Birds of America* stolen from the Schaffer Library, Union College, Schenectady, NY. The thief, an ex-convict, was held for trial under $100,000 bail.[6] The following year police apprehended two thieves who had been burglarizing the Lincoln Library in Springfield, IL for more than a year.[7] In 1973 the two "self-styled unfrocked Byzantine priests" who had stolen rare books from Fordham, Harvard, Yale and numerous other libraries were arrested.[8] The thief who devastated northeast academic libraries, removing Winslow Homer prints from 19th century journals, has not yet been caught. Cornell University lost 156 prints.[9]

Whether spurred on by love or greed, book theft has become a serious, costly problem and one that is not easily solved. Studies indicate that electronic security systems can be effective book theft deterrents, but alternative theft prevention programs have also been successful. Evaluation of theft control programs is in a state of flux. The only program librarians unanimously find unworkable is the honor system. In 1968 the Tarlton Law Library in Texas left legal treatises on open shelves to test the honor system. At the end of one year over $4,000 worth of material had been lost.

Because no single theft prevention program is ideal for all libraries, devising a program becomes a matter for the individual institution. The following questions should provide the basis for devising a theft prevention system compatible with long-range library goals, library budget, philosophy of service, and staff and collection size.

1. What is the extent of overall collection loss attributable to theft?

2. What is the annual loss rate attributable to theft?

3. What materials are most susceptible to theft?

- current imprints
- books in particular subject fields
- journals

4. How much is theft costing the library? Take into consideration:

- the percentage of books missing because of theft that the library would actually replace
- additional interlibrary loan transactions necessitated because of theft
- additional reference hours wasted because of theft

5. Are losses significant enough to warrant a theft prevention program?

6. What funds are available for devising and maintaining a theft prevention program?

7. Which theft prevention program is most suited to the library budget, library staff, library building design, and the nature and extent of losses sustained?

Every theft program has its shortcomings. Anyone who has watched a tired library guard wave crowds of exiting library patrons through check-out lines without checking for date due cards or looking through briefcases knows how the guard system can be compromised. Electronic security systems range from 70% to 95% effectiveness and all of them can be compromised in some fashion. (The most common way is to remove from books the sensitized tags that could otherwise trigger alarms.)

Clearly, then, there is no definitive solution to the problem of theft. There are, however, a number of ways to reduce losses significantly. With few exceptions, a dedicated, security-conscious staff insures the success of any theft prevention program. Confidence of that kind, however, results from having chosen the program which best suits the library's individual needs. To assure that the confidence is well placed, all programs should be evaluated after a year of operation.

ELECTRONIC SECURITY SYSTEMS

In the early 1970s, electronic security systems — systems which electronically survey exiting patrons to detect improperly checked out library materials — became very popular. A 1973 survey by R.M. Broadhead summed up the general attitude: electronic systems were "more effective in cutting book theft" than other systems.[10] A few dissenting voices were raised, but, by and large, the literature heralded the 1970s as the decade of electronic security.

Responding to this literature, librarians began asking which electronic security system is the best? Such a question assumes that electronic security systems provide the best protection and that one electronic security system is better than another. Neither assumption is necessarily true. The best question to ask is which theft prevention program or system is most suitable to the type and magnitude of loss the library sustains.

First a library must determine that on the basis of budget, annual losses, long-range goals and philosophy of service, an electronic security system is the most suitable program for its needs. The following review of the systems currently available should then help to identify the system which particularly fills those needs. Six questions are asked about each system:

- Who distributes it?
- How does it work?
- What does it cost?
- What will it protect?
- How is it installed?
- What are its special features?

Systems are discussed alphabetically by manufacturer or distributor in the following order:

Checkpoint Systems/Checkpoint Mark II
Gaylord/Gaylord Magnavox
Knogo
Library Bureau/Book-Mark
LPS International/Stop-Loss
3M/Tattle-Tape and Spartan
Sentronic

A final section outlines methods of cost-benefit analysis and major distinctions among the systems.

Before presenting details, however, a few generalizations about the two basic types of systems, their safety aspects, and their compatibility with automated circulations systems are in order.

Bypass and Full-circulating Systems

All electronic security systems operate in the same basic way. Treated detector tags are placed in library materials; when those materials are taken past sensing screens, strategically located by the circulation desk, they trigger an alarm. If a library book is properly charged out, however, no alarm will be triggered.

In a bypass system materials charged out of the library are passed around the sensing screens of an electronic security system; they bypass the system. Such a system is less costly, but is suitable only in libraries where patrons do not return with previously charged-out items very often. Bypass systems are used most frequently in public libraries. They usually employ a detector tag which is different from the tag used in full-circulating systems; bypass tags are permanently sensitized.

Full-circulating systems accommodate libraries in which users frequently return with previously charged-out materials, like school libraries. They are more costly because special units are required to deactivate and reactivate the detector tags which are placed in library materials.

Safety

Two health questions regarding the use of electronic surveillance equipment have been posed. Do the systems interfere with the operations of or endanger the users of pacemakers or hearing aids? Is the radiation they emit a danger? To answer the first question, most companies have submitted their equipment to testing, and only Knogo reports that equipment may interfere with, but never endanger, pacemakers. Nevertheless, patrons in libraries using other systems have reported that hearing aids often pick up a slight buzz.

The second question is more difficult to answer. In 1973 the U.S. Senate held hearings on the effects of low level electromagnetic radiation (EMR) on the environment. Thereafter, the Office of Telecommunication Policy directed an extensive research program on the matter. The results indicated that small amounts of EMR affected both behavior and the nervous system. Neither government interest prior to this investigation (P.L.90-602 on Electronic Product Radiation Safety), nor after it (1974 Radiation Control for Health and Safety Act), however, has altered the accepted U.S. standard for power density, which is 10mW/cm. square.

Most of the systems reviewed here use less than the maximum-allowed power. (Sentronic and Book-Mark, which operate on magnetic principles, use none.) Nevertheless, even those amounts exceed the standards of some European countries. As a result, several of the systems listed are not marketable in those countries.

Compatibility with Automated Circulation Systems

At present, practical field experience indicates that security systems operating on the electromagnetic principle (Stop-Loss, Tattle-Tape, Knogo and Gaylord/Magnavox) are not always compatible with automated circulation systems. For example, the Biomedical Library at UCLA has experienced difficulties interfacing the 3M Tattle-Tape security system with the CL Systems LIBS 100 automated circulation system. Radiation emitted by the circulation system's cathode ray tube interfered with the operation of the 3M system, keeping sensitized targets from triggering alarms. The Biomedical Library's problem was rectified by representatives from 3M and LCSI working together cooperatively. The solution to the problem is relatively easy; sensing screens are simply moved farther away from CRTS.

CHECKPOINT SYSTEMS/CHECKPOINT MARK II

Who Sells It?

Checkpoint Systems, Inc.
110 E. Gloucester Pike
Barrington, NJ 08007
(609) 546-0100

Checkpoint Systems, Inc., which was formerly a subsidiary of Logistics Industries Corp., was spun off from that company in 1977 and is now independently owned. Checkpoint specializes in electronic theft detection systems and automated library circulation systems.

In the mid-1960s Peter Stern, engineer at Logistics Corp. and active member of the Cheltenham (PA) Library board, developed the Checkpoint Mark I book theft detection system. This first system, a metal detection, bypass system, was installed and tested at several branches of the Free Library of Philadelphia in 1968. It was deemed successful, but false alarms were numerous. In 1973 the Checkpoint Mark II system, a bypass or full-circulating system operating on the principle of radio frequency, was introduced. Checkpoint Systems claims that the new system, which is unique in several ways, has *no* false alarms; most users concur.

How Does It Work?

The way books are charged out in the Checkpoint System is different from the way books are charged out in other systems. Checkpoint's detection tags, called checklabels, are always active. For this reason, a library staff member must either pass books around the sensing screens from behind the circulation desk or deactivate books by placing a specially treated date-due card, called a checkcard, over the checklabel. The checkcard shields the checklabel; it does not deactivate it. In all other full-circulating systems detector tags are deactivated. One implication of this difference is that the Checkpoint system requires less equipment than the others. There are two basic components in the Checkpoint system: sensing screens and an operator's control unit.

The overall dimensions of the sensing screens are 1 foot, 2-3/4 inches wide by 5 feet, 6 inches high by 5-1/4 inches deep. The upper portion of the screen is made of Plexiglas framed in aluminum channels. The usual aisle width between screens is 36 inches. An unlimited number of sensing screens may be installed to protect large exit areas; each additional screen requires another turnstile or gate.

The operator's control unit is the system's power source; it also contains an alarm indicator light, a volume control for the audible alarm, a manual alarm feature, primary and secondary circuit breakers and a reset button. It measures 10 inches high by 7 inches wide by 3 inches deep.

In addition to a gate or turnstile, the system has one other feature for libraries which want to re-check a patron who has triggered an alarm: a portable detector. The portable detector is a hand-held, lightweight electronic scanner that a staff member holds near an individual to locate the concealed checklabel that is causing the system to alarm. The detector measures 7 inches wide by 11-7/8 inches long by 1-1/4 inches deep, and it weighs 23 ounces; its maximum detection range is 16 inches. When a checklabel is detected, the portable scanner emits a muted audio signal. It is rarely used in libraries, however, being found most commonly in retail store installations.

Checklabels have an adhesive film coating that requires no moisture, heat or other preparation prior to or after application. They are simply peeled off a sheet of release paper and applied. If they are part of a bypass system the labels can be placed on the inside front or back cover, on any page, under a book jacket cover, under a bookplate, inside or under a book pocket, or they can be printed and used as bookplates. In a full-circulating system the labels must be affixed under a book pocket, inside a book pocket or on the back cover – i.e., in a place where they can be shielded by a checkcard.

Checklabels measure 2-1/2 inches (plus or minus 1/10 inch) by 3 inches (plus or minus 1/10 inch) by 1/100 inch thick with adhesive coating. Special labels are available for cassette tape and phonodisc protection.

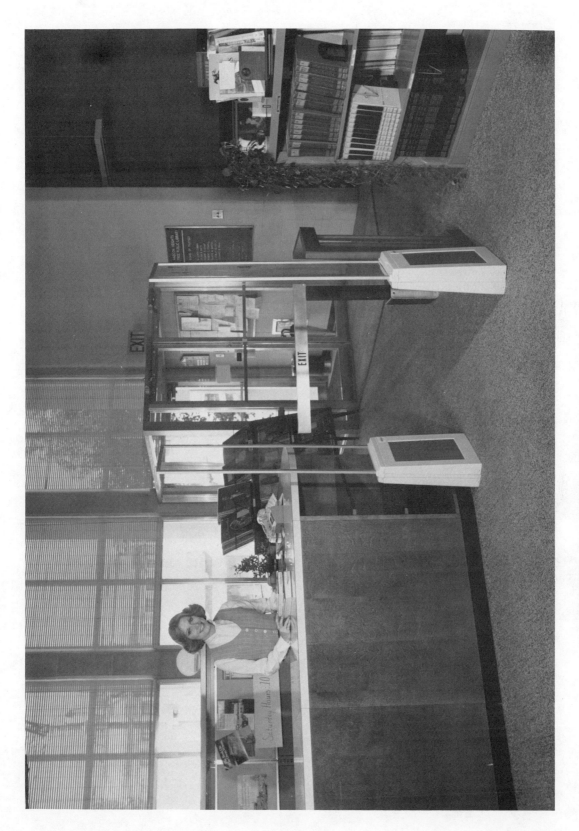

EXIT GATE with Checkpoint sensing screens. (Courtesy Checkpoint Systems, Inc.)

What Does It Cost?

<u>Equipment</u>

Systems:	Single Exit	$4,400
	Dual Exit	6,600
Turnstiles:	Manual Entrance	550
	Electric Exit	650
Gates:	Manual Entrance	550
	Electric Exit	650
Portable Verifier:		500

There is an all-inclusive first year warranty; a service contract is available in second and subsequent years for purchase and lease-purchase programs.

<u>Rental Agreements</u>

1. Straight rental $140/month
2. One-year lease   126/month
3. Three-year lease   126/month
4. Five-year lease   117/month

<u>Lease Purchase Plans</u>

1. Two-year plan $280/month
2. Three-year plan   210/month
3. Five-year plan   154/month

Service is included in all straight rental agreements; a maintenance service contract is purchased after the first full year's warranty on lease purchase agreements.

<u>Detector Tags</u>
Checklabels

Quantity	Unit Price Checklabel	Printing Add per Color
5,000 - 9,999	$ .17	$ .02
10,000 - 14,999	.14	.015
15,000 - 19,999	.12	.015
20,000 - 29,999	.105	.01
30,000 - 49,999	.10	.01
50,000 or more	.095	.01

Replica checklabels (no circuit)

Quantity	Unit Price	Printing Add per Color
5,000 - 9,999	$ .04	• $ .025
10,000 - 19,999	.035	.015
20,000 or more	.03	.01

Printing

For initial printing orders, a one-time preparatory artwork and printing plate charge of $75.00/color is assessed. The minimum order for printing is 2500.

Checktabs

1-1/2 inches by 2 inches, unprinted, pressure-sensitive on rolls — $8.00/thousand.

Checkcards

3 inches by 5 inches, available in white, green, buff, cherry, blue and salmon colors. Printed in date due grid or 1/2/3/4.

Quantity	Style	Unprinted	Printed two sides
5,000 or more	White	$30.00/M	$35.00/M
	Color	35.00/M	40.00/M

Treated Bookpockets (with Checklabel affixed to back of pocket)

$6.00/thousand, plus Checklabel cost

Checklabels for cassette tapes and phonodiscs

Quantity	Unit Price
*1,000 - 2,999	$ .015 (plus checklabel cost)
3,000 or more	.010 (plus checklabel cost)

*Minimum Order Quantity

Terms

Net 30 days, F.O.B. Barrington, NJ 08007 (prepaid and billed on invoice). Prices exclude foreign import duties, federal, state or local taxes.

What Will It Protect?

Checklabels can be applied to books, unbound periodical issues, phonodiscs, phono-disc jackets, cassettes, cartridges, paintings, prints and reels of film if the hub is large enough. When affixed to unbound periodicals the checklabel can be placed on the front cover with a printed non-circulating sign, or it can be affixed to a subscription form inside the journal. If the latter technique is used the checklabel can be saved and reused. Checklabels cannot be placed on cassette cases.

How Is It Installed?

Installation entails anchoring the sensing screens, gates or turnstiles, and guide rails. The entire process can be completed in a few hours. The customer is responsible for supplying the 117 volt, 60 cycle, AC convenience outlet near the location of the sensing screens. While the actual installation may be done by maintenance staff, Checkpoint personnel or outside contractors, Checkpoint employees supervise the process, make the final electrical connection and place the system in operation.

What Are the System's Special Features?

- Some systems use one tag for bypass systems and another for full-circulating systems. Since Checkpoint uses one tag for both systems, conversion is easy from one to the other.

- The Checkpoint full-circulating system is tailor-designed for circulating systems using date-due cards. Additionally, the company has recently designed an automated circulation system with which the book theft detection system is compatible.

GAYLORD LIBRARY SYSTEMS/GAYLORD/MAGNAVOX

Who Sells It?

Gaylord Library Systems
Division of Gaylord Brothers, Inc.
P.O. Box 61
Syracuse, NY 13201
(315) 457-5070

The Gaylord/Magnavox Book Security System was first marketed in 1976. In June 1976 five systems were in use. A year later 44 were installed and were operating: 16 in public libraries, 15 in high schools and 13 in colleges. Between 12 and 16 new installations were projected by the end of 1977.

The system was designed by a well-known electronics and integrated circuitry company, Magnavox, and a company with over 80 years experience in library supplies and furniture, Gaylord Brothers, Inc. Most librarians now using the system were attracted to it because of Gaylord Brothers' record of service.

How Does It Work?

The Gaylord/Magnavox Book Security System works on an electromagnetic principle. When library materials with detector tags are taken past sensing screens at the circulation desk, a physical, acoustical and visual alarm is triggered. A turnstile or gate locks and either a muted acoustical sound is emitted or a light appears. When patrons leave, the sensing screens, by means of a small electronic field, search for a detector tag.

Basically, the system has four components. A detection unit (two sensing screens) looks for concealed books; an electronics module provides power for all components; a remote control module resets the system after an alarm; a circulation unit (needed in full-circulating systems) deactivates and activates detector tags.

The two sensing screens that make up the detection unit are smaller than comparable units of other systems. The standard height is 4 feet, 5-3/4 inches, and the standard width is 1 foot, 11-7/8 inches. Each column is 5-5/8 inches thick. The aisle width is 2 feet, 3-3/4 inches. Screens and outer surfaces are finished in Honeytone Teak and the ends and tops are in Gold Leather Finish. Other Formica designs and colors are available at additional cost.

The electronics module, which interprets signals received from the sensing screens, is the main power source for all of the system's components. Since it activates the whole system, it is usually located on a shelf at the circulation desk, at either side of the sensing screens. The system is ready for operation five minutes after the switch on the left front side of the module has been raised to the "up" position.

The remote control module, which releases a gate or turnstile after an alarm, may be placed wherever the librarian wants it. It has two controls. A switch in the center selects one of two alarms. If a staff member switches it to the right, a visual alarm will occur — to the left, an acoustical alarm will result. Depressing the "push" button to the left turns the alarms off, releases the turnstile or gate, and resets the system.

The circulation unit, which activates and deactivates tags in a full-circulating system, must be located at the circulation desk. It may be either on the desk's top or built flush into the desk top. When books are being charged out (i.e., deactivated), the librarian pushes down the switch and wipes the book across the unit's top surface. When books are returned and the tags need to be activated, the librarian pushes up the switch and again wipes the book across the unit's top surface. When the unit is not being used the switch should be in a center position.

The Gaylord/Magnavox Book Security System uses the same tags for both its bypass and full-circulating systems. This makes conversion from one to the other easy. The tags are 3-1/4 inches by 3-1/4 inches by 3/20 inch thick and come with peel-off adhesive backings. They can be placed under book jackets, under book pockets, inside book pockets,

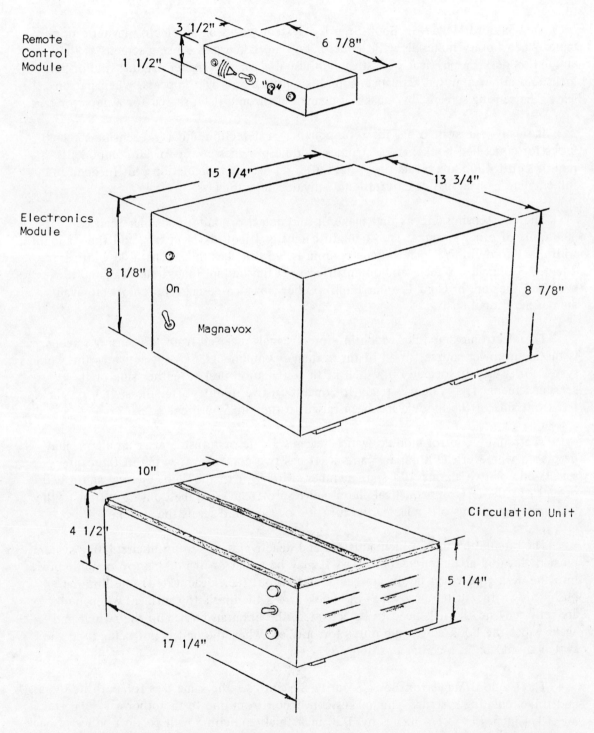

Remote Control Module

3 1/2"

6 7/8"

1 1/2"

Electronics Module

15 1/4"

13 3/4"

8 1/8"

On

Magnavox

8 7/8"

Circulation Unit

10"

4 1/2"

5 1/4"

17 1/4"

COMPONENTS of the Gaylord/Magnavox Book Security System, Gaylord Library Systems

or they can be used as printed bookplates as long as they are inserted within 1-inch thickness of the cover. A special tool is needed to apply tags only if they are placed inside book pockets; otherwise the release paper is removed and the tag is applied. A 2-inch pressure roller, included in the initial tag shipment, can be used to assure smooth, uniform adhesion.

In addition to the usual 3-1/4 inch tags, detection pieces are also available in 3/8-inch wide, 500-foot rolls. Like detector tags, strips have adhesive backs; unlike detector tags, however, they can be placed in gutters, spines and margins of books. Since the strip's length determines detectability, 4-inch long strips are recommended, and two 4-inch strips at right angles afford maximum detectability.

What Does It Cost?

Equipment	Full Circulating	Bypass
Detection Unit	$5,000	$5,000
Circulation Unit	500	—
Exit Turnstile or Gate	550	550
Entrance Turnstile or Gate	525	525
Installation	750	750
	$7,325	$6,825
Monthly Rental	$ 165	$ 157
Annual Service Contract after first 12 months	$ 300	

With a lease/purchase agreement 60% of payment is applied to purchase and there is no service charge. In five years equipment will be owned.

Detector Tags	Unit Cost	
	Plain Tags	Printed Tags
1,000	$ .13	—
5,000	.12	$ .13
10,000	.11	.12
25,000	.105	.115
50,000	.10	.11

One roll of detector tape strips (3/8 inch by 500 feet) costs $60. The cost per inch is $ .01.

What Will It Protect?

The Gaylord/Magnavox Book Security System detector tags can be affixed to books, unbound periodical issues, phonodisc jackets, cassettes, cartridges, paintings, prints and reels of film. The tag is placed in the cartridge, cassette or film container. The only items which cannot be protected are phonodiscs.

The company suggests that magnetic tapes not come into contact with the circulation unit; if they do, loss of content will result. Magnetic tapes are not harmed if carried through the detection unit, however.

How Is It Installed?

A mounting plate is used to install the sensing screens; this eliminates fastening screens to the floor. Because the mounting plate contains the wires which connect the two screens, no electrical conduit is required either in or on top of the floor. Therefore, floor alterations are unnecessary. Both the mounting plates and ramps are covered with carpeting.

The library is responsible for providing outlets required for security system equipment. A standard 115 volt AC single phase, 15 amp, dual receptacle properly wired with safety ground located within 6 feet of the sensing screens is essential, and is usually placed under the circulation desk. Full-circulating systems require an additional outlet for up to two circulation units.

What Are the System's Special Features?

- Gaylord/Magnavox uses one detector tag for both bypass and full-circulating systems; therefore, conversion from one to the other is easy.

- The circulation unit may be built in flush to the circulation desk surface.

KNOGO

Who Sells It?

> Knogo Corporation
> 100 Tec St.
> Hicksville, NY 11801
> (516) 822-4200

Knogo's sole business is the manufacture and leasing of anti-pilferage detection systems. The company was incorporated in New York in 1966 as the Monere Corp. and adopted its present name in August 1969. In 1972 it formed Knogo International, Ltd., a domestic international sales corporation, and at present it has two subsidiaries: Knogo International, Ltd., and Knogo Europe, Ltd.

Currently, over 2000 systems are in operation in retail stores, industrial plants and libraries throughout the world. In 1976 only 10 systems were in libraries; however, by late 1977 26 were in full operation and 10 more were being installed.

Knogo has been sued by 3M over rights to its system. The plaintiff claims its patents are infringed; Knogo denies any infringement, and is counter-suing, alleging antitrust violations. Negotiations were underway for an out of court settlement as *Book Theft and Library Security Systems, 1978-79* was being prepared.

How Does It Work?

The Knogo Book Detection System, available as a bypass or a full-circulating system, works on an electromagnetic principle. The company states that the system produces no harmful radiation, and that no equipment emits microwave radiation.

When materials with detector tags are not properly charged out and are taken past the sensing screens, a chime or a light and a locked exit gate or turnstile result.

The system has three major components: sensing units, charge/discharge units and a master control panel. The two sensing screens are 5 feet high and 5 feet wide. If traffic is particularly heavy, a dual corridor is available. If libraries are using a bypass system, a sensing screen much narrower than the standard unit may be ordered to facilitate the pass-around procedure. Aisle width is 30 inches and screens can be ordered in an all-wood design.

A library has three choices for charge/discharge units. The standard unit for full-circulating systems is the book verifier, a portable desk-like console which activates and deactivates materials. It is 6-1/2 inches high, 14 inches wide and 15 inches deep. The librarian controls which function the machine performs by the use of a switch not accessible to patrons. It is called a verifier because, regardless of function, a red light on the front of the unit lights up (verifies) when a book with a sensitized tag is inserted.

The book check unit, like the book verifier, is a portable desk-like console, measuring 6-1/2 inches by 14 inches by 15 inches, which activates and deactivates books. Again, the librarian controls the function the unit performs by a switch which is not accessible to the patron. No verifying light is included, however.

The final charge/discharge unit is the universal unit. In addition to activating and deactivating books and journals, it also activates and deactivates phonograph records. It is rectangular and, unlike the other two units, has a flat top surface.

The master control panel activates the system and controls the alarms. Normally it is located behind the circulation desk and can be supplied with any of the following features:

- *Reset Button,* used to turn off audible alarm, open the turnstile or gate that is locked (upon alarm), and restore the system to its normal operating mode.

- *Audible Alarm,* an electronic solid state tone-producing apparatus used to notify library personnel that the system has sensed the presence of a sensitized tape.

SENSING UNITS for the Knogo Book Detection System. (Courtesy Knogo Corp.)

- *Volume Control,* to raise volume during peak noise periods such as heavy use of copiers, vacuuming of carpets, etc.

- *Duration Control,* similarly controls duration of alarm tone.

- *Initiate Button,* to allow library personnel to lock gate or turnstile when desired.

- *Alarm Light,* red light to signify alarm condition. It is to stay on until Reset Button is pushed.

- *Power On Light,* green light to show system is working.

- *Power Switch,* to permit turning off power to the electrically operated turnstiles or gates under emergency conditions.

- *Counter(s),* a resettable digital readout showing number of patrons using library.

Knogo also has a mass target sensitizer available. This unit can sensitize large numbers of books at one time.

The Knogo Corporation refers to its detector tags as the heart of its system. The standard target is 1/8-inch wide, 7 inches long and 1/100 inch thick; it is also available in 4-inch lengths. Whether permanently sensitized or in sensitizable/desensitizable form, tags come with adhesive backs protected by release paper. They are usually placed in the spines of thick books or on two randomly selected adjacent pages of a book or unbound periodical. However, they can also be put under hinges, within the boards of a book, under the bookplate and under the book pocket. If tags are inserted in spines, a 16-inch long and 1/8-inch wide wire is needed; otherwise, tags are placed in a gutter, release paper is peeled off, and pages are pressed against the adhesive.

Special patent-pending, semicircular tags for phonograph records and tape cassettes increase the system's usefulness. These 2-inch wide adhesive-coated, crescent-shaped tags are placed between the label area and end groove of a record and are covered by a protective black annular label that makes detection or removal of the tag difficult.

What Does It Cost?

Equipment	Cost	Monthly Rental
Sensing Unit and Control Panel (single corridor)	$4,800	$150
Sensing Unit and Control Panel (dual corridor)	7,500	250
Book Verifier	1,500	40
Book Check	900	30

Installation (single corridor)	550	
Installation (dual corridor)	750	
Gates and Turnstiles	—	20

A one-year warranty is given on all electronics.

Should the renting library opt to buy, approximately 70% of rent paid is applicable to purchase.

Subsequent to the first year annual service approximates $300 for a single corridor unit and $450 for a dual corridor unit.

Detector Tags

Knogomatic Detection Strips	Book Detection 4" Strips Unit Cost	Book Detection 7" Strips Unit Cost	Record & Cassette Detection Strips Unit Cost
min. 500 - 999	$ .095	$ .14	$ .20
1,000 - 2,499	.09	.13	.18
2,500 - 4,999	.085	.12	.17
5,000 - 9,999	.08	.11	.16
10,000 - 24,999	.075	.105	.15
25,000 - 49,999	.07	.10	.14
50,000 - 99,999	.065	.095	.13
100,000 or more	.06	.09	.12

What Will It Protect?

The Knogo Book Detection System's tags can be affixed to books, unbound periodicals, phonodiscs, phonodisc jackets, cassettes, cartridges, paintings, prints, reels of film, calculators, typewriters, pictures and art pieces. Magnetic tapes will be wiped clean if they are deactivated, but will suffer no damage if walked through the sensing unit.

How Is It Installed?

Installation is handled by Knogo personnel. Normally only two to three days are necessary; this includes fine tuning. It is the library's responsibility to furnish a dedicated line for the sensing unit (nothing else on that line) and regular outlets for other equipment.

What Are the System's Special Features?

- Knogo provides tags which were designed for audiovisual materials and which can be applied directly to those materials rather than to cases and jackets. (Sentronic also offers a range of detector tags.)

- A mass target desensitizer which can deactivate large numbers of books at one time is available.

LIBRARY BUREAU/BOOK-MARK

Who Sells It?*

Library Bureau
801 Park Ave.
Herkimer, NY 13350
(315) 866-1330

The Book-Mark system was originally marketed by the Library Bureau of Herkimer, NY, which had licensed the system from Sentronic in 1971. In 1977 the system was sold to General Nucleonics, the parent company of Sentronic. Although negotiations are underway to have Library Bureau distribute the system, at present all requests and questions should be directed to:

Sentronic International
Division of General Nucleonics, Inc.
P.O. Box 116
Brunswick, OH 44212
(216) 225-3029

Sentronic plans to improve the present Book-Mark system by adding a discriminator, but at present, the system described below is the same as that formerly offered by the Library Bureau.

How Does It Work?

Library personnel attach encoded paper-thin labels to library materials. Materials are then put through an activating unit. If a patron takes an item that has not been deactivated past exit columns which contain sensitive probes, the light and audible alarms at the control point are triggered, the light alarm at the exit is triggered, and gates and turnstiles (if used) lock.

The system comprises six components: a combination activator/deactivator, a control console, a magnetometer and a probe set, two exit columns, a cabling and connector set, and a perceptor. The combination activator/deactivator is a portable unit which is mounted on a roll-around table that measures 2 feet wide by 3 feet high. The unit's job is to magnetize and demagnetize detector tags. It comes with a three-position switch that selects mode of operation. Indicator lights and a 6-foot electrical cord are also included. Overall, the unit's measurements never exceed 14-1/2 inches long by 8 inches high by 18-1/2 inches deep.

---

*Library Bureau sold the system from 1971 to 1977.

The control console contains the power supply and the controls for the exits. A counter and reset control are included in the front panel which can be connected to an exit turnstile or gate to record traffic volume. The console has a metal cabinet housing and never exceeds 7-1/3 inches high, 19-1/4 inches wide and 10-1/2 inches deep. It can control up to three exits. Exit columns measure 6 feet high, 1 foot, 6 inches wide, and 5-3/4 inches deep. The exit platform has an 8-foot long, 3-foot wide and 1-1/4-inch thick wood base. There is also a hand-held unit, the perceptor, to locate the source of an alarm without a physical search.

A magnetometer is contained on a plug-in printed circuit card which is installed in the control console unit. The six sensing probe pairs are concealed in the sensing or exit columns; these sensors will set off an alarm when someone carries an item containing active magnetic strips through the exit columns.

Book-Mark has three different detector tags. The bookplate tag measures 2 inches by 3-1/4 inches and has pressure-sensitive adhesive on two sides. The strip tag measures 3/8 inch wide by 7 inches long and has adhesive on two sides. It is placed in the spines of books or between two pages of a book or periodical. The spine tag, measuring 1/2 inch by 6 inches, has adhesive on only one side; it is designed for insertion in the spine tube of bound volumes.

What Does It Cost?

Equipment

Combination Activator/Deactivator	$ 950
Control Console	1,277
Magnetometer and Probe Set	2,285
Exit Columns	300
Cabling and Connector Set	195
Perceptor	36
	$5,043
With Locking Exit Turnstile	1,058
	$6,101
With Entrance Turnstile	425
	$6,526

Detector Tags

Minimum sales are lots of 1,000.   Price per Tag

	1,000 to 10,000 lots	11,000 to 25,000 lots	26,000 to 50,000 lots
Bookplate Tag	$ .13	$ .12	$ .11
Strip Tag	.14	.13	.12
Spine Tag	.12	.11	.10

What Will It Protect?

Book-Mark tags will protect books, periodicals, phonodiscs, phonodisc jackets, cassettes, cartridges, paintings, prints, reels of film, audio and video projection equipment, artifacts, office equipment and files.

How Is It Installed?

All systems are installed by the manufacturer, who promises that service personnel will be located no more than 75 miles from an installation and will provide service within 24 hours (holidays excluded). The library should provide a separate 100-120 volt AC 15 amp three-wire, grounded outlet for each console and is additionally responsible for any essential hole drilling or moving of existing fixtures. Guides, railings, partitions and emergency exit gates will be provided by the library after the system is installed.

What Are the System's Special Features?

- Book-Mark is a magnetic system and emits no radiation.

- Activators/deactivators can be placed in book chutes, making the activating/deactivating tasks automatic.

- Charging desk need not be located at exit.

LPS INTERNATIONAL/STOP-LOSS

Who Sells It?

> Loss Prevention Systems
> LPS International, Ltd.
> 6065 Roswell Rd.
> Atlanta, GA 30328
> (404) 256-0297

LPS International owns the original patents which the 3M Tattle-Tape system is licensed to use. Only a few systems have been produced in Europe, where they are marketed under the name Stop-Loss.

In the U.S., LPS is stressing retail applications for its system. It hopes to conclude an agreement whereby a company specializing in the library field will distribute Stop-Loss to libraries. However, to date it has not reached such an agreement. LPS claimed at the end of 1977 to have 12 orders from libraries, but as the company would not reveal the names of any customers, this statement could not be verified.

In the absence of any installations in the field, the specifications released by LPS, and detailed below, should be carefully verified by any library considering the system.

How Does It Work?

LPS, available as a bypass or full-circulating system, operates on the electromagnetic principle. An encoded paper-thin label is attached to library materials. When materials are carried through a control area without being checked out properly, an alarm is triggered. The interrogator and detector cabinet, exit control panels and de/reactivator are the system's major components. The system employs electronic logic to monitor signals in order to avoid triggering false alarms.

The interrogator and detector cabinet is the system's power supply. The unit is 19-1/2 inches high by 20 inches long and 15-3/4 inches wide. The design of LPS exit control units is highly flexible. If a floor plan is submitted to the LPS Engineering Department, a design can be constructed to fit any desired requirements. The commercial units usually measure 5 feet, 6-1/2 inches high tapering to 2 feet, 10-1/2 inches by 5 feet long by 2-3/4 inches wide. The company would not provide exact dimensions for library units.

The manual de/reactivator, for use in full-circulating systems, activates and deactivates the LPS detector tag. The unit measures 1 foot, 4-3/8 inches high by 1 foot, 6-1/2 inches long by 1 foot, 1-3/4 inches wide. It weighs 30 pounds and its opening measures 4-5/8 inches high by 13-3/4 inches long by 10-1/2 inches wide.

The LPS system uses two kinds of detector tags (sensors). One-way tags are permanently sensitized. Removed in the retail industry when a protected item is sold, they are the basis of protection for non-circulating materials such as reference books as well as the basis of protection for all materials in a bypass system. Two-way tags, shipped in an active state, are used in full-circulating systems.

Tags are 2 inches long and 1/8-inch wide. They can be applied with adhesive, staples or pins, or through sewing and heat sealing. Libraries would be most likely to use adhesive-backed sensors. Those pieces could be placed in book covers and book spines or they could be printed as labels. No special tools are needed to insert tags. LPS also makes detector tags which are 7 inches long; special tools must be used to insert these strips.

What Does It Cost?

Equipment

LPS would provide no breakdown of individualized costs; however, the current purchase price of the system is $5600. This includes a year's warranty on parts and workmanship. Installation and service costs vary with location.

Detector Tags

2-inch detector tags cost between $.04 and $.08 each.
7-inch detector strips are $.10 each.

What Will It Protect?

LPS detector tags can be affixed to books, unbound periodicals, phonodiscs, phono-disc jackets, cassettes, cartridges, paintings, prints, reels of film, furnishings and manu-scripts. Tapes should not be passed through the de/reactivator unit.

How Is It Installed?

The following electrical requirements are necessary: 115 volts, 60 cycles, 8 amps. Also available: 220 volts, 60 cycles, 4 amps or 220 volts, 50 cycles, 4 amps.

What Are the System's Special Features?

- One detector tag is extremely small, only 2 inches long.

- The company claims that use of electronic logic in the system eliminates the triggering of false alarms.

3M COMPANY/TATTLE-TAPE AND SPARTAN

Who Sells It?

Tattle-Tape Brand Book Detection System
3M Company
Library Systems Building 220
3M Center
St. Paul, MN 55101
(612) 733-2851

The 3M Company is a major industrial corporation which operates 94 plants and 122 sales offices throughout the United States and 94 plants in 23 foreign countries.

The 3M Company produces a variety of products and services: electrical products, abrasives, adhesives, building service and chemicals, graphic systems, advertising services, protective products, recording materials, photographic printing, industrial graphics and nuclear products, and health care products and services. The Tattle-Tape Brand Book Detection System was first marketed in 1970.

How Does It Work?

The Tattle-Tape Brand Book Detection System is available as a bypass, full-circulating or combination system. It operates on an electromagnetic principle. A low frequency electrical signal is triggered when a thin metallic detection strip, concealed in library materials, stimulates an alternating electromagnetic field. If a patron attempts to pass the detector with material not checked out or not cleared for circulation, a chime sounds and the gate locks. At present, two models are available; another is in the planning stage. The first model is the Tattle-Tape model; the second, designed for the lower traffic requirements of high school libraries, small public libraries and small junior or community colleges, is the Spartan model.

The basic components of the Tattle-Tape system are the sensing unit and the detector, the book check unit and the circulation desk control panel. The sensing unit controls exit traffic. On the Tattle-Tape system it stands 6 feet, 6 inches high, 11-3/8 inches wide and 4 feet, 5-1/4 inches long. Directly across from it, not more than 31 inches from its base, is a 9-1/4-inch square pillar. The pillar, or detector post, stands 5 feet, 7 inches high. Together, these units "search" each exiting patron for library materials improperly checked out.

On the Spartan system the sensing unit is 6 feet, 5 inches high, 8-1/4 inches wide, and 4 feet, 9 inches long. The detector post is 10 inches shorter than the Tattle-Tape detector post.

The book check unit activates and deactivates library materials. It measures 20 inches long by 18-1/2 inches wide by 6-1/2 inches deep. A signal light to the left indicates whether the strip is sensitive or nonsensitive. To activate or deactivate library materials a staff member pushes a switch, setting the unit to perform only one of these functions. Then the staff member slides the book through the unit, with the book's spine against the unit. An audible thump means the machine has performed the desired task.

The circulation desk control panel on the Tattle-Tape system activates the entire system and resets it after an alarm. The panel has five elements: an amber indicator light, a green indicator light, a normal/stand-by switch, a patron counter and a red alarm light.

The amber light indicates that the power is on. The green light indicates the system is malfunctioning. The normal/stand-by switch is set at "normal" during usual working hours and placed on stand-by thereafter. If a staff member pushes the switch to stand-by position the system's power remains on but the physical and acoustical alarms are turned off. Visual alarms continue; the red light flashes momentarily instead of staying on. The stand-by position is ideal if a system malfunction occurs.

The patron counter which operates on a stand-by basis is activated electrically when patrons interrupt the invisible, infra-red photocell beam across the exit passageway. Since there is no way to set it back to zero, readings must be taken daily. Finally, the red light switch indicates an alarm and resets the system after an alarm. The duration of the alarm can be adjusted within the range of 3 to 18 seconds.

The Spartan model houses a control module, containing the chime and the patron counter, at the base of the sensing unit. It has a separate remote control unit at the circulation desk which performs the following functions:

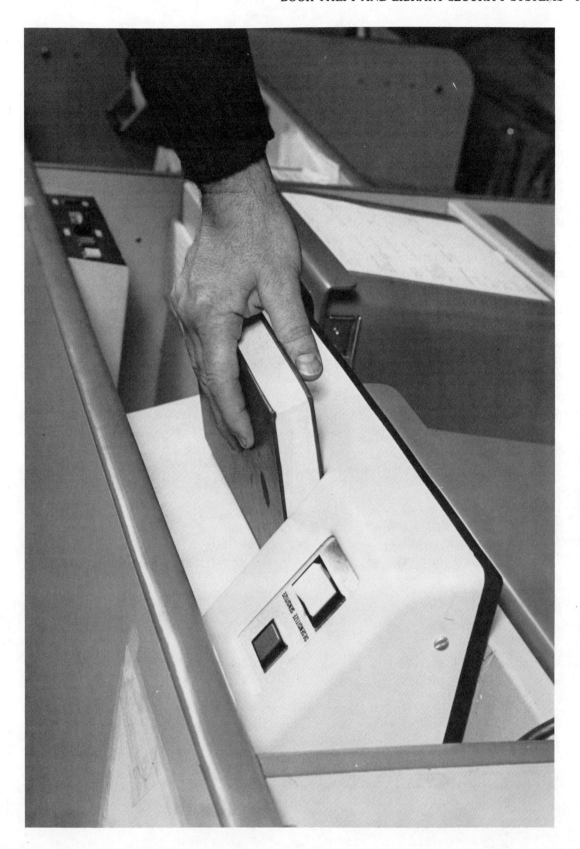

THE TATTLE-TAPE system's book check unit. (Courtesy 3M Co.)

- alarm activation
- gate unlock mechanism
- stand-by switch

Two kinds of detection strips are available for use with the Tattle-Tape and Spartan systems: permanently sensitized, single status strips (SS) and sensitizable/desensitizable, dual status strips (DS). SS strips are used in bypass systems; they also protect non-circulating materials in full-circulating systems. DS strips are used in full-circulating systems. Strips are no thicker than 1/100 inch. SS strips are 7 inches long and 1/8 inch wide; DS strips are 7 inches long and 3/16 inch wide.

They come with a pressure-sensitive adhesive backing and an extended liner which is 9 inches long if adhesive is only on one side and is 14 inches long if adhesive is on both sides.

Strips with adhesive on only one side are placed in the spines of books and in bound periodicals. A thin metal tool is needed to insert them. If adhesive is on both sides, the strip is aligned in the book's or unbound periodical's gutter, the extended liner is removed, and the pages are pressed against the adhesive.

What Does It Cost?

Equipment

	Cost	Monthly Rental
Tattle-Tape		
Sensing Unit (single corridor)	$6,950	$210
Sensing Unit (dual corridor)	9,950	300
Book Check Unit	1,600	50
Gates or Turnstiles	565	18
Spartan		
Sensing Unit (single corridor)	$4,600	$150
Sensing Unit (dual corridor)	8,750	270
Book Check Unit	1,600	50
Gates or Turnstiles	565	18

Detector Strips

DS 1 (single adhesive); DS 2 (double adhesive) green
SS 1 (single adhesive); SS 2 (double adhesive) white

	Price per Strip	
Quantity	green	white
1,000 - 1,500	$ .14	$ .10
2,000 - 7,000	.12	.09
7,500 - 14,500	.10	.08
15,000 - 24,500	.095	.075

There are 500 strips per box and a minimum of two boxes must be ordered. Pricing for larger quantities available on request.

What Will It Protect?

Tattle-Tape and Spartan systems protect books, unbound periodicals, phonodiscs, phonodisc jackets, cassettes, cartridges, paintings, prints and reels of film. The strip is affixed to cassettes, phonorecords, and cassette liners. Magnetic tapes must bypass the system; they should not be discharged in the book check unit.

How Is It Installed?

The library must provide the following electrical circuits: 110-120 volts AC for single corridor system at circulation desk, two-three for a dual corridor system; 110-120 volts AC for each book check unit; 110-120 volts AC for remote entrance gates. Installation takes from four to eight hours.

SENTRONIC

Who Sells It?

Sentronic International
Division of General Nucleonics, Inc.
P.O. Box 116
Brunswick, OH 44212
(216) 225-3029

Developed in 1963 and installed in 1964, Sentronic was the first theft detection system on the market. It and its licensee, Book-Mark, are distinguished from other systems because they operate on the principle of magnetism. There is no radiation emitted by either system. In 1976 over 100 Sentronic systems were in use; 14 were in libraries.

Tyco Laboratories, Inc. acquired the assets of General Nucleonics, Inc. in 1967. General Nucleonics is part of the industrial equipment and materials group of Tyco Laboratories, a research, manufacturing and development organization serving high technology industries as well as commercial and consumer markets.

How Does It Work?

Unlike other electronic security systems which use electromagnetic or microwave radiation, Sentronic employs magnetism as an energy form. In other systems patrons are surveyed or interrogated by radiation whenever they pass by sensing screens at the library's exit passageways. Detector tags in these systems cause an alarm, but the system is "on" whether or not these tags are present.

In magnetic systems, however, detector tags trigger the alarms; there is no other interrogation or surveillance.

Apart from its energy form, Sentronic, a full-circulating security system with bypass possibilities, operates much the same as other systems. Sentrons (magnetic targets, placed in library materials) produce an alarm if materials are not deactivated before being taken past sensors in exit columns. The alarm is visual, audible and physical (the turnstile locks).

Sentronic offers four models. Although full-circulating, bypass and a combination of both systems are available, the two basic models are the S-64 and the S-76. The S-76, the ScanScope system, visually pinpoints the location of a concealed item; the S-64 is the conventional system. Both systems are comprised of sensing columns, control consoles and charge/discharge units.

Tapering from a base of 1 foot by 5-1/2 inches to 6 inches by 4 inches, the two columns which form the exit pathway are at least 4 feet, 10 inches high. Special finishes are available at extra cost; metal, molded polymer and specially concealed sensing columns are additionally available.

The control console contains the power supply for the system and the electronics for producing alarms and resetting the system after alarms. The S-64 console measures 8 inches by 16 inches by 12 inches. The ScanScope console, the S-76, measures 9 inches by 11 inches by 16 inches.

Sentronic users have a range of charge/discharge units from which to choose. Units may be portable or permanent, manual or automatic. Most equipment is permanent; however, one model activator is portable. The portable activator is an automatic piece of equipment; that is, it performs only one function. It is mounted on a wheeled table, measures 2 feet by 2 feet, 2 inches by 2 feet, 6 inches, and is comprised of an on/off switch, indicator lights and an 8-foot electric cord and plug.

Other automatic units are permanent. The automatic activator is mounted in the book-return chute. It measures 11 inches by 20 inches by 5-1/2 inches with a 4-inch by 13-3/4-inch opening. When books are returned through the chute they are automatically deactivated. That unit's counterpart, the automatic deactivator, whose dimensions are 14 inches by 14 inches by 4 inches, is operated a little differently. When library materials are checked out, a library staff member presses a foot switch and slides books over the circulation counter. The deactivator is concealed under this counter.

The Control Console

The new, optional ScanScope feature now includes the figure of a human silhouette for
revealing the exact location of concealed or
shielded theft in addition to the audio-visual
signals from the detection and apprehension
functions.

Turnstile Control Optional

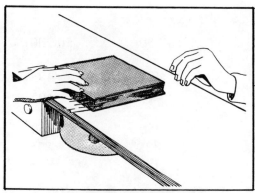

Books being automatically deactivated during normal charge-out function at circulation desk.

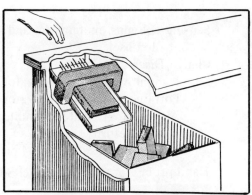

Books are energized or activated
when initially treated or following
their return to the library by patron.

SENTRONIC'S S-76 model, with ScanScope feature. (Courtesy Sentronic International.)

If the manual unit, which performs both activating and deactivating tasks is being used, library staff press one of two buttons. A red button activates materials and a green one deactivates them.

In addition to these components, a hand probe is available for use with model S-64. The hand probe detects the source of alarm. Sentronic's plans include making available a discriminator: an automatic feature which will identify the particular field emitted by a sentron instead of a foreign magnetic field by some object that might have been magnetized accidentally or intentionally by a patron.

Sentronic detector tags are available in seven different forms: three for books, two for tapes and two for phonodiscs. Special types and sizes can be made to order for any application. Book detection tags come as follows:

- 2-inch by 3-1/4 inch by 1/100-inch tags with two pressure-sensitive sides, for attaching bookplates or for attaching book pockets to inside covers of books

- 2-inch by 3-1/4-inch by 1/100-inch tags with no adhesive, for inserting in covers during rebinding

- 3/8-inch by 7-inch by 1/100-inch strips with adhesive on two sides, for concealing in gutters of books and magazines

Tags for cassettes and tape decks are thin labels with one pressure-sensitive adhesive side for application on the actual tape. Tags for phonodiscs are circular, label-like tags with adhesive on one side. One is for 33-1/3 RPM records; the other is for 45 RPM records.

What Does It Cost?

Equipment	Model S-64	Model S-76
Sensing columns, metal base, and control console	$4,750	$6,200
Charge/Discharge Units		
Manual Activator/Deactivator	495	495
Portable Automatic Activator	865	865
Automatic Activator, mounted in book return	850	850
Automatic Deactivator	825	825
Hand probe, for use with Model S-64	195	—

Detector Tags

	Price per Tag
Books	$ .10
Magazines (book gutters)	.10
Tape cassettes	.20
Phonodiscs	.20
Magnetic tape decks	.20

What Does It Protect?

Sentronic detector tags can be used to protect books, unbound periodicals, phono-discs, phonodisc jackets, cassettes, cartridges, paintings, prints, reels of film and EDP materials; no tags are needed to magnetize office equipment, hand tools, typewriters and other equipment which incorporates some ferromagnetic material susceptible to a magnetic charge. Magnetic tapes may be activated and deactivated without damage.

How Is It Installed?

Sensing screens are mounted on a rigid, but portable base. No special preparations are necessary.

What Are the System's Special Features?

- Automatic charge/discharge units are available.

- There are a variety of detector tags; some are specially designed for phono-discs and cassettes.

- The hand probe, comparable to Checkpoint's portable detector, locates where a book is hidden.

- The ScanScope system visually locates where a book is hidden.

SUMMARY COMMENTS

The choice of which electronic security system to employ depends on a library's objectives and its budget. Briefly, if a library wants a bypass system now, but envisions the need for converting to full-circulating later, Gaylord and Checkpoint make conversion simple.

If fear of radiation's effects is a primary concern, the library may wish to choose the Book-Mark or Sentronic system, which emit no radiation. Sentronic points out that while electromagnetic systems operate within the current U.S. standard for radiation frequency (10mW/cm square), this standard is 1000 times greater than the standard established by many European countries. Stop-Loss, for instance, was not marketable in Switzerland because its radiation level was too high; Checkpoint was not marketable in Denmark and the United Kingdom for the same reason.

If protecting audiovisual materials is important, Knogo makes special detector tags for these materials, and Sentronic and Book-Mark are the only systems in which tapes can be deactivated safely.

If absolute assurance of theft is essential, Sentronic, Book-Mark and Checkpoint provide instruments which determine where an item is concealed. Additionally, Stop-Loss, Knogo and Tattle-Tape offer the least detectable strips; users indicate Checkpoint has the fewest false alarms, the other electromagnetic systems have a few, and the magnetic systems have the most; all systems give a choice of either turnstiles or gates with the exception of Sentronic which, finding gates unsafe, provides turnstiles.

None of the systems is, or can be, 100% effective. In all systems a common problem is that patrons can locate detector tags and remove them. If this happens, of course, a book can be carried out through the sensing screens without triggering any alarm.

In the Checkpoint system, checkcards, the date-due cards which shield detector tags by being placed over them, can be removed and then used to remove other books from the collection. In electromagnetic systems, magnets can be used to increase the level of magnetism in sensitized tags; such increased levels will not trigger alarms. What this means is that patrons can foil the system simply by carrying a small magnet with them when they take books through the sensing screens.

These shortcomings of electronic security systems, combined with the persistent problem of false alarms, suggest that the technology is far from perfect. Observers point out that if the equipment were really reliable, large companies like 3M would emphasize retail applications, which represent an enormous potential market, rather than the rather small library market. As it is, concerns about the reliability of equipment and about being sued over false arrest have deterred suppliers from pursuing retail installations in a large-scale way.

FOOTNOTES

1. Florine Fuller and Irene Glaus, "To Have or Not to Have a Security System," *Tennessee Librarian* 26:41 (Spring 1974).

2. William J. Greaney, An Investigation into the Problem of Lost and Damaged Books in the Senior High School Libraries of Suffolk County, Thesis.

3. Donald L. Ungarelli, "Excerpts—Taken from a Paper Entitled *The Empty Shelves,*" *Bookmark* 32:155 (May-June 1973).

4. "Book Theft On The Upswing," *Library Journal* 100:2208 (December 1, 1975).

5. *National Inventory of Library Needs* (Washington, DC: National Commission on Libraries and Information Science, 1977).

6. "News Notes," *AB Bookman's Weekly* 48:370 (1971).

7. "Police Recover Rare Books Stolen from Lincoln Library," *Library Journal* 97:1232 (1972).

8. "Library Security Roundup," *Library Journal* 98:1533 (May 15, 1973).

9. "Libraries Hit by Book and Art Thefts," *Library Journal* 102:1446-1447 (July 1977).

10. R.M. Broadhead, "Comment," *New Library World* 74:236 (1973).

Bibliography

"AAP and Authors Counter CNLA Copyright Stand ." *Advanced Technology/Libraries* 7:1,5 (January 1978).

"A.B. Dick/Scott Outfits Newspaper Morgue with Updatable Microfiche." *Advanced Technology/Libraries* 6:7 (July 1977).

Advanced Technology/Libraries, April 1975; November 1976.

"The Age of Miracle Chips." *Time* 111:44 (February 20, 1978).

Ahern, Dr. Michael J. III. "A Comparative Study of Microform and Hardcopy as Methods of Presenting Career Information Materials." *The Journal of Micrographics* 9:184 (March 1976).

Allison, Anne Marie, et al. "The Impact of OCLC on Cataloging Departments — A Study." *Network* 2:11-16 (January 1975).

American Libraries, April 1978.

Atherton, Pauline and Roger Christian. *Librarians and Online Services.* White Plains, NY: Knowledge Industry Publications, Inc., 1977.

Automated Circulation Systems in Public Libraries. McLean, VA: Mitre Corp., June 1978.

Avram, Henriette D. *MARC: Its History and Implications.* Washington, DC: Library of Congress, 1975.

BALLOTS Center. *Status Report on BALLOTS.* Stanford University: BALLOTS Center, April 1978.

Becker, Joseph. "The Rich Heritage of Information Science." American Society for Information Science. *Bulletin* 2:11 (March 1976).

Blake, Fay M. and Edith L. Perlmutter. "The Rush to User Fees: Alternative Proposals." *Library Journal* 102:2005-2008 (October 1, 1977).

Books: A MARC Format. 5th Edition. Washington, DC: Library of Congress, 1972.

"Book Theft On The Upswing." *Library Journal* 100:2208 (December 1975).

Bowker Annual of Library and Book Trade Information. New York: R.R. Bowker Co., 1971 and 1977.

Broadhead, R.M. "Comment." *New Library World* 74:236 (1973).

Brown, Connis, O. Jr. "Computer Output Microfilm and the State Archivist: Opportunity and Responsibility." *The Journal of Micrographics* 9:37-41 (September 1975).

Butler, Brett. "The State of the Nation in Networking." *Journal of Library Automation* 8:200-220 (September 1975).

_____. "Updating the Reference Book Through Microform Supplements." *Microform Review* 3:30-33 (January 1974).

"Butler Says 800 Libraries Involved in Automation." *Advanced Technology/Libraries,* October 1975.

Chronicle of Higher Education, September 19, 1977.

"Closing the Card Catalog." *Advanced Technology/Libraries* 6:4,5 (November 1977).

The Computerized Data Base Market. New York: Frost & Sullivan, 1977.

Conversion of Retrospective Catalog Records to Machine-Readable Form. Washington, DC: Library of Congress, 1969.

Cooper, Michael D. and Nancy A. DeWath. "The Cost of On-Line Bibliographic Searching." *Journal of Library Automation* 9:195-209 (September 1976).

_____. and Nancy A. DeWath. "The Effect of User Fees on the Cost of On-Line Searching in Libraries." *Journal of Library Automation* 10:304-319 (December 1977).

DeGennaro, Richard. "Copyright, Resource Sharing, and Hard Times: A View From the Field." *American Libraries* 8:430-435 (September 1977).

"Detroit Urges Use of Teletypewriters." *Library Journal* 52:1190 (August 1951).

Diaz, Albert J., ed. *Microforms and Library Catalogs: A Reader.* Westport, CT: Microform Review, 1977.

_____. *Microforms in Libraries: A Reader.* Westport, CT: Microform Review, 1975.

Dranov, Paula. *Automated Library Circulation Systems, 1977-78.* White Plains, NY: Knowledge Industry Publications, Inc., 1977.

Edgerton, Curtis. "The Mine Map Repository — A Service of Mine Map Data." *The Journal of Micrographics* 8:235-240 (May 1975).

Edwards, Mary Jane. "Microforms: A View from the State Library of Pennsylvania." *The Journal of Micrographics* 8:247 (May 1975).

Franceschi, Harold J. "On-Line Microfilm System for Medical Records." *The Journal of Micrographics* 11:15-21 (September 1977).

Freedman, Maurice J. "Cataloging Systems: 1973 Applications Status." In *Library Automation II: State of the Art.* Susan K. Martin and Brett Butler, eds. Chicago: American Library Association, 1975.

Fuller, Florine and Irene Glaus. "To Have or Not to Have a Security System." *Tennessee Librarian* 26:41 (Spring 1974).

Gaines, Katherine. "Undertaking a Subject Catalog in Microfiche." *Library Resources and Technical Services* 15:297-308 (Summer 1971).

Geller, William Spence. "Duplicate Catalogs in Regional and Public Library Systems." *Library Quarterly* 34:59-60 (January 1964).

Greaney, William J. "An Investigation into the Problem of Lost and Damaged Books in the Senior High School Libraries of Suffolk County." Thesis.

Greene, Robert J. "Microform Attitude and Frequency of Microform Use." *The Journal of Micrographics* 8:133 (January 1975).

_____. "Microfilm Catalogs and the *Lends* Microfiche Catalog." *Microform Review* 4:30-34 (January 1974).

Grosch, Audrey. *Minicomputers in Libraries 1979-80*. White Plains, NY: Knowledge Industry Publications, Inc., 1978.

Hock, R.E. "Providing Access to Externally Available Bibliographic Data Bases in an Academic Library." *College & Research Libraries* 30 (May 1975).

"'Home Brew' Saves $$ in Georgia." *Library Journal* 102:673 (March 15, 1977).

Industry Survey: Computer Output Microfilm. Silver Spring, MD: National Microfilm Association, 1974.

"Information Center Profile, Institute for Scientific Information." *Information Hotline,* March 1977.

International Organization for Standardization. *Documentation — Format for Bibliographic Information Interchange on Magnetic Tape*. Geneva, Switzerland: ISO, 1973; ISO 2709, 1973 (E).

King, Donald. "Statistical Indicators of Scientific and Technical Communications, 1960-1980." National Technical Information Service, 1976.

Knapp, Sara D. "The Reference Interview in the Computer Based Setting." *RQ,* Summer 1978.

"Libraries Hit by Book and Art Thefts." *Library Journal* 102:1446-1447 (July 1977).

"L.A. County PL Establishes a Series of Firsts." *Advanced Technology/Libraries* 6:2,3 (September 1977).

"Library Launches On-Line Distribution Service." *Library of Congress Information Bulletin* 37:49,52-53 (January 20, 1978).

Library of Congress. *Annual Report of the Librarian of Congress for the Fiscal Year Ending September 30, 1977*. Washington, DC: Library of Congress, 1978.

Library of Congress. MARC Development Office. *Books: A MARC Format*. 5th ed. Washington, DC: Library of Congress, 1972.

Library of Congress. Subject Cataloging Division. *Library of Congress Subject Headings*. 8th ed. Washington, DC: Library of Congress, 1975.

"Library Saves $370,000 on System Conversion." *Computerworld,* May 1, 1978.

Library Security Newsletter 1:10 (March 1975).

"Library Security Roundup." *Library Journal* 98:1533 (May 15, 1973).

Lynden, Frederick C. "Replacement of Hard Copy by Microforms." *Microform Review* 4:19 (January 1974).

MacQuarrie, Catherine and Beryl L. Martin. "The Book Catalog of the Los Angeles County Public Library." *Library Resources and Technical Services* 4:211 (1960).

Malinconico, S. Michael and James Rizzolo. "The New York Public Library Automated Book Catalog Subsystem." *Journal of Library Automation* 6:3-36 (March 1973).

———, et al. "Vernacular Scripts in the NYPL Automated Bibliographic Control System." *Journal of Library Automation* 10:205-225 (September 1977).

Markuson, Barbara Evans. "Granting Amnesty and Other Aspects of Automated Circulation." *American Libraries,* April 1978.

_____. "The Ohio College Library Center." *Library Technology Reports* 12:13 (January 1976).

Martin, Susan K. *Library Networks, 1978-79.* White Plains, NY: Knowledge Industry Publications, Inc., 1978.

Mason, Philip P. "Archival Security: New Solutions to an Old Problem." *The American Archivist* 38:484 (October 1975).

McCarn, Davis. "Trends in Information." *Information Utilities.* American Society for Information Science, 1974.

National Inventory of Library Needs. Washington, DC: National Commission on Libraries and Information Science, 1977.

"News Notes." *AB Bookman's Weekly* 48:370 (1971).

New York Times Co. *Annual Report.* New York, 1977.

OCLC Newsletter 1, 1970; 93:1 (January 14, 1976); 97:1 (April 2, 1976); 115:3 (April 7, 1978).

Ohmes, Frances and J.F. Jones. "The Other Half of Cataloging." *Library Resources and Technical Services* 17:321 (September 1973).

Olson, Edwin E., Russell Shank and Harold A. Olsen. "Library and Information Networks." *Annual Review of Information Science and Technology* 7. Carlos Cuadra, ed. Washington, DC: American Society for Information Science, 1972.

"Online Circulation: Costs Pegged." *Library Journal* 102:33 (April 15, 1977).

"Police Recover Rare Books Stolen from Lincoln Library." *Library Journal* 97:1232 (1972).

"Protocol for Computer-to-Computer Communication." *Journal of Library Automation* 9:167-176 (June 1976).

Radwin, Mark S. "Choosing A Terminal." Parts I & II. *ONLINE Magazine,* April, June 1977.

Rather, John C. "Filing Arrangement in the Library of Congress Catalogs." *Library Resources and Technical Services* 2:240-61 (Spring 1972).

Risner, Dr. M. Thomas. "Micropublishing Helps Increase Availability of Non-Book Media References." *The Journal of Micrographics* 9:31-34 (September 1975).

Ross, Joan. "The Great Output Race: COM Joins the Winners' Circle." *The Journal of Micrographics* 10:11-15 (September 1976).

Salmon, Stephen R. "User Resistance to Microforms in the Research Library." *Microform Review* 3:194 (July 1974).

Shera, Jesse H. "The Book Catalog and the Scholar." *Library Resources and Technical Services* 6:214 (Summer 1962).

Schleifer, Harold B. and Peggy A. Adams. *"Books in Print* on Microfiche; A Pilot Test." *Microform Review* 5:10-24 (January 1976).

Schwartz, Philip J. "Use of Color Microfiche as a Replacement for Slides in a University Elementary Accounting Course." *The Journal of Micrographics* 11:217-219 (January/February 1978).

Tauber, Maurice F. and Hilda Feinberg. *Book Catalogs.* Metuchen, NJ: The Scarecrow Press, 1971.

Thorson, A. Robert. "The Economics of Automated Circulation." In *The Economics of Library Automation.* J.L. Divilbiss, ed. Clinic on Library Applications of Data Processing, 13th. Urbana-Champaign, IL: University of Illinois, Graduate School of Library Science, 1977.

Ungarelli, Donald L. "Excerpts — Taken from a Paper Entitled *The Empty Shelves." Bookmark* 32:155 (May-June 1973).

University of California. *Union Catalog of Monographs Collected by the Nine Campuses From 1963 Through 1967.* Berkeley, CA: Institute of Library Research, 1972.

University of Toronto Library Automation System. "Collection Inquiry Reporting and Control System." Toronto: UTLAS, 1977.

"Viewdata Sparks Interest at OCLC and Telenet." *Advanced Technology/Libraries* 7:1 (July 1978).

Wanger, Judith, Carlos A. Cuadra and M. Fishburn. *Impact of On-Line Retrieval Services: A Survey of Users 1974-1975.* Santa Monica, CA: System Development Corporation, 1976.

Weber, David C. "A Century of Cooperative Programs Among Academic Libraries." *College & Research Libraries* 37:205-221 (May 1976).

West, Martha and Brett Butler. "Microreadings: Easing Obstacles to Library Distribution of Information." *The Journal of Micrographics* 8:17-22 (September 1974).

Whalen, Richard. "Microfilm in the Secondary School? Definitely!" *The Journal of Micrographics* 8:153 (January 1975).

Wilde, Daniel U. "A Comparison of Costs Between On-Line and Fast-Batch Searching." Paper presented at American Society for Information Science Annual Meeting. Boston, MA, October 29, 1975.

_____, and B. Snodgrass. "The Value of Searching Multiple Data Bases." In *The Value of Information.* Collected papers of American Society for Information Science midyear meeting. Syracuse University, May 1977.

Willemse, John. "Microfiche as a Means of Providing Students with Literature." *Microform Review* 3:26-29 (January 1974).

Williams, G. "The Preservation of Deteriorating Books." *Library Journal* 91 (January 1966).

Williams, Martha. "Computer-Readable Data Bases." *ALA Yearbook, 1978.* Washington, DC: American Library Association, 1978.

_____. "Data Base and Online Statistics." American Society for Information Science. *Bulletin,* December 1977.

_____, and Sandra Rouse. "Computer-Readable Bibliographic Data Bases." Washington, DC: American Society for Information Science, October 1976. Updated April 1977 and April 1978.

Wooster, Harold. *Microfiche 1969 — A User Study.* Springfield, VA: Clearinghouse for Federal Scientific and Technical Information (AFOSR - 69-1847 TR), 1969.